Helen Britt
May 1st 2012
I bought this Book when
Becky + I visited Uncle Ducky
+ Aunt Janice while Uncle D. Was
a pt at Wayne Mem. Hospital

"A glorious blend of story, tutorial and the words of prayer warriors who have gone before. . . . A powerful and personal book about prayer."

Publishers Weekly

"Other books on prayer give 'how-to' advice. Patricia Raybon takes a different and much more daring approach. She embeds prayer in real life: surgery, family conflict, anger, prodigal children, race, memory. The result is raw—and for that reason, comfortingly real."

PHILIP YANCEY

Author, *Rumors of Another World, Reaching for the Invisible God,* and *Soul Survivor*

"This book, filled with raw honesty, serves as a powerful argument for the healing nature of prayer."

ROCKY MOUNTAIN NEWS

"Patricia Raybon's memoir of learning to pray is wonderfully written and a delight to read. She is honest and clear as she struggles with who God is, how to pray, and what to pray for. On her journey, Patricia discovers how her love for Jesus does not separate her from people of other faiths, but deepens her respect for them. Her story integrates prayer into every aspect of living. In fact, Patricia Raybon's school of prayer is life itself."

REVEREND JANE E. VENNARD

Adjunct faculty, Iliff School of Theology; spiritual director; retreat leader; author, *Praying with Body and Soul: A Way to Intimacy with God*

"Patricia Raybon has written a beautiful book with a beautiful message. She tells her story honestly, bravely, and with a good dose of humor. A very satisfying and illuminating book!"

CARLEEN BRICE

Editor, *Age Ain't Nothing but a Number: Black Women Explore Midlife*

"Patricia's powerful, personal story becomes our own as we recognize similarities in our families, marriage, and life. Just as powerfully, her lessons about prayer become our own as we follow her journey closer to Jesus."

CAROL KUYKENDALL
Author; director of leadership development, MOPS International

"With clarity of purpose, Patricia exposes her inner self and the challenges of her life. She brings the reader in childlike faith to trust more, love more, and wondrously develop the delightful experience of being able to listen and talk to God."

THE REVEREND LONZIE SYMONETTE
Adjunct professor, Fuller Colorado Theological Seminary;
assistant minister, Payne Chapel African Methodist Episcopal Church

"Patricia Raybon has written a power-filled yet gentle book about her journey to spiritual maturity. She allows the reader to overhear, envision, and identify with her deeply personal experiences and faith development. Her mantra of "God is bigger" permeates the prayer lessons she examines in the sweeping pages of this text. The creative vulnerability of her writing establishes her as one of the cutting-edge voices in all of spirituality."

TERESA L. FRY BROWN
Associate professor of homiletics, Candler School of Theology, Emory University

"This wonderfully written book reaches across racial, denominational, and cultural lines, as Raybon discovers that prayer is a deliberate discipline which draws the prayer warrior into a life-changing relationship with God."

FORBES BOOK CLUB

"More personal than formulaic, this book is nonetheless filled with gentle tips for energizing your own prayer time."

Today's Christian

I TOLD
THE MOUNTAIN
TO MOVE

Learning to Pray So Things Change

Patricia Raybon

SALT**RIVER**®

AN IMPRINT OF
TYNDALE HOUSE PUBLISHERS, INC.

Visit Tyndale's exciting Web site at www.tyndale.com

TYNDALE is a registered trademark of Tyndale House Publishers, Inc.

SaltRiver and the SaltRiver logo are registered trademarks of Tyndale House Publishers, Inc.

I Told the Mountain to Move: Learning to Pray So Things Change

Copyright © 2005 by Patricia Raybon. All rights reserved.

Cover photograph copyright © by J. A. Kraulis/Masterfile. All rights reserved.

Author photograph copyright © 2004 by Nicholas DeSciose. All rights reserved.

Designed by Beth Sparkman

Published in association with the literary agency of Ann Spangler and Company, 1420 Pontiac Road S.E., Grand Rapids, MI 49506.

Library of Congress Cataloging-in-Publication Data

Raybon, Patricia.
  I told the mountian to move / Patricia Raybon.
    p. cm.
  Includes bibliographical references.
  ISBN-13: 978-0-8423-8797-2 (hc)
  ISBN-10: 0-8423-8797-8 (hc)
  ISBN-13: 978-0-8423-8798-9 (sc)
  ISBN-10: 0-8423-8798-6 (sc)
  1. Prayer—Christianity. 2. Raybon, Patricia. I. Title.
BV210.3.R39 2005
248.3'2—dc22   2004025262

Printed in the United States of America

11   10   09   08   07   06
  7   6   5   4   3   2

*This book
is dedicated to
my mother, Nannie,
and to prayer warriors
in every corner
of the world.*

FREE Discussion Guide!
A reproducible discussion guide for
I Told the Mountain to Move
is available at
ChristianBookGuides.com

SaltRiver Books are a bit like saltwater: Buoyant. Sometimes stinging. A mixture of sweet and bitter, just like real life. Intelligent, thoughtful, and finely crafted—but not pretentious, condescending, or out of reach. They take on real life from a Christian perspective. Look for SaltRiver Books, an imprint of Tyndale House Publishers, everywhere Christian books are sold.

SALT**RIVER**®

Intelligent. Thought-provoking. Authentic.

w w w . s a l t r i v e r b o o k s . c o m

⊰ CONTENTS ⊱

Listen to me!
You can pray
for anything,
and if you believe,
you will have it.

Mark 11:24

PART ONE

Climbing

Climbing

June 2000

I was unbearably young when I first learned to pray. Barely a year old, sitting in a high chair before a bowl of cooked cereal at breakfast time, I offered up my hands while my mother pressed them gently together— in the position of prayer—then leaned toward me to coo: "Say your grace, precious." Then, in my one-year-old babble, I would "pray"—just as my mother and father did before they ate breakfast and lunch and every other meal ever taken at our house.

And of course I didn't remember any of this. What does a one-year-old remember well enough to recall when she is grown?

So I watched closely now as my mother repeated this same scene with my grandchild, a baby just barely one.

Mama at eighty-four, sitting at my kitchen table, pulled her chair close to my visiting grandbaby's chair. She pressed this little girl's hands together—in the position of prayer. Then my mother cooed: "Say your grace, precious." And my first grandchild, in her little child's babble, started to pray:

"Babba ab ba babba," she said, bowing her head and leaning into her hands, smiling up at my mother. She wanted to get this praying thing down right. Then the baby, hurrying to finish, added with a flourish her closing touch: "Ahhh-men!"

My mother, agreeing with her, closed with her own flourish, a loud

3

and sturdy "*Ah*-men." Then Mama, with full approval, added, "Okay, now we can eat our breakfast." Then she handed my grandchild her unbearably small spoon.

This is how it started, my blessed journey—this unlikely quest to learn how to pray. I didn't know of such beginnings until that summer of 2000, when my long-widowed mother was comfortably aging and I, at fifty-one, was far into life myself.

I'd always thought that Daddy, not Mama, was the teacher of everything in our house. Everything spiritual, that is, would have started with Daddy. He was a daddy in the fifties, after all, and I was his youngest child. So his word was law. His wishes were granted. His dinner was hot when he walked through the front door after work. And his table was quiet while we ate. No horseplay from my sister and me. No talking back. No childish, crazy foolishness.

But foolish me, sitting at the dinner table one Friday evening, yelled like crazy across his dinner plate at my sister, who had just given me a sly and delicious look.

I can't remember why. But big sisters can do this. At ten years old, my sister could goad and tease and look innocent all at the same time. We both did this, in fact, eyeing each other across our family's kitchen table, rolling our impudent eyes on the sly while our parents laughed and talked. Knowing this, I saw my older sister's look and I responded. I yelled. "You better stop that, Lauretta!"

Daddy, still eating, said, "Stop!" He didn't look over. Didn't have to. He was Daddy. One word did it. So *stop* should have been enough.

But here was another look. A delicious tease. At five or six years old, I couldn't let it pass. So I yelled again.

"You better stop looking at me like that, Lauretta!"

Daddy put down his fork—one movement.

His eyes found mine, flashing and speaking. Then Daddy cleared his throat to *really* speak.

Of course, I heard him. How could I miss that sound? And how could I *not* listen? My handsome, proper father—still wearing his starched white shirt from work, his dark silk tie, loosened at the collar—was so painfully lovely to behold. His lean brown face was always shaven, his hair always barbered, his mouth never slack, his eyes always vigilant, his diction ever perfect.

His presence alone was enough to shift my attention, to focus my awakening ears.

But listening is hard when you're just starting out to pray.

Yet Daddy had something to say.

"If you open your mouth one more time . . ."

But who can figure? I was five. I kept talking.

In fact, I said something childish and stupid, something like: "Well, if you'd just look at *her* and not be looking at me . . ." Then: *WHAM!*

Lightning! Daddy's backhand. Landing hard across my mouth. Tasting like fire. Feeling like power and truth and God in one hard blow. I flew off my chair and hit the floor, my bottom lip ballooning to twice its size and bleeding.

A five-year-old gets dramatic.

"*Waaawww . . .* Daddy!" I started to bawl. Loud and insulted. "*Waaww!*" I cupped my bleeding lip with both hands, crawling—chastised—back to my chair. "*Wa-aa-aw!*" I was wailing, panting and snotting up, gasping dramatically for air.

Daddy was past patience, however.

His face was an inch from mine, his soft ebony eyes now hard and sharp with straining.

"Stop that racket *now*—or I'll give you something to cry about!"

He was glaring now. His look was driving home the message: In *my* house, talk right. In *my* house, don't sass. In *my* house, keep quiet. Be good. Obey. Don't question. Stay in your place. Toe the line. Rules clear?

Don't remember? *WHAM!*

Daddy didn't think twice about punishment. He just got right down to it, that backhand flying. Not all the time, of course. But enough for me to be on guard. So that's how I lived, careful and watching, always vigilant, ever keeping a healthy sense of fear.

Looking back, however, Daddy seemed fearful the most—afraid of not teaching me right, terrified that if I didn't learn how to toe every line, something bad could happen. Even to a Christian girl, bad things could happen. And with every passing year, the stakes seemed to get higher. Coming home after work to find a wild-haired daughter dancing and gyrating in the kitchen to *American Bandstand* sent him into a kind of despairing rage.

"Stop that foolishness!" he would shout. But me, I kept dancing—eyes closed, snapping my fingers, singing the Motown words—digging the thumping music. So he shouted again. "Stop that foolishness."

Then beyond patience, he reached down and grabbed me by the arm, his beautiful eyes boring into mine. "*Patricia! Didn't you hear me?*"

A perfect question for a prayer warrior. And this *is* a Christian journey. But I put off my answers, then I made peace with my daddy—so he could make peace with his God. Those backhands and shouting soon ended, in fact. So I grew to honor my father—even to revere him, maybe even to adore him. Then I launched my life, daring to move on—vowing to believe that life's hard moments, and the problems that frame them, were over and done with, now and forever *amen*.

But here was something else, these fifty years later. Another beautiful man, my husband, Dan, this time—shouting even louder, *yelling* with all of his beautiful heart from upstairs.

"Why'd you leave this door open! Who closed this window! This house is too hot! This TV's too loud! Who emptied the gas tank! Why can't you fill it up! Why won't you answer? *Patricia! Can't you hear me calling you down there?!*"

Still a good question. But I closed my heart to my husband's shouting, unsure how to answer hard questions. In fact, my husband wasn't yelling hard things. But he sounded odd because his complaints sounded small. The only thing smaller was my modern life. Indeed, the soul of our household seemed to be shrinking under mountains every day.

So our oldest daughter now had a baby but had never been married. Our youngest daughter, gone from the church, was looking for God in "false" religions—or that's how they looked to me. My aging mother's health, meanwhile, was slowing—but so was our love. She needed my help and love, sometimes in the same hour. But "we cannot give to the outside what we don't have on the inside," the saintly Mother Teresa said. So I made my nightly calls and sounded cheerful. But cheerful calls to two strong-willed daughters and an eighty-four-year-old widowed mother aren't truly love, and I knew they must have known it.

I had failed us all, it seemed. And this failing of us stung. On many nights, I sat in the dark in my bedroom and I grappled for God—falling to my knees, begging God to fix our torn, worn places—especially to fix my torn, small life.

Then I sang a small song: *Poor me*. That was my theme. So I hummed it and rolled it around in my head, tossing it about my shoulders like a wet wool scarf. And everybody knows what wet wool smells like.

Well.

Satan likes us like this.

He likes us small and tossed and groaning and weary. He likes our lights turned off and our hope turned down. He likes us reeling and fearful and cast out and empty, and pretty much useless because of it all.

But not even Satan was counting on a fifty-something woman, finally worn out on small songs and hard memories, digging up enough good common sense to call on God. That kind of woman cinches on her whole armor and gets busy working with the Master.

That sounded good, at least. The truth was something else. In truth, Satan had me mesmerized—eyes glazed over—still believing that my life was torn and small and hardly worth the time, when my life was just buried, deep under shadows.

To make matters worse, however, I did a hard thing. I turned to the head of the family—that is, I turned again to God—and I asked for help.

And God? The Big and Silent One?—at least that's how God seemed during that long, hard summer. God seemed big and cold and distant— as silent as death, as soundless as the grave. God seemed a great and distant emptiness, saying nothing, *doing* nothing, mocking and empty and *not there*. So God was my *Deus Absconditus*—the God who is hidden, as the ancients would have called him. In fact, the words looked like I was feeling. *Deus Absconditus*.

Or as the psalmist put it in his ever-honest way: "O my God, I cry out by day, but you do not answer."

Chuck Swindoll, talking on my radio, described it in a question: "Have you ever heard the silence of God?" Swindoll's deep, confident voice rolled out of the speakers. I turned up the volume. So Swindoll asked the question again, his voice slightly lower, sounding even closer.

"Have you ever heard the silence of God?"

I nodded. Yes! I have heard that silence.

But I didn't know that ages before Saint John of the Cross had called God's silence "the dark night of the soul."

For scholar Howard Macy, it was "the withering winds of God's hiddenness."

For preacher-warrior Renita Weems, it was the "long silence between intimacies" and the "winter months of faith" and finally "the period pulls into darkness."

Indeed, for Richard Foster, the soulful Quaker, it was the "icy cold of . . . nothing" and "the purifying silence." In fact, in one such eighteen-month-long trial, Foster said his great lesson was "the intimate and ultimate awareness that I could not manage God. Neither . . . could I conquer God. God was, in fact, to conquer me."

I wasn't as eloquent. But I understood the work of waiting on God and not getting answers. At my job, I saw a revolving door of ever-evolving students—other mothers' son and daughters, other people's lovely prayers and dreams. Often they looked beautiful and unfinished and distant, indeed. I surely looked that way to them, in turn.

But nobody was more beautiful and unfinished and distant that year than my beautiful and distant husband.

Once we had laughed and loved and whispered and dreamed. We had joked and hoped and, my goodness, we had touched. We would come home from work, put dinner on, reach for each other in the kitchen and then we just kissed. We wrapped our arms around each other and leaned in and didn't pull away.

But that feeling of closeness and warmth, of leaning in and mutual good will—of just the two of us together, bonded in life and holding on right there in our very own kitchen—had evaporated. My big fear was that we would sit across the breakfast table one day and have nothing left to say.

And here is something:

It didn't matter that we were a good Christian family; living our earnest lives; going to our good, earnest church. It didn't even matter then that we were black, or African American as folks say now. In fact, we were a modern American family—a bit tossed about, a bit uncertain, a lot unglued. But mostly we were broken—and we couldn't figure out how to put ourselves back together again.

Even the Oprah book I bought at the grocery store warned this was a problem. "The tragedy," said a preacher in Cry, the Beloved Country, "is not that things are broken. The tragedy is that they are not mended again."

To top off my tragedy, however, I was aware of the oddest feeling—not of anger so much, but of betrayal. It was as if God himself had stopped my mending. Then God had dropped my case, and to seal the deal, God had stopped, closed and locked a door.

And God?

God was there, standing behind the gate, inside the shadows, just out of sight, enormously quiet.

Silent as a coffin.

It struck me that way halfway into summer, as the skies in Colorado went dark with dry lightning and sparse rain. Then a kind of thunder roll rumbled with a crash and I threw off my wet wool and I sat straight up. I was aware, that is, of a ridiculous understanding: God was real. But God was waiting. Waiting on *me*. So God wasn't moving. If anything, to get to God, *I'd* have to make all the adjustments. Not God, but *I* would have to shift *my* position. Is that what Jesus meant? When you pray, pray like *this*—that is, get in the right position? Or as the straight-shooting Frederick D. Haynes III put it: "When our hands are tied, *then* they are positioned for prayer."

So here I was now:

Family unraveling. My hands were tied. In position. So the prayer words just eased from my mouth.

"I want to pray."

I was on the phone, talking almost in a whisper to my oldest daughter, Joi, not sure I should say such hard words out loud.

"You want to pray? Is that what you said, Mom?"

Joi sounded busy. Her hands were full, raising a baby and running the small bookstore she owned in a struggling black part of town. And now I wanted to *pray*?

"I want to *learn* to pray," I said. "I want you to get me some books—on prayer."

"By black authors? Is that what you need, Mom?" she asked.

"No, for once, this isn't about race," I told her. Joi is an angel daughter. But she didn't get it just yet. She didn't see that her good mother's Christian life had buried me, even while a great Christian life had eluded me. She didn't really know that her mother wasn't living right—that I still hadn't learned enough hard, smart lessons.

I was in a standoff with a marriage gone dry, with a life drained empty. But this go-round, instead of pushing back, I would look up to heaven and surrender. Finally now I vowed to learn, as Richard Foster put it, the *real* way to pray:

Pray so things healed.

Pray so things stopped.

Pray so things started.

Pray so things changed.

I was desperate, indeed, to learn all of prayer's little secrets, to master all of its hidden methods.

But prayer isn't a skill, as Andrew Murray said. Prayer is an art. And maybe more than that, it is a calling.

"The highest part of the work entrusted to us, the root and strength of all other work," Murray declared. Nothing, he insisted, should we study and practice more than the work of praying. And this praying, he said, which at first "appears so simple," turns out to be the hardest thing of all, because it's about developing a relationship.

So praying would be tough. For me—who found relationships tricky and so dismaying—real praying would be maybe impossible. Or something far beyond what I had been doing. I had always prayed, from my little child's Now-I-lay-me-down-to-sleep prayers, right up to my O-Lord-help-me-Jesus prayers.

Not only that, I'd heard a lifetime of prayers. In the black church, on any given Sunday, a preacher might moan one of those James Weldon Johnson kind of prayers: "Oh Lord . . . we come this morning, knee bowed and body bent."

Or as only Johnson could put it: "Bow our hearts beneath our knees, and our knees in some lonesome valley."

Well, yes. I knew about *those* kinds of prayers.

But even that kind of groaning, longing, desperate praying wasn't unlocking God's delicious silence.

But I was ready to be schooled. Just put me in your school, Jesus. That's all I asked now. Then I'd be like Andrew Murray, whose challenging treatise *With Christ in the School of Prayer* was praised as a classic prayer guide. Jesus has opened a school, Murray wrote, "in which He trains His redeemed ones, who specially desire it, to have power in prayer."

I didn't necessarily feel redeemed, whatever "redeemed" actually meant. I'm sure I didn't know then. But I knew this: My prayers lacked power. When I prayed, I sometimes got a little portion of peace, but it was fleeting. When I prayed, my daughters' lives sometimes changed, but not by much. When I prayed, my husband's love sometimes warmed, but it didn't burn.

And I missed the burning. Even a Christian can miss the burn of good married love.

I also missed laughing with my daughters, as we did when they were girls.

I missed my mother's touch and whatever closeness we once knew.

In contrast, I also realized, from years of sitting in Sunday school lessons—or maybe from some fresh new awareness—that when Jesus prayed, *big* things happened.

Sick folks got well.

Blind folks got sight.

Lame folks walked.

Dead folks found life. Even cold and moldy Lazarus, already four long days in the grave, got up from death when Jesus prayed. The Bible didn't lie.

Jesus wept. "Then Jesus looked up and said, 'Father, I thank you that you have heard me.'"

Thanking God *before* the miracle of Lazarus. That was Jesus—the schoolteacher—thundering and confident, crying and shouting at the grave.

"Lazarus! Come out!"

And there came Lazarus, stumbling from his tomb, wide-eyed, shocked to be breathing again—pulling in the fresh, good air, blowing out the stale. Stunned at suddenly hearing the crowd's raucous roar, shocked to smell the unwashed crowd's earthy smells, dumbfounded to be back in the land of the noisy living, and maybe not too happy about it.

Death to life. It was incredible, but when Jesus prayed—wiping the tears from his sad, indescribable eyes—I believe heaven opened.

Well.

I'd never prayed like that in my life. Odd to be past fifty and finally really see that. Crazy, indeed, to waste not just months but *years* praying with little ever changing. Odd, indeed, to see that the problem wasn't just in the effort, it was in the praying. I had been doing it all wrong.

I was a beggar at prayer. *Please, Jesus, please.* But begging wasn't prayer. With prayer, surely more was at work—especially the first thing: that prayer isn't about getting things; prayer indeed is about getting changed.

"We work, we pull, we struggle, and we plan until we're utterly exhausted," Evelyn Christenson wrote. "But we have forgotten to plug into the source of power. And that source of power is prayer."

That sounded right. So around midsummer, I took the plunge. I ordered Joi's books on prayer, and I read them. Well, I underlined the good parts and pondered the hard parts. I got off my knees. Instead I *wrote* down my prayers. Then I studied my prayers, looking at their shape, listening to their sounds. Then sure enough, over time, the prayers were less like cold lists and more like warm letters. Then they were more like love letters.

"Our dear heavenly Father," I wrote, "thank you for being who you are."

So they were praise letters.

"You are magnificent and sovereign and wonderful and great. You can do the impossible. . . . "

I began to feel that God not only expected this adoration. In fact, God needed it. So I felt, for the first time ever, my heart growing warm and soft toward God, the Creator of the universe. He *was* big, in fact. But he still needed something from me: my praise.

So I gave it.

"Our wonderful heavenly Father: You are Love. You are wise. You are perfect. You are gracious. You are matchless. You are just. You are every-thing. . . ."

So July ended and August came.

Then slowly, as September rose and then waned, I began to perceive—ever so slightly—that God was hearing me. That is, I felt that if I took the time to be still with God, that this was prayer. Indeed, to pray was to be still. As prayer scholar Steve Wingfield said, prayer primarily is "enjoying the presence of God." And here it was—God's presence.

So I luxuriated in it.

I closed my bedroom door. I tuned out my husband's trouble, his ham-mering irritations, his odd complaints—and I moved inside with God.

And it was true. Prayer was to sit and to listen, to wait with silent joy for the Most High God. Prayer was to approach the Holy of Holies and to *enter*. Prayer was to sit down, not at the feet of the Creator of the universe, but to sit in his lap and rest.

So I went in and I rested. I laid my head on his big chest. I leaned back. I felt the big embrace, letting it hold me up, letting me lean, inviting me to rest, encouraging me to stay.

Then the big thing would happen—and this *was* big—God would deem to speak.

The Big Silent One would talk, spirit to spirit, heart to heart, the way a caring, patient parent communes with a beloved but unruly child. This was Father-love, as Andrew Murray described the presence of God. And I was astonished by it—that *he* had been there all the time. Our Father God was just waiting for me to turn from the irritable chaos of my empty, weary life and to sit down long enough to hear him.

So we sat, God and I, as summer turned to fall. I listened to God's presence. Then I dared to tell God everything he already knew: about my husband's complaints and my mother's aging distance and my daughters' hard choices and their busy and seeming indifference, and I was astonished. I could feel God listening.

The more I focused on God, in fact, the less I worried about my household's ongoing and never-ending dramas and irritations and problems.

That seemed to be a big prayer principle: Magnify God. Make him bigger than any problem by focusing not on the problem but on him.

Then pay attention while he told me what to do and how to pray.

Pray long enough, indeed, to stop talking and start listening.

God's still, small voice would break into the chaos. I could hear it. Spirit to spirit. A whisper. Divine breath barely glancing my soul. Not often, but enough to know that it was there and it was real. The silent God does speak.

This was a breakthrough.

Cool. *Very* cool indeed.

By October, I was pleased with myself, to tell the awful truth. I was ready now to soar with the great and almighty God, because finally it seemed—at long last—I had discovered the keys to the Kingdom. I was ready now to claim my abundant and problem-free and peaceful and redeemed Christian life.

⊰∄⊱

Then this: "Where's the Excedrin?"

My husband.

Dan was sixty and a few heartbeats past retirement. It was mid-October. There had been parties, at least three, just a few weeks before. There were presents and photographs and a fancy ice sculpture some four feet high and a live jazz combo and speeches and flowers and kisses.

And then: "Where's that Excedrin?" Dan asked again. "My back is killing me." He grimaced. "And my neck." He grabbed the nape of his neck, which did actually look—oddly, in fact—as if something was pulling it off center toward his left shoulder, which was also aching horribly, he said.

"Stress," I told him. "You're just struggling with retirement. You need to relax. You have to adjust. It just takes awhile."

That's what I said. But what I thought was that my husband had turned into a whining, self-absorbed malcontent, and his retirement was going to be a test and a trial.

But instead of saying such things, I got the aspirin. I even rubbed his neck, although there wasn't much love in the aspirin or in the rubs.

Then, of course, the hurting didn't go away. Then it got worse. Then it got hard. Then it got evil. Then on a cold, blustery day in late October—the night before Halloween, in fact—my malcontented husband's face turned an odd gray and his eyes went dull.

Then, looking a bit confused and surprised, he said: "I can't walk."

I looked at him.

"You can't walk?"

Dan was leaning into the doorframe of our hotel room in Grand Rapids, Michigan. We had traveled there to present a series of workshops at a state university.

Now on a bitterly cold evening, he had returned from his evening workshop after struggling to give the program from a folding chair.

"I tried to stand," he said. "But my legs . . . they wouldn't hold me. They wouldn't work."

In fact, following the workshop, after getting dropped off at the hotel, he'd had trouble walking from the hotel lobby to our room.

"I had to hold on to the wall the whole way down here," he grumbled. He leaned for a desk near the door, then reached for a chair, finally letting his body fall onto one of the double beds.

I watched him struggle. He was crumpled and kind of sweaty. His necktie, loosened, dangled around his neck. He asked for help taking off his coat, pulling off his shoes, shrugging out of his sweater vest, one of dozens he routinely wore.

He started barking instructions.

Get me the Excedrin. Plug in my heating pad. Stop fumbling with that bottle. *Can't you just open it?*

I did those things, then turned away from him and shut my eyes, inhaled a deep breath. Here we go—another grouchy, nitpicky, self-absorbed night. Yet more proof that Dan's retirement-stress "thing," whatever it was, had finally hit the limit.

Now he couldn't walk?

It was ridiculous. And I'd had enough—enough of his grouching, complaining, griping dramatics. As soon as we got back to Colorado, we'd have to have a long talk. No, a hard talk.

Dan turned with some theatrics on the bed, then groaned a bit.

I shoved the Excedrin back in his briefcase, plugged in his heating pad and positioned it around his back, thinking the whole time that not only was he lousy at playacting, he didn't even sound all that sick.

It was all I could do not to mimic his pathetic moan.

⊶⊰⊱⊷

So—no, I wasn't a good wife. A good wife thinks *emergency*. She rushes her husband to a hospital. At the very least, she summons a hotel doctor.

But I will just tell this truth.

That night I did not feel much compassion or pity—or hardly much love—for my husband.

He had picked and pushed and put me down all summer. He did this, I would learn later, when he couldn't explain that something in his body was very wrong, and he rarely got sick. But now his back was rigid and hot, burning and angry with pain. Sometimes he could barely move. Often the pain drove him to his knees. Once he lay all night on the hard bathroom floor, trying to get relief. But it wasn't just back pain. Something terrible was happening. But he didn't know what or understand why.

So he was terrified.

But he wouldn't admit it. Instead, he barked at me. And I was sinking under his disdain, more weary with every put-down. I only noticed that my husband wasn't himself anymore—no longer his joking, carefree, husband-boyfriend-best-friend, regular, everyday self—enjoying his blessed life. Instead, every day the temper tantrums got worse. Who left the dryer on? Who drank all the milk? Stop moving all my pens. I can never find a pen. *Who took my pen?!*

The irritable griping of a terrified, sick man. Dan, once my prince of shared dreams and big hopes, had become an angry stranger. And now he couldn't walk?

Here is the short version: A rushed flight home from Michigan after an early morning emergency-room visit yielded no answers, just more questions. Then, back in Denver, a scramble to University Hospital prompted an MRI, followed by an angiogram. Then a long consultation with neurosurgeons and cardiologists and radiologists and other sober physicians in white coats and somber shoes ended a hard day.

Then too soon the neurosurgeons had a name. But it didn't matter that it was arteriovenous fistula—because I'd never heard of arteriovenous fistula.

I only understood that it was a problem with the blood flow in Dan's spinal cord—right next to his brain stem. A tangle of malformed veins—in place since birth but never troubling him before—now were engorged like a tourniquet and were hemorrhaging. This mess of swollen vessels was pressing without mercy inside Dan's spinal cord. His spinal canal was ablaze with inflammation. So from his head to his feet to his calves to his waist he couldn't feel anything. His pants were wet because he couldn't control his bladder.

He also looked horrible. He was gray and clammy and undeniably sick. Worse, he looked afraid. He also looked surprised, as if this odd thing was happening and he hadn't seen it coming.

We called my mother. I held the phone to Dan's ear while my husband whispered to his mother-in-law that something was wrong. *I can't walk.* And to make matters worse he still didn't exactly understand why. *Arteriovenous fistula.*

Of all the ridiculous things.

Months would pass before I fully understood what an "a.v. fistula" meant, that the malformation on the spinal cord was rare, and that its location meant the results could be catastrophic. His breathing could stop. With the brain stem involved, he could lose his speech or his memory, or suffer irreversible paralysis.

I didn't know this. Moreover, I couldn't find an easy way to talk about it.

"Well, is it a stroke?" our friends would ask.

"No," I'd mumble, trying to explain about malformed connections involving veins *blah blah blah,* which was a mouthful but didn't seem to help anybody understand.

"That's like an aneurysm?" somebody would ask. "Or like a heart attack?"

The questions came and I would stumble over my explanation.

A sick husband is one thing. A sick husband whose condition is hard to explain is even worse.

This a.v. fistula sounded like some made-up, frivolous, psychopathic, TV talk-show disease. And when I said the words to people, they'd get a strange look, as if I enjoyed spouting medical terms that sounded sort of important instead of just telling them what was going on.

Maybe that's why I kept smiling.

In the emergency room at University Hospital in Denver, the neurosurgeons gathered at the foot of Dan's bed. And while they looked more sober than any doctors I'd ever seen in my life, all I could manage was a smile.

A nice wife's grin. We smile when we want to scream. Christians do this. Christians who are wives may do it best.

A sixty-year-old husband on a hospital bed looks small and cold and thin under a white sheet. Dan looked all of that and less on that dank first day of November.

His retirement year, the beginning of a new life—*our* new life. That's what I had hoped for: A life without complaints and griping, maybe with peace and perhaps a portion of occasional joy. But now he was dying.

This, as one doctor deftly put it, "is a serious situation."

His name was Dr. Breeze. An unlikely name for a man wearing such a grave look. Not once during the examination did a "breeze" or anything like it cross his face.

Dr. Breeze, in fact, insisted that I go home—to get some "real rest."

Real rest—for what?

His stoic look said it all: For the ordeal of trying to keep your husband alive.

And still this truth did not register.

So I asked: "Are these surgeries serious?"

Dr. Breeze looked at me, solemn. The surgery would take all of the next day, he answered. Then, as he put it: "We'll be working around expensive real estate."

He pointed to the back of his skull. Just a hair from the brain stem, he said. As he pointed with one graceful finger, I had to catch my breath.

This doctor's hands were exquisite. Small for a man's. Refined. Graceful. Smooth and so delicate they could have been a child's, wrought from fine porcelain.

He was saying that the surgery couldn't be more serious. And so was my husband's condition.

But while he was talking, I stared at those hands. I pictured the lovely refined fingers moving across my husband's exposed brain. These hands would fight to unravel vascular, microscopic outlaws and make everything okay again. They would do this, I knew, even as Dr. Breeze said the challenge was dire.

Then the doctor looked at me, seeing the wife's smile. He had seen it before.

He was going home to rest, he said, to prepare for a long day of surgery. So rather than camp out in your husband's hospital room, you should consider going home yourself, he said again.

This was a perfect moment for him to smile. I don't think he did.

Maybe a man with graceful hands, who puts such hands onto the moist, fragile tissues around the human brain, couldn't afford to crack jokes, even if his name was Breeze.

So I smiled at him again. I wanted him to know that he had been clear. Then I myself turned breezy.

"Be back first thing in the morning," I sang at Dan, "before . . . well, before everything."

Dan barely nodded his head. To tell the truth, he didn't even really look at me. It wasn't like the TV movies where the husband grasps the wife's hand. Then their eyes meet and the music rises.

Instead, my husband turned his face and was silent. So I gathered up my keys and purse. I said good-bye to the doctors. I clomped down to the hospital parking garage. But I was moving by some force outside my own. Finally, I understood. Dan was *dying*.

The doctors' hands made it so. So did the doctors' sober looks. They were grave, almost like a funeral was waiting to start. But only their solemnity and skill could put the funeral off.

A light snow was falling, like sugar, melting the instant it touched the windshield of my aging Nissan.

Driving home, I was aware of moving through traffic and passing familiar streets and avoiding familiar potholes and stopping at red lights and proceeding at green ones. But every mile of the thirty-minute trip passed like an odd dream. Roads passing beneath me. Snowflakes dissolving in front of me, the car heater blowing warmth onto my chilled wife's smile. All a dream, except I couldn't wake up.

Dan was *dying*?

Was this how a marriage ends? With bickering and sparring, then somebody gets sick and dies?

I pulled into our garage, next to my husband's old blue convertible— a hunk of blue-metallic junk he'd planned to restore during his retirement. Then the truth broke in.

I collapsed into wailing sobs. *Oh God! Oh God!*

My body was shaking, giving in to hopelessness. But I didn't bang my fist against the steering wheel because what good would that do?

I sat in the old Nissan, turning off the engine. The tears raged in sheets. With one foot, I pushed open the car door, forcing my body from the car, almost crawling now through the garage. But every step took me on a parade past my husband's beloved "car stuff": his balled-up T-shirts for car buffing, his Simoniz wax tins, his jars of nails, his wrenches, and his other garage tools. At the sight of each thing, I sobbed harder, crying out to God.

Dan was *dying*. But his junky car and his junky nails and his Simoniz wax were still here. Waiting for what—a man who might not come back? I groped my way through the garage, still sobbing from my insides out.

Inside the house, it was worse: His faded jacket, waiting on a hook across from the washing machine. His teacup, cold and half-empty on the kitchen counter. His beat-up sneakers, lumped at the foot of the stairs. Our house was an archive of my husband's artifacts. But the truth was he might not return to them.

And no chance to make things right again. To work our way back to the place where we'd started together, whispering and hopeful and believing.

Upstairs in our room, I opened the linen closet where he kept his clean socks and undershirts and fresh towels. At the sight of them I literally collapsed—tears still raging—onto this pile of clothes.

I pressed them to me, inhaling my husband's laundered-underwear smell and crying even harder while I bunched his clothing to my face.

What else to do, indeed, but cry? Our life together had spiraled downward, and now he was sick unto death. And I was angry about it because I still loved him.

But I hadn't acted like I loved him. And now he might die. And death would ruin everything by taking him away.

So gulping back tears, I curled up in a ball on our bed, pulled up the covers. Then still hugging one of my husband's clean undershirts, I fell asleep.

⊰⊱

Then 3 A.M.

In November, of course, the house was dark but also cold. I opened my eyes in the dimness and suddenly sat up straight, shivering.

God was talking.

That is, God's Spirit was talking to my spirit and I recognized the voice. Not an out-loud voice, of course. But I could *hear* the words in my head— or in my heart?—as if they were spoken aloud. That is, my spirit could hear the words. They were as plain as plywood. Simple and even and plain, and there were four of them: Stop crying. Start praying.

Stop crying? Start praying?

I yanked the covers back and sat still in the dark.

I heard it again.

Stop crying. Start praying.

I had not been shaken by the shoulders or drenched in cold water. But these words penetrated my heart as if I'd been thrown headfirst into a cold, deep lake. And I can't swim.

I was wide-awake.

I switched on the lamp on the nightstand next to the bed.

A pile of books, each one on prayer, was stacked there helter-skelter, just as I had left them days earlier.

"Jesus," I said out loud.

My husband needed prayer. *Real* prayer. His side of the bed was empty, and it would stay empty if I didn't get up right now, wipe my tears, and get to *work*.

God was ordering me to get moving, to start praying, and to believe that he would hear and that he would answer. Not only that, God was ordering me to be the big and good and and substantial person that I longed to be, and to believe that he would help me do it.

I grabbed a book. It had a yellow jacket, and the author was Richard Foster.

I read the title to myself: *Prayer: Finding the Heart's True Home*.

Such a nice Christian title.

But right now I needed something flashy and dramatic and real. I needed *How to Pray for Your Dying Husband at Three O'Clock in the Morning*.

But the yellow book was there. So I flipped quickly to the table of contents and stared at the longest list of prayer categories I'd ever seen in my life.

"Simple Prayer." Wrong one.

"Formation Prayer." Wrong one.

"Covenant Prayer." Wrong one.

"Meditative Prayer."

"Contemplative Prayer."

Foster listed twenty-one different kinds of prayer. But finally, way at the bottom, there it was. Chapter 17: "Intercessory Prayer." I fumbled for the page and started reading out loud.

"If we truly love people . . ."

"No, no!" I groaned out loud. Then: "Yes! Yes, God, I love my husband," I shouted at the book, probably looking and sounding foolish. Then I got quiet.

Calmly, I said out loud: "Yes, heavenly Father, I love my husband, Dan, and he's sick and he needs me to pray for him and he needs you to hear it. So, dear God, help me tonight to pray right."

I asked for forgiveness, indeed, for being so unloving.

Then I scoured the chapter, reading out loud but looking for what—advice? The right words? The right method? I wasn't sure. But finally, after searching page after page, I turned one more page and there it was. A chapter called "Healing Prayer."

I took a deep breath and started to read. "Healing prayer is part of the normal Christian life."

The calm, sure words of a faithful man rose off the page. They seemed to reach out and embrace me, leading me page by page—not to a method or a technique—but to a calm assurance that God was there.

So the calm words took me by the hand, and I sat on the side of my bed, reading. Listening.

⟡

Four A.M.

I rushed down the hall to my office and flipped on the light.

Within seconds, I had booted up my computer and started typing, fingers flying, as I searched for e-mail addresses for friends and family and even coworkers—anyone I suspected of being a believer—to join me in praying for Dan.

So like the prayers I had written out just weeks before, I wrote out a prayer for Dan. Only this time it felt like a gift. It felt as if God, who had shown himself to me so beautifully in the past weeks—when I was hungering to learn to pray but didn't know why—was now here with me.

I talked to the Father. I wrote for an hour. Maybe longer. And during that time, I stopped to be still. I listened. I praised God, knowing that if I had ten thousand tongues, they wouldn't be enough to thank him for hearing these words of prayer.

By 5 A.M., the prayer was finished. I pasted it into the e-mail space, then hit the Send button and propelled a prayer for my dying husband into eternity. It was a prayer but maybe it was also a song:

> Oh dear God, in the name of Jesus, your healing Son, and by whose stripes we are healed of every infirmity, we pray right now.

That's how it started. I didn't know how the words were coming, but I kept typing, daring to list *by number* the things we should pray for.

Number 1: The complete healing of the fistula at the base of Dan's brain stem. Number 2: The restoration of every function and sensation in his body. Number 3: The discernment and skill of every medical person involved in Dan's case. Number 4: The reversal of any inflammation and swelling in and around Dan's spine. Number 5: The cessation of any pain in his shoulders and neck.

The prayer went on for pages as I asked people to *visualize* Dan's healing:

> . . . *seeing in our minds and believing in our hearts, Lord, your powerful reordering to correction of every problem in his body right now!*
>
> *God, we see the swelling and inflammation going down and going away. We see the veins and artery connections returning to normal. And we even see Dan healed, restored to his feet and walking again with total normal function, with joy, and without pain—all for your glory! Hallelujah.*

Going on like this, I urged the prayer circle to pray for every patient in the surgical ICU to be healed.

> *I can't remember them all, Lord, but you know them—even the number of every hair on their heads.*

I went on, insisting:

> *By the blood of Jesus, we hold captive every negative thought around these and Dan's situations—especially any well-intentioned but ineffective, wrong-centered, or wrong-minded prayers by any of us for Dan, and especially any fears or any evidences of faithlessness in you by any of us.*

Then I prayed for us to loose in heaven—by the power and authority that raised Jesus from the dead—*every positive and heavenly power to heal Dan completely.*

> *Oh, God, we see it!*
>
> *We believe it, and like Bartimaeus in the good Gospel of Mark, we receive Dan's healing on his behalf, and in Jesus' mighty and precious name, by faith—itself a marvelous gift from you.*

The sum of it all was this: We were inside the secret chamber with God. We were praying by faith. We were praying with authority. We were praying with insight. And this was the crazy but holy thing—we were praying God's prayer for Dan back to God.

In fact, Jesus himself, the Bible promised, "ever liveth" to pray for each of us.

Jesus—praying for Dan?

I'd had maybe four or five hours of sleep, but I was riveted by the promise that Jesus, not to mention my sleepy, ragtag band of prayer warriors across the country, was praying for my husband.

Praying together. Praying in faith.

Praying to cheat death.

Praying to heal our own souls.

We prayed over the next critical days, and then the beautiful and the unlikely: Miracles began to happen.

First, before the sun came up that night, the peace came. Peace that flooded my spirit. I'd never felt such peace, as if the peace itself was a real, physical entity, holding back some torrent of terror and anxiety that threatened to pour in and overwhelm everything. There was enough happening soon, a nearly eight-hour surgical ordeal that could kill my husband or leave him permanently paralyzed and speechless. And these things should have terrorized all of us. But the peace that came had its own presence. I could have reached out and grabbed it.

Then came the second round of unexpected miracles. Within a day, the prayer circle began to report back with miracles.

> "I've been blessed so much by praying for Dan. I can't explain it. . . ."
>
> "Just wanted to tell you that the changes in my life while I've prayed for Dan have been remarkable. . . ."
>
> "Thank you for inviting me to pray. What a blessing it has been. I can't tell you how much."
>
> "Something has happened! This prayer time has changed so much in my life, and the lives of my family around me. . . ."

The stories kept trickling in, phone call after phone call, e-mail after e-mail.

It seemed miraculous. Then it seemed crazy. How could I, a run-down Christian—with just a few weeks given to the study of prayer and a lifetime record of *unanswered* prayer—inspire this?

Or as one of the prayer members asked: "How did you learn to pray like *that?*"

The question stunned me. What did I really know of the deep secrets of prayer? I was just a scratched-up, middle-of-the-road Christian, working halfheartedly at a state university, where the very idea of praying to an unseen God, let alone the act of praying, could get me laughed off my campus if not out of a job.

But this prayer journey had already started.

That's what the pages of this book would become: a walk through half a life that started with innocent and rote and mimicking prayer—*Now, I lay me down to sleep*—a life that took many detours, that traveled many roads, then ended with me back on my knees.

I'm there on my knees tonight as I think about my beloved husband who would face the biggest hurdle of his life: the fight to stay alive.

I'm there on my knees as I think about my younger daughter—who, at the moment of my husband's surgery, had left our Christian faith to embrace another. Her choice had sent me reeling. So I pray.

I'm there on my knees as I think about her sister—a single mom, struggling on that morning to run her own small business, even while she believed that the Lord would strengthen and keep her. So on her behalf, I pray.

I'm on my knees, to be sure, as I think about my widowed mother who had already survived the worst—the death of my father, the loss of all her siblings and many friends, a cancer diagnosis, and the frustration of a daughter (that would be me), who, no matter what I did, seemed to keep failing to honor her and help her through her graying days.

Indeed, I'm on my knees, trembling indeed, as I dare to believe that a prayer memoir like this might move others to vow to learn to pray.

So this can't be an idle journey.

Prayer, as Richard Foster said, "is the deepest and highest work of the human spirit." In real prayer, Foster added, we think God's thoughts. We desire the things that God desires. We love the things that God loves. We will the things that God wills.

But there is more, I learned. Isn't there always?

In real prayer, we go places we don't want to go. We learn lessons we don't want to learn. We tell secrets we don't want to tell. We walk bridges we don't want to cross. We face battles we don't want to fight.

Then we change the world.

We stand at the door to heaven and then we rush in.

But as we go, we change ourselves. "To pray is to change," wrote Foster, and with those few words he pulled together the deep essence of it all.

Renita Weems said the point of a journey is the going, "the movement and the traveling, not just the arriving."

I just wanted to save my husband's life and then get a life that mattered.

But as I travel, I get ahead of myself. Like real prayer, real journeys take time.

Mine can start here.

Mine can start now.

PART TWO

The School of Prayer

Call to me and I will answer you and tell you great and unsearchable things you do not know. JEREMIAH 33:3

It's Easy

For my yoke is easy to bear, and the burden
I give you is light. MATTHEW 11:30

God desires honesty. So I will start with the easy truth.

I was afraid of God at first. As a child, that is, I was afraid. Well, perhaps not Deuteronomy afraid—as in "Fear the Lord your God, serve him only and take your oaths in his name." True, that is a good way to live and a wise rule for anybody to keep.

As a child, however, I was afraid of what hanging around God could do to a person. Primarily I was afraid I might grow up to become like one of the stewardesses at Cleaves Memorial Christian Methodist Episcopal Church in Denver, Colorado. In fact, I loved these women and still do.

But as a child, I was afraid I might grow up to *look* like one of the stewardess sisters at Cleaves. That meant wearing a starchy white dress, a square black cap on my head—held down with black ribbons tied in a bow under my chin—and, even worse, those plain, black brogan shoes, not to mention the white stockings. Nobody but a prune-hearted sad sack would wear white stockings and brogan shoes. Well, isn't that right?

I didn't know. Fear can make us guess wrong. But the getups were standard uniform back then for stewardesses at Cleaves, and the women wore them every Sunday, sitting so starched and ready on the first two rows in the center section of the overheated sanctuary. Wearing brogans and black caps, however, wasn't the worst part of being close to God, as I saw it. The worst part was the shouting.

All that hollering and running up and down the front of the church: "Jesus! Jesus! Oh, thank you, Jesus! Thank you, Jesus! Thank you, Jesus!"

They were like women possessed. The last thing I wanted to do was to grow up and be possessed by God. If possession is nine-tenths of the law—or whatever the legal fraction is supposed to be—I knew I'd never surrender myself to a God who would slay me in the Spirit, then steal my self-control. Throwing up my purse while my hair bun unraveled, shouting "Thank you, Jesus! Praise you, Lord" was one step too far.

That is what I said then anyway. So, yes, things change.

At the time, however, there was something else. The stewardesses looked old. No, older than old. And I never, ever wanted to look that old. Even when I got old, I didn't want to look that old—even though at the time the women were, at the most, just middle-aged and not that old after all.

But to a child like me they were ancient. Some of them looked as if every drop of blood had been drained from their sanctified bodies. And the only thing left was thinning bones and dry, colorless skin. And, yes, these were *colored* women—Negro women. But some of them had the countenance of sad, colorless life. Too young to understand their sadness, I focused on their clothing—the colorless dresses, the black bonnets, the sad brogans—as they fell and fainted together in front of the altar.

This is where I started out in religion: Worried about looks in church more than my heart. And the stewardess sisters, more than other people at the church, looked "religious." They left me terrified.

In contrast, Cleaves had its ushers. *Much* better to become one of them. And much better still to *look* like one of them. Ushers sported trim black skirts. Kick pleats in the back. Silky white blouses jazzed up with lacy white handkerchiefs tucked inside the breast pocket. High-heeled shoes—black pumps with pointy toes. Some ushers even wore pumps with open heels, showing off the back of their smooth feet, feet surely lotioned and pumiced and oiled so they could wear the best thing of all: sheer black stockings. So with the trim black skirts with the kick pleats and the stylish black heels, those sheer stockings were the limit. Their legs were beautiful.

But that wasn't all.

Ushers also wore perfume, some of them. You could smell it when they hugged the saints good-bye after church—the scent of Wind Song or Topaze or L'Air du Temps wafting up from the V in their blouses or rising off their caramel-colored necks and their pretty ear-bobbed ears.

The whole effect of their aura was a joyful combination of feminine hospitality. As they stood smiling at the double wooden doors, the ushers' warm demeanor said *Welcome! Come on into God's house.* Standing there, wearing white cotton gloves, each usher held a neat stack of church bulletins—the ones with airbrushed colored people on the cover—and handed them out so primly one by one, while they tapped the toes of their pumps to the gospel piano pounding away at the front of the church. The ushers could have been hosting a big party.

Their red-lipstick smiles looked like candy.

The best thing about ushers, however, was that they hardly ever fell out, slain by the Holy Ghost. They were too busy passing out bulletins, collecting dollar bills and coins in the shiny, gold-tone offering plates, welcoming visitors, and passing out the mortuary fans to revive the stewardess sisters—many of them laid out, sometimes prostrate on the carpet in front of the altar, by the sheer energy of praising God.

Sitting so close to the front of the church like that, the stewardess sisters were awash in the music, the preaching, the rustle of the minister's robes as he passed their pew on his way to the rostrum.

He would begin to sermonize, speaking slowly and softly at the beginning, then letting his voice grow until, at the end, he was fairly roaring from the platform—"And then GOD, I say *God Almighty himself* will deliver *you*"—and those final words just did it.

The stewardesses leaped to their feet, clapping their hands, jumping up and hollering, "Thank you, Jesus! Thank you, Jesus!" Or they would be overcome unto unconsciousness, slumped lifeless in their seats, their black hats knocked sideways or knocked off completely, while the pretty ushers fanned away happily, trying to revive them.

So I looked at this contrast and decided that I did not want to be a shouting, fainting stewardess woman. Instead, I'd be an usher. I'd learn their secrets, and when the time was right, I would grow up and develop into a woman who looked and acted just like one of them.

I was about four years old.

One Sunday it happened that the head usher invited me home after church to have a Sunday dinner with her. My parents had known her for years, so they said yes.

After church, she gathered up her purse and white gloves, took me by the hand, steered me out of church, and helped me into her Pontiac sedan. We drove the four or five blocks to the apartment building where she lived properly alone in a second-floor walk-up.

As we climbed the stairs, located on the outside of the building, I felt first grown-up and then free. No parents around. Nobody to say no, stop, don't—as my parents often did. So I skipped lightly up the stairs, trailing the pretty head usher, following her lovely black high-heeled shoes, eager to see the secret rooms of her life, this head usher's *apartment*.

To me, this was like traveling to Paris, wherever that was. Yes, my mother kept Evening in Paris perfume bottles on her dresser top. Walking the stairs to this apartment felt like spraying on some of that, which I secretly did once, then going out. Or maybe this was even better. I wasn't going to a house with grass around it, like our house—and like the homes of my parents' friends. Instead, climbing painted wooden stairs on the outside of a three-story building on my way to an apartment—without my parents— was *better* than traveling to Paris.

When we got to the second-floor landing, passing doors with numbers on the outside, my little heart was pounding. Then we finally arrived at the usher's place—her door, of course, nicely painted. Next to the peephole, the door wore some kind of religious plaque. Later I would learn what it said: "As for me and my household, we will serve the Lord."

This usher's household was only her, however. She was a divorcée, as my mother described it, putting the accent on the final *e*. This usher's boys were all grown—one maybe in prison, I had heard. Despite everything, she was holding on. And she was crazy about little girls, but she had never had any. So here I was.

She unlocked the painted door and led me inside. I held my breath, longing for a scene of exotic beauty. But behind the door was a plain, clean room. Ordinary furniture. Sofa, table, lamp. Some magazines, a few books, a Bible on a bookshelf, a hardwood floor, bare but clean. The usher smiled at me.

So I joined her in her tiny kitchen, easing through the small doorway, watching her complete our meal. She put plates of cold chicken and potato salad and glasses of lemonade on dinner trays and we sat down in a little sitting area. The usher blessed the food.

We ate and she talked to me.

"Do you like Sunday school?" she asked, chewing but dainty.

I told her that I did.

"I like the stories," I said, chewing but dainty too.

"What's your favorite?" she wanted to know.

I didn't know. There were so many.

"I like all of them," I said.

The usher laughed.

"I like them all too," she said.

"Which ones?" I asked.

"Daniel in the Lions' Den," she said.

"What else?" I asked.

So the usher went down her list, and it turned out we liked the same stories: Elijah and the raven, Jesus feeding the five thousand, the Good Samaritan.

Then she asked me if I had any favorite songs.

"I can sing 'Jesus Loves the Little Children,'" I said. "Want to sing it?"

Good idea, she said. So we sang a chorus of "Jesus Loves the Little Children." Then we sang it again because she said that I had a sweet voice.

Then she cleared away our plates, and a few minutes later, she brought in dessert—a slice of buttery pound cake with sliced strawberries marching around it, all of it sitting on a pretty plate. It was maybe the nicest ending to any dinner I'd ever eaten in life.

Years later, when I did become an usher myself, I would read the usher's guide and meditate on the ministry of hospitality. That perhaps is what drew me to the usher boards, their glad service and their welcoming ways. This woman put a face on Jesus, and it was pleasant and loving. So we ate, pleasant and loving, not talking, but content.

Then soon she told me to get my things, and she led me, hand in hand, back down the wooden steps to her Pontiac sedan. Then she drove me safely home.

She was, in that way, the hands and face of God.

I thought for years that I met God in church, and that church is where God lived and where he stayed and where you prayed to him, by shrieking and hollering and falling out and crying, "Thank you, Jesus!"

This was talking to God, or so I thought. I saw folks talking to God every Sunday. And it looked hard. For years, in fact, I thought prayer was the hard moaning and the shouting and the falling out and the fanning with the mortuary fans.

And look what I didn't know—that prayer was just taking time to be with God, and that his presence, so unseen and so present in the very same moment, was not unlike a refreshing taste of pound cake before you swallow it, chased by a compote of red strawberries sitting lightly on your tongue.

This is being with God. It is like eating cake. Sweet and pleasant and easy.

Church had made God look so hard to get to—forcing you to fold yourself inside out and turn into a crying, shrieking woman done up in brogans and white stockings before he would hear you say thank you. Now it turns out that God doesn't mind the crying and the hollering, or even the brogans and the starchy dresses and the white stockings. But he doesn't need them.

God just wanted me to come over to where he was and to sit down. To take a walk up some painted wooden stairs and stay awhile.

He was that good. He was that big.

So God was bigger than the details of church, bigger than whatever "going to church" itself meant. God was deeper and higher and wider than the Morning Hymn and the Responsive Reading and the Old and New Testament lessons and the offering in the gold-toned plates.

Those things were like little moments of human strain and effort to get God's attention and maybe to look a bit like God.

But maybe God didn't even go to church himself, not all the time anyway. Or maybe while we were praying and shouting and pounding our gospel tambourines and sashaying around in our choir robes, while we were cutting our eyes at the soprano hitting the wrong note, God was cutting out to go someplace else. Maybe he took off for a minute for the other side of town. Or maybe he was down the street, four or five blocks over.

Or maybe he was eating supper in a walk-up apartment with a pretty mother whose boys were all grown, a lovely servant of God who still liked to wear her high-heeled shoes. Even though some people in church gossiped about her, whispering that she had no business clicking all over the sanctuary in those patent-leather shoes—and with her heels out too— God liked her in those shoes. He liked seeing her there in the sanctuary. He knew she liked his stories and he liked hers.

Talk to me, he said.

And late at night, when the woman opened her Bible and looked at the pictures of her grown boys that she kept in there—even the one who was in prison—God listened. They were friends.

Praying is like *that*. Sometimes, anyway, it is as easy as picking up the phone and calling a good friend. When the friend answers and you say, "Girl, you sitting down?" this friend laughs and says yes, already chuckling with you. So you lean back in the moment and just talk. The two of you.

Prayer is like that.

If you know what you are doing, it is like that.

If you know the One you are talking to, it is like that.

If your motives are right, it is like that.

Two good friends—just talking.

God Is Bigger

Then all the kingdoms of the earth will know that
you alone, O Lord, are God. 2 KINGS 19:19

So the sun was shining the morning of my husband's surgery. Good, warm
sun. A loving and easy thing.

That's how things felt—vivid and dazzling and loving—as I drove to the
University of Colorado Health Sciences Center for my husband's critical
surgery. But traffic seemed light. So I arrived just before seven, early
enough to visit with him, hug him, hold him, see his warm and easy face.

I was tired. But I also felt refreshed, in an odd and illogical way, almost
as if I'd slept like a blanketed, happy baby all night. I felt content and
loved—if, in fact, that's how a blanketed baby feels.

Also, I felt alert. All senses seemed galvanized. Or magnetized. Or elec-
trified—so wired for action that I could shoot off like a rocket, flying
through the heavens, soaring through the dazzling sky and in an instant
reach that easy sun. I was that primed, that pumped. A lit fuse. So I wasn't
lolling around, looking for crystal-colored frost glistening on the sidewalk
under my feet. But I saw the frost now, each glistening shard a shining gem
of natural beauty, each step on that sidewalk a precise and purposeful
crunch, moving me onward, sharpening my pace.

So I wasn't looking for brilliant sunshine creasing a big, cloudless sky.
But, wow, I could see it now. My dark sunglasses, normal for Colorado,
couldn't hold back the piercing morning sun. So I squinted, shielding my
eyes with gloved hands.

I thought of the office secretary on my campus, who just up and quit one day, announcing she was moving to Seattle or Portland or some other rainy place because "there's just too much sun in Colorado. Almost *every single day,*" she added, holding a palm over her eyes as she stood behind her desk to complain.

At the time, I had thought her logic was odd—the gripe of a moody, sour whiner. What kind of person hated sunshine?

But maybe she was right. The sun's rays here were intense, resplendent, acute. On this morning, however, the sun felt like a blessing. I opened the top button of my coat and let the heat pour in.

I needed the warmth to burn off my lingering fear, or the threatening terror, about this day. Despite God and all of his promises, all of his sweetness of the night before, this day could go bad. Surgery could go wrong. The worst could happen. My husband, lying inside the tall brick hospital at the end of the street, could find this day to be his last. I knew it. He knew it.

But I was also aware of God, and of spending the long night with him. So while I should have been half-crazy with terror, I felt almost cozy with confidence. I felt bigger than my fear. I felt bigger than the facts.

I felt prepared—as ready as I knew how—for what I didn't know and what I couldn't see.

I had taken a quick, hot shower, in fact, before I left the house to make sure I was awake but mainly to wash off anxiousness from the day before. Also, I wanted to look beautiful for my husband. To look like health. Like the time I had surgery and my mama visited me in the hospital the next morning. She floated into my room in a hot-pink velour running suit, carrying pink azaleas and waving a funny card.

She was uncanny and beautiful and glowing, like the flowers she offered—petals abloom with perfume and hope. By the time her visit ended, I couldn't wait to obey her funny card that said: Get well soon.

On Dan's surgery day, I wanted to look as velvety and cheerful and lush and healthy and hopeful as my mother and her pink azaleas. So I would wear, let's see. Yellow? *Sunshine* yellow. Good color on me. Maybe even a great color. Soft and pleasing, maybe even loving. So God knows I needed to wear yellow and plenty of it. And lipstick, red lipstick. I'd wear a clean pair of soft jeans. I'd also wear the only yellow thing I could find, which looked so right even though it sounds so wrong: a clean University of Colorado alumni sweatshirt—yellow here to yonder—with sharp black CU letters emblazoned across the front. *Yeah* and *Go Buffs!*

I laughed out loud. This was good. This was God. Only God would know that wearing a CU alumni sweatshirt to the University of Colorado Hospital on the day when my husband's life hung in the balance would be a good thing.

I had drenched myself in the shower, dressed fast, and grabbed my purse and a book on prayer—Andrew Murray's challenge: *With Christ in the School of Prayer.* Learning prayer secrets, Murray warned, "can only be learned in the school of much prayer, for practice makes perfect."

Yes, so true. But I was in a hurry, so I had tucked the book in my bag. Grabbed my cell phone. Hustled up some bottled water. Grabbed my Bible. Folded slippers into my bag.

This might be a long day.

⁘

At the hospital's big, automatic main doors, I took a deep breath. Hospital sounds met me too fast. Swishing doors and opening elevators and gurneys and wheelchairs with rubbery wheels on overly waxed linoleum floors all screamed *hospital.* A sprawling floor mat inside the door bore a huge motto: "Far Beyond the Ordinary."

In a couple of years, this hospital would relocate to new property in Aurora, Colorado, assuming a fresh and modern atmosphere in new buildings. Far beyond the ordinary, indeed.

For now, however, this was still the old University Hospital, and it possessed a worn-hospital look, its brick facade fortresslike and fading.

Young medical people rushed by, looking sober and intelligent and tired, but mostly looking young. Medical schools were graduating babies these days. Well, very smart babies—bright and earnest and hardworking and wearing serious occupational shoes. But even with their thick-soled clogs they looked young.

An elevator lifted me wearily to ICU. The waiting room was almost empty. A woman with red hair slept under rumpled blankets on a corner chair. An Asian couple, silent and staring, sat side by side, holding hands on a couch.

I pressed the button and was buzzed into the patient area.

In ICU, the young nurses looked up briefly as I entered. Nobody smiled. They were focused on patients. No one said much more than good morning. So I took off my coat and in my bright yellow sweatshirt walked toward Dan's big ICU room, the last one on the corridor.

Along the way, I passed the lineup of critically sick patients, each displayed behind the window of a big room for all of the nurses to see.

These patients were sick, indeed. And they looked so exposed. Women without makeup, hair askew. Balding men without their teeth. This was somebody's spouse, a wife or husband. Somebody's daughter or somebody's son. Someone whole and lively was, by illness or accident, now reduced to a still and silent bundle under piles of white sheets. A young man lay exposed to his waist, bare chest pierced with tubes and needles, a ventilator machine raising and lowering his bare shoulders as it breathed in his life for him, then pushed the breath back out.

In the room next to Dan's, a young Asian woman was lying silent on her bed, eyes partially open in a sedated stare, black hair splayed on the sheets. A car crash hadn't killed her. So she hung on, her room darkened, the lights dimmed, the morning sun held at bay by closed drapes on outside windows. A tower of monitors—measuring each breath, every heartbeat, any rise or fall in temperature, every variation in blood pressure and blood gases and every other vital measurement—was positioned by her bed.

This wasn't the hospital wing of newborn babies, so rosy and cute in little newbie cribs, pink and blue balloons everywhere and happy families all around.

In ICU, balloons didn't fly. Instead, I saw the unbearably sick. My husband, Dan, was one of them. The glass wall around his room was closed off with vertical blinds. Inside, my husband lay on his own exposed bed, connected to his own needles and tubes—saline drip, antibiotic, and one other liquid, silent and clear, flowing into his veins. The bedsheets covered him, disheveled a bit and brilliant white. I bounded in the doorway.

"It's so cold outside," I said, greeting him. "But the sun is brilliant." I smiled big, wanting to give off sunshine and health. This was my wife smile, big and welcoming, red lipstick on cheerful lips. But Dan stayed silent. So I stashed my coat and bag. I turned so he could see my cheerful yellow sweatshirt: University of Colorado alumni. *Go Buffs!*

I adjusted my sweatshirt. I waited.

Dan looked up at me briefly but still was quiet.

"Did you sleep okay?" I finally asked, still smiling.

He closed his eyes, slightly shaking his head, meaning no.

"It's worse," he mumbled, eyes still closed. I could barely hear him. His voice, usually so forceful and confident and deep, was trapped inside of him, like something big was smothering him.

My stomach tightened.

The look on Dan's face was straight fear. A real terror. I could see it in his eyes. He was trying to grapple with whatever swift, dangerous thing had overcome his body.

Some slick, tricky enemy—an enemy I thought I'd overwhelmed overnight by prayer—stared back.

Now Dan was telling me that despite my praying, he had actually gotten worse.

"Still can't feel anything?" I asked with surprise.

He shook his head no, looking over at me quickly, the fear full and obvious.

So I looked back at the fear, not understanding how a night of praying could leave me feeling so good and leave Dan feeling so defeated.

I thought prayer conquered evil enemies. It does. But on that morning, I didn't yet know two big things about prayer: that real prayer is persistent and that God is sovereign. God can grant peace, and at the same time, God can withhold promise. God decides how it goes. That's because of one true thing: God is God.

And me?

I was a beginner at knowing God—and at praying. Even after years of going Sunday after Sunday to the colored C.M.E. church and now to our A.M.E. church. Even after all of that—after singing in the choir and watching the sisters in their white-dress stewardess getups fall out in the Spirit and hearing the gospel music and basking in the good, preached Word of God—I was still a novice when it came to prayer.

One good night of great praying was just one first, small step.

We had miles to go.

I could see the distance in my husband's eyes.

⊰⊱

Two doctors came in, leaving the door open.

They wore name tags and I looked at them.

One said Dr. Breeze, the name from yesterday. The other I never learned. But I couldn't forget his kind, cheerful ways. They were the neurosurgeons I had met in the emergency room. But today they looked rested and focused. Everything about them looked keen and ready.

They looked, indeed, like surgeons. Today it was their eyes.

Dr. Breeze, tall and dark haired with a few hints of gray, was fine boned and elegant looking with piercing eyes that didn't veer for even a second off my husband. He moved around the room, but with every step he aimed his eyes at Dan. Looking. Studying. Looking.

Looking. The man was looking as if he could see right through him.

The other doctor, in contrast, was rounder—going toward plump—with a balding, once-blond head and an open, confident face. He wore a mustache and a smile, and it welcomed me. It said, *We're together in this. You're on our team. You're one of us.*

Yes, I wanted that, to share their confidence, be one of them.

But I didn't have their eyes. Or their beautiful, smooth hands. So I stepped back, leaning against the wall, as the doctors moved forward and circled the bed. Dan's breath was shallow as the doctors moved in to press and prick his body, asking him questions. Finally, one turned to me: "Your husband's loss of feeling continued to worsen overnight. He's really not feeling any sensation now, nothing from his feet on up to his shoulders. Right, Mr. Raybon?"

"So he's worse," I said, interrupting.

"We're getting him into surgery as soon as we can," the doctor said.

"I was hoping he'd be better," I said, and both doctors gave me a wan look.

But that's not what I wanted to see from them. And it's not what I wanted to say: *I was hoping he'd be better.* No, in fact, I wanted to *shout: I was praying all night! I was praying AND I was listening. I was listening to God Almighty himself. And now, praying people all over the city—no, all over the country—are opening up e-mail and lifting their hands and their hearts for Dan in prayer. Folks are praying, indeed. And God is answering.*

But the medical men were talking to each other. They used unbearable medical terms. They discussed the surgery, set to start as soon as they scrubbed, then reconnoitered their team downstairs in the operating room.

They gave me a kind look, both touching Dan on his shoulder in a comforting doctor gesture. Then they left the room, not bothering to close the door.

⁂

Dan closed his eyes. He was still breathing fast, going to the thoughts that a dying man has. But he wasn't sharing them with me. He looked gray and vulnerable under his pile of white sheets. He groaned a bit. I moved to check on him. Just then a dozen or so medical students stopped at the doorway with their rose-faced professor, a bald, clean-shaven man in a starched white coat.

The professor gestured toward my husband. "Okay, we've got a sixty-year-old male. Arteriovenous malformation, located in the spinal cord."

And with that, the entire student group came to attention, uttering together a low, dramatic moan. "Oh *no*." Then I could hear, one by one: "Wow, tough luck."

"Poor guy."

And on down the line. Maybe that was for their professor's sake. Or maybe they were genuinely horrified that Dan was so sick. But their groans, uttered together, consumed too much space. They seemed wrong.

Their professor picked up his litany: "Rapidly deteriorating loss of feeling and . . ."

I walked to the door and shut it.

We were surrounded by good medical people who saw the worst. Maybe they had to see the worst to make it better.

But Dan needed a more hopeful vision and he needed it now. I'd have to do what a good wife does: speak life when others saw death, use faith when others spouted fear.

I grabbed a chair and jerked it toward the bed. The chair legs scraped the floor and not too quietly. But I didn't care. I sat down facing Dan, lowering my face to his.

"Listen to this," I said to him.

He opened his eyes, still silent, but he was paying attention.

"Listen, sugar pie, I've been praying. Praying for you all night long."

He seemed to swallow hard, continuing to listen.

"I was praying and other people are praying for you too." I named names, listing good friends and praying partners. "Dale and Michelle, and Cleo, Delaris Carpenter, and the men in your choir. The Johnsons, the Materres, Lauretta and Cat, and all the people down in Atlanta."

I could see Dan's eyes water. There was something about knowing that people who love you are praying for you—not randomly, but praying in particular for you—because you need it. These were people who prayed like that, and Dan understood.

I had his full attention now and I wasn't letting go.

Now, in fact, I was a Christian wife talking to her Christian husband. I would have sounded kooky religious to anybody else, but not to him. He knew he must understand. He was paying attention.

"The Lord spoke to me last night," I said. Dan didn't bat an eye. I went on.

"I asked him to give me a word to give you." I paused. "And . . . I kept hearing it—that God is bigger."

I said it again. "God is bigger, sugar pie."

I knew Dan was scared, and I knew he wouldn't admit that. So I said it again: "God is bigger, bigger than anything you will face today in that operating room."

Dan nodded to show he understood.

"Whatever they bring your way, just tell yourself 'God is bigger.'"

Dan moved his mouth and I could hear him, barely a mumble. "God is bigger."

I put my face closer to his and rubbed his cheeks with my hands. "God is bigger, sugar pie," I whispered. "God is bigger and he loves you."

I love you too.

I didn't say it. We had argued so much over the summer. We had stopped touching. We had stopped hugging and comforting, and we had stopped loving. So how could I say I love you now and have it come out right? It would sound insincere and wrong and downright cheesy.

It would have sounded like what it was: An empty statement spoken too many weeks and months too late. I kissed Dan on the forehead, lingering there. I didn't know if he understood, but I wanted to think he did.

Then, as I held the phone to his ear so he could pray with our pastor before the surgery, the nurses started coming in.

⧏⧐

Intensive-care nurses are soldiers and angels, wrapped in armor and deep knowledge about hospital procedures and healing insight and care.

Dan's nurse on this morning was Heather, a ponytailed pack of no-nonsense power with business and healing on her mind.

She looked at me. She looked at my CU alumni sweatshirt. "Mrs. Raybon?"

I stood at attention.

"Downstairs, first floor, you've got to sign your husband in to surgery."

I didn't understand. He was already here in the hospital, waiting for surgery. Then the nurse explained that in yesterday's rush to get Dan from the emergency room into ICU, hospital staff had skipped one key step—actually admitting him, officially, to the facility for surgery.

"Look for the door marked 'Day Surgery Check-In,'" she told me. "Surgery can't start until you get down there and sign all the forms."

I grabbed my purse and book, gave Dan one more hopeful smile, then headed out of ICU for the elevators, past the nearly empty waiting room, beyond the red-haired woman, past the somber couple.

I was moving. I had a task to do. But I was walking on legs that felt like lumpy cotton, barely attached to my body. The effect was nerves and disbelief all jumbled together. Physically I was starting to feel it. A big and critical milestone was right around the corner. Dan would face a scalpel that could change our life—his life, for certain. Or maybe the scalpel would take his life. I didn't know the outcome, but I had to sign the papers to get the process started.

This isn't as bad as signing the okay to turn off a loved one's life support. That, surely, must be the hardest choice a wife or husband would ever have to make, or so it seemed. Still, I felt inadequate. Who was I to sign over my husband for surgery that could forever change everything?

I left the elevator at a fast clip. But each step was set in plaster. It didn't help that when I walked into Day Surgery Check-In, a TV attached to a wall was playing too loud and the room was already crowded.

The check-in nurse greeted me. Then she thumbed through a stack of files to find our name, Raybon. A stack of forms, paper-clipped together, emerged along with a pen. The nurse, whose name tag said Dianne, smiled efficiently, pointed to the spot on the first sheet where I was to sign. I placed my belongings on the counter in front of her and started through the stack of pages, signing here, initialing there.

Suddenly, the nurse put down her pen. Something had caught her eye.

It was my Andrew Murray book on prayer.

"You're reading that book?" she asked.

When I nodded yes, her smile brightened.

"Oh, I love Andrew Murray," she said. "I just finished studying *Abide in Christ*, another book by him. My mother sent it to me. I just loved it."

I was surprised. Andrew Murray is well-known in theological circles, but I'd never met a single other person who'd read one of his books—not anybody at my church or any other friend or Christian acquaintance.

As for *School of Prayer*, the book jacket said in the past seventy-five years only some 200,000 had read the book. That's on average 2,700 or so folks a year picking it up to read—hardly a runaway blockbuster by anybody's standards.

Maybe it was the language, all those *thous* and *thees*, *haths* and *hath nots*, *willsts* and *willst nots*. Every sentence felt seventy-five years old, not to mention looked too long. So I often had to read a line twice, like this one: "In Abraham, we see how prayer is not only, or even chiefly, the means of obtaining blessing for ourselves, but is the exercise of his royal prerogative to influence the destinies of men, and the will of God which rules them."

But after a couple of rereadings, I got the drift—that prayer isn't mainly to ask for our own blessings. Instead, prayer is a privilege, a sacred right, established in Abraham's case by his stature through his connection to God.

Thus: "We do not once find Abraham praying for himself," Murray wrote. "His prayer for Sodom and Lot, for Abimelech, for Ishmael, prove what a power a man, who is God's friend, has to make the history of those around him."

So Murray says prayer can change our loved ones' circumstances. This is our destiny, sealed by our lineage with God, he insisted. Then Murray's punch line: "Prayer is not merely the cry of the suppliant for mercy; it is the highest forth-putting of his will by man, knowing himself to be of Divine origin, created for and capable of being, in king-like liberty, the executor of the counsels of the Eternal."

Wow.

That's what I'd written in pen on this page of Murray's book: *Wow*.

Here was Murray, in his impossibly stuffy wording in his incredibly stuffy book, saying simply to ask. *Ask*.

Ask—because we're royal. We were born to the highest family in the universe. We spring from God's royal house. We are God's family. If we bear God's image, we can bear God's rule. So God can trust us with the privilege of asking in prayer—and *getting*—what the world, or any one person in the world, might need.

This was just one lesson in the Murray school of prayer, and the book had scores of them. Indeed, when this nurse, Dianne, said she'd been studying a Murray book, I understood that she meant *study*.

More important, here she was, in her cramped hospital office, right in front of me. God was presenting her to me. She was a gift. A prayer partner. A fellow believer. An intercessor, she was seated before me on the very morning that my husband needed intercession in ways that I couldn't imagine.

But nurse Dianne could imagine.

"Does your husband need prayer?" she asked.

Her question pierced my soul.

"Yes," I whispered.

"What's his name?" She looked at his folder. "Jesse?"

"No, it's Dan." I explained: "We use his middle name. Jesse's his first name. But we call him Dan."

Dianne looked at me evenly. She stood up. "That's my husband's name: Dan." As she said it, a pained look crossed her face.

I reached across the counter and grabbed her hand. She grabbed mine and squeezed.

"I'm going to pray for Dan," she said, offering a smile.

"He needs it," I said.

And me? I needed more Murray. More lessons. More practice. Murray said as much, that intercession is "part of faith's training school."

And suddenly, here I was in boot camp.

I had thought in recent weeks that I'd learned a few choice things about prayer. But I was just a babe in prayer. A little baby wearing a yellow CU alumni sweatshirt. *Yeah, go Buffs.*

⁜

Dan was lying on a gurney in an anteroom next to the surgery ward when I returned from signing the hospital papers.

I walked over and put my hand on his shoulder. White blankets were pulled to his neck. He lay very still, looking up at the row of lights in the ceiling. He smiled at me a bit. I laid my hand on his forehead.

I introduced myself to the nurse. She was full faced and pleasant looking, her cheeks rosy with busy efficiency. She wore starched blue scrubs and a puffy, baby blue skullcap that covered every inch of her hairline.

She was checking Dan's vital signs. His blood pressure was elevated. She rested her hand on Dan's as she checked his IV tubes. She was chatting softly, explaining to Dan the step-by-step procedures up to the surgery itself.

She told me she and others would be in touch with me during his operation. She checked my hospital beeper. She was assuring; she was comforting and caring.

Then the anesthesiologist, draped in a long coat, came around the corner and stopped at Dan's bed. Dan's blood pressure and pulse rose, flashing the higher numbers on the monitors at the side of his bed.

The anesthesiologist had read Dan's chart. He asked the questions we'd answered before. The questions were a litany:

"Mr. Raybon, are you allergic to any medicines?"

"Mr. Raybon, are you allergic to any foods?"

"Are you . . . ?"

Dan, at some point, shut his eyes. Maybe he couldn't hear this. Or maybe he was talking to God and didn't want to be bothered. I turned to the anesthesiologist and this doctor understood. He finished up his questions with me.

Then Dan's surgeons, looking serious and alert, entered the room. One of them spoke, loudly I thought. But he wanted to make sure we understood.

He had yet more papers for us to sign, giving the hospital permission to do the surgery, despite the risks. They were bad. To put it bluntly, Dan could die. His chances were about fifty-fifty, the doctor said. Bad odds. A cup half-full. A cup half-empty. Dan opened his eyes for this, maybe listening as I was with tuned ears. But I am positive that we weren't really hearing this. We were hearing it, but we didn't *want* to hear it, even if it was imperative that we hear it.

So what next?

If he survived, the doctor said, he could be paralyzed from the neck down.

Dan blinked hard. I listened, nodding, but I wanted to scream.

This wasn't idle information. Dan could only hear it from some place of great emotional distance. I could only listen, from that same indescribable distance. But neither of us could respond. I could only nod and Dan couldn't even do that.

The doctor kept talking. He said again paralysis could mean that Dan would not regain function from the main location of the surgery, which would be near the nape of the neck, right down to his feet. The odds of this, he said: About fifty-fifty.

More bad odds.

So what next?

If he survived and wasn't paralyzed, he could still face brain injury—from mild to severe.

Then: If he survived, wasn't paralyzed, and didn't have any brain injury, he would still face extensive rehabilitation. He'd have to learn to walk again, of course. He'd have to learn again how to control bowel and bladder function. He'd have to overcome the emotional trauma of battling a serious illness.

And on and on.

So what next?

If we agreed to the surgery, after knowing all of this, I should sign here. The doctor handed me a pen.

I signed my name.

Then other nurses and doctors gathered, a team of people now preparing to move Dan's bed into the operating room.

I leaned toward my husband, put my face close to his, and I didn't just smile, I gave him a laugh.

"God is bigger," I told him. I shrugged. Nothing more did he need to know.

"Just keep saying it," I whispered.

I kissed Dan again on the forehead, letting my lips linger there. Then I kissed him on the lips.

He kissed me back.

Look for Jesus

Simon Peter answered, "You are the Christ,
the Son of the living God." MATTHEW 16:16

My husband's sister, Diana, was on her way. Thank you, God.

She was his sole living family member, in fact. So she dropped everything in New Jersey, where she lived with her husband of thirty years
and where she was an award-winning elementary school principal and
a devoted mother of two grown children. She would fly now to Colorado
to be with her beloved only brother, Dan.

To say Dan and Diana were close doesn't capture it. Their mother died
of cancer in her fifties, always too young. Their father died at eighty-one
after a long fight with emphysema—and after a longer, disastrous second
marriage to a woman whom Diana and Dan honestly hated.

To say "hate" in a Christian family is a hard thing. But when it came
to their father's second wife, they never minced words. They couldn't
abide her.

The truth is the truth.

So there was more. Dan's father, a beautiful and generous man, also was
a drinker. Dan and Diana didn't hide this. They grew up watching him,
knowing his daily habits. His scotch on the rocks. His crazy-looking rye.
His endless chain-smoked cigarettes. His long-necked beers in the morning. His scotch on the rocks in the afternoon.

As grown kids, they vowed to help him. But when he married again, he
chose a woman who would join him at the bottle, match him cigarette for

49

cigarette, argument for argument. So nightly, by the end of dinner, the living room reeked of liquor and smoke. That's when the arguing started. Then more booze. Then more booze and more arguing. Then arguing and *more* booze. *More* arguing and booze. More cigarettes and arguing. Long into the night. Long past Leno. Way past Letterman. Still arguing and booze. And too much smoke for anybody to half-breathe.

Dan and Diana worried in agony about their beloved father. Their childhood home never had seen such chaos, not when their mother was alive. Their dad, now in his seventies, deserved better. Besides, he was their prince. Or maybe, as Dan always said, he was a man in search of a kingdom—a place to rule and to be more than who he was, a retired postman. Still, he was their king, their Sir Lancelot–Robin Hood–Prince Charming. He was a dad who brought home candy and cold pop and bubble gum when they were kids—and forget about the cavities, he said. If your teeth fall out, we'll buy you some new ones.

He made them laugh. He took them to movies on Saturday mornings. He bought them cheeseburgers on Saturday afternoons at the Negro grill across the street. If they needed money for something big, and he didn't have it, he hunted through their basement to find a treasure to sell: old jazz records, his mother's antique dresser, old guns, barely used cameras, a box of first-edition books somebody had given him. He didn't sweat it. If his kids needed something, he made it happen.

This is love.

For better or worse, this is love.

Dan and Diana both, indeed, embodied perhaps their father's best quality: generosity. Or maybe it was his worst quality. Even when he wasn't asked, he was pulling money from his wallet, clothes from his closet, furniture from his basement, shoes from his feet, and the shirt off his back.

Dan and I argued about these gifts from him—the money especially.

"*Another* check from your father?"

I could condemn like a champ.

So Dan became defensive.

"What difference does it make? If he wants to send money, why's that *your* problem?" Dan stuffed the check in his wallet and turned to walk off.

"The difference," I said, not letting go, "is that he's a retired mailman on a fixed income. And I don't understand how you can take money from a retired mailman."

Dan turned back, looking sober.

"He's my father!"

"So? That makes it okay?"

"More than okay," Dan shot back.

This is where condemnation leads. To bitter words and harder hearts. Still every month, I questioned. That's how often the money would come.

Then we argued, ignoring what marriage experts say: Conflicts are likely to end on the same note that they began. So my "start-ups"—as psychologist John Gottman calls the opening words of marital bickering—were always harsh.

I nagged, refusing, as Richard Foster put it, to "lay down the everlasting burden of always needing to manage others." Or, as Foster also said, "When we genuinely believe that inner transformation is God's work and not ours, we can put to rest our passion to set others straight."

I didn't understand that. And yet we took the money. We always needed it. It always came. So we always argued.

So one hot summer, there we were, visiting Dan's sister in New Jersey. She had an idea. Let's hit the mall. Take the kids. *This is good,* I thought. Walk the mall. Buy Icees. Drive back home. A nice, cheap outing for the children. But for Diana, the mall was a pleasure palace with chances to buy—without a second's hesitation—T-shirts and candy and cute purses and little plastic jewelry and Hot Wheels and jelly shoes and sunglasses and hair bobs or whatever else the kids were craving. She rarely said no.

Once I asked her about it. Her answer was quick. She laughed. "Dad bought stuff for us all the time. I don't even think about it."

She zipped her wallet and dropped it in her purse. "If somebody in my family wants something, and I can afford it, I buy it."

Our trips to St. Louis to see their father looked the same. Dan always left carrying good suits, straight out of his father's closet, and new shirts his father had just purchased, fresh from the store. Tags still flapping. Receipt in the bag. But his father pressed Dan to take them, always with the same argument: "I won't even use it. Here, take it."

As we climbed into Dan's blue Volkswagen hatchback, loaded down for the drive back to Colorado, Dan's father would always open his worn leather wallet. "Got enough for gas, Danny?"

He'd pull out three, four, five twenty-dollar bills—and Dan would take them. I'd grimace, wanting Dan to say, "Oh *no*, Dad. I wouldn't think of it. I can't take cash from a parent on a fixed income." Maybe I even thought it was sin to take the money.

Or maybe I thought that this family I'd married into didn't understand money. Their way looked wrong to me. But now I know why. I wasn't looking for the good in it. I hadn't learned Paul's lesson to be "generous to those in need, always being ready to share with others."

With the generous Raybons, it was, indeed, buy and spend and give—and for Dan's father, all of this came from a meager pension from his years as a St. Louis mailman. Sure, he'd owned a tavern once—his training ground for booze, in fact. But any profit from that business was long gone. Sure, after retirement to make ends meet, he took a job as a doorman at a fancy St. Louis condo. He was in his seventies. He wore a maroon jacket and opened doors for rich, busy people. At Christmas, the busy people gave him tips: ten dollars, twenty dollars, once a hundred-dollar bill from a Missouri senator who lived in the penthouse.

How could Dan accept such hard-earned money? Moreover, how could his father give it away—and with a laugh, no less? He just raised his high-ball with a wink and took a sip. "Cheers," he'd say, putting his wallet away before beginning to argue again with his second wife in a house that often needed repairs. His son, indeed, seemed destined for the same life, never having enough because he, too, gave away so much of the little he had. Handing out cash to any student on our campus who acted or looked in need when our own bills at home were overdue.

"*Two hundred dollars?*" I had shouted once at Dan. "You gave some kid *two hundred dollars*—to pay a bill—and we've got our own bills?!"

"It was an emergency," Dan answered, unconcerned.

Besides, money was for spending, not keeping. That's how he saw it. So spread it around. Use it, especially to help somebody. And helping was their family way. Their giving looked like Jesus, if I had been looking for Jesus then. But I couldn't see Jesus in my husband. Didn't think to look for Jesus in a spendthrift man.

In fact, I wanted Dan to be different. To be like *my* father.

My goodness. An accountant by training, my father could account for nearly every penny he'd ever earned. My father had invested wisely and well. Mutual funds. Annuities. Savings accounts. Life-insurance premiums. The odd savings bond or two. His house was paid in full. So were his cars. He was, in fact, utterly and aggressively debt free.

Anybody who still thinks black people are lazy and poor never met Brother William Amos Smith. Not only did he work nearly every day of his life, he saved all his life. Moreover, he invested most of his adult life, and all of this saving and working and investing and putting away paid off. For a civil servant, who labored thirty-four years for the federal government, he was flush with the proceeds of saving and working.

Then he died. He was too young, just sixty-eight. A bout of pneumonia turned aggressive, and he couldn't rally. So my daddy went to the cemetery, and the savings—all of it, earned so hard and counted and watched for so long—stayed right here.

In fact, when my father died, he left my mother without a financial worry in the world. She wanted him here with her, still alive. But for consolation, such as it was, she could forever buy whatever she wanted in life.

In contrast, when Dan's father died at eighty-one, most of what he had owned was long gone. A garage sale disposed of the remainder of his possessions.

When he passed, his family itself was a remnant. He left only one distant cousin—whom nobody could find—his children, Dan and Diana, and three stunned grandchildren. At his funeral, the brother and sister clung to each other in sober grief. Their mother was gone. Their father was gone.

And now this: Dan was himself sick unto death and Diana was in an airplane, rushing to be with him.

⁘

Diana would be praying.

Well, actually, I wasn't sure of that.

I hoped she'd be praying. But I just didn't know how. She and I didn't talk much about religion—about faith, that is. In fact, we were sisters-in-law, but in truth we weren't very close. Family by marriage can be awkward.

Moreover, we were young when we first met. I was just twenty-five, still trying to figure out how to figure out life. Diana was barely thirty. I wouldn't speak for her, but I came to our relationship with baggage. So I looked at her on the outside: A light-skinned black woman—pretty with long "good" hair, a beautiful new home in New Jersey, a lovely petite figure, an engineer husband with a good job and a seemingly great income. Always enough to buy.

I had none of that, nothing to compare. A brown-skinned woman—fifteen pounds past perfect and average-looking with short, coarse hair, that was me. I was divorced with a child and now married to Diana's brother. He, a junior administrator. Me, a grad student. We lived in a rented apartment and never seemed to have enough dough to bake our life.

So I was pious. Fear and jealousy breed it. I was the Bible-quoting, hand-clapping, Sunday-go-to-meeting, born-again Christian—so self-righteous, I don't know how she or anybody else could stand me. Church was my sanctuary. So when we visited New Jersey, I was up early on Sunday morning, eager to roll. Then there we were, entering my sister-in-law's quiet, cool church—a Catholic parish named for a mystic I didn't know: St. Bernard of Clairvaux. And hoity-toity to me too.

My hair was five minutes from frizz in the New Jersey damp. But the church was blessedly cool—and not hoity-toity.

"Forty-five minutes," Diana's husband, Mac, told us. The summer Sunday service would be quick, he said.

"In and out?" Dan asked, laughing.

"In and out," Mac agreed, laughing himself.

Meantime, Diana was beautiful: long, black hair curling around her shoulders, bouncing down her back. Her children were beautiful too: my new niece and nephew, two cute and precious kids.

I sat down on a hard wooden pew, next to my daughter, Joi, holding her hand. Dan sat on my other side, holding my hand. Maybe he was hoping, as I was, that if he held me down my hair wouldn't rise up to Afro before the forty-five-minute service ended.

But what a service. My first Catholic "church" experience. No real gospel music, not here anyway. Instead, a modest-looking woman played acoustic guitar and sang sweetly, her voice skipping over the pews.

I followed the songs and liturgy in a little book, pleased to see familiar sacred words. Then came the passing of the peace: "Peace be with you. And also with you." So refined. Shy people and soft voices and softer handshakes. Dan and Joi and I shook hands gently with strangers, offering our vacationer smiles.

Then a priest in white robes mounted the rostrum and delivered the shortest sermon I'd ever heard in my life. It evoked St. Bernard of Clairvaux (which means "clear valley," I learned). As a child, the priest said, the French-born Bernard looked one Christmas into a crèche at his family's church and saw the face of Jesus. The moment changed his life. The holy face taught him "to stop magnifying small transgressions," as one historian put it, to concentrate on the greater work "of forming devoted followers of Christ." So Bernard, with his clear-minded vision, did just that.

Well, I was enchanted. Even without a black gospel choir backing the preacher, the homily lifted my heart, smoothed out my mind, maybe even relaxed my hair. We got in line to take Communion—and a surprise and shock—the shining purple liquid was *wine*.

Then one final song. That was it. Sing amen and see you next Sunday.

"Forty-five minutes," Dan said, pointing to his watch.

Diana's husband broke into a laugh.

"What'd I tell you? In and out!"

The priest was shaking hands by the big doors out front.

"What a wonderful message," I told him. "I just loved it."

"And you are . . . ?" the priest asked.

Diana stepped in to introduce everybody. A polite, warm exchange. Everybody smiling. Soft handshakes.

"Come back when you're in New Jersey next time," the priest said.

"Absolutely," I told him.

But back in the car, Diana seemed unsettled.

"You didn't like it, Diana?" I asked.

"Church is okay, but it's so . . . bor-ing," Diana said. She is a bright woman, an award-winning educator. So she knows spiritual places can also be joyous and illuminating. They don't have to be dry. Besides, "boring" is too easy a way to define a religious experience that doesn't feel right. So she explained: "I'd rather commune with God in a beautiful park on a Sunday morning. But church?" She shrugged, dismissive.

I listened to this. But I didn't know how to answer.

Church, for my family, was a rich salve, better in some ways than being in our own home. At church, I could lean back in the building's plush, red, secondhand movie seats and let the gospel music from the Sunday choir wash over me in sloshing, warm waves.

A tenor might wail: "We are soldiers! In the army! And we have to fight, although we have to die!"

Saints would be on their feet then, waving arms, clapping hands, tapping toes to the thumping gospel piano, wiping tears from their glowing brown faces, soaking up the words.

"Yes! We have to hold up the bloodstained banner. Oh! Have to hold it up! And fight on—anyhow!"

On Sunday, always, our daddy would carry us to that music. He drove his '54 Dodge Coronet, the first car he ever owned. So the car was shining like a star—and at church, my father was transformed. At church, he was beautiful and starry and so we were beautiful and starry too—despite knowing that the world back then said we were, like all colored people, awful and ugly.

But at church, my sister and I were "sweet." We were "cute," of all the unlikely things. At church, my mother was important—teaching Sunday school and even running the Sunday school at one point, getting appointed by the pastor himself as Sunday school superintendent, with her name in the bulletin every Sunday. And Daddy?

At church, Daddy was magnificent.

At church, he stepped into a public personality that was expansive and wise and generous and kingly, and on him it looked royal. To some, Daddy *was* the church. He was Brother William A. Smith, trustee and chairman of the finance board and chief man in the pews, and he sang solos in the senior choir—"How Great Thou Art" and "Precious Lord" and "I'll Fly Away."

So at church, after all of this singing and beauty, our family would remember that we loved each other and act like it again, at least for a while until the week ran us down and the next Sunday would wait to come around again.

On Sunday, we returned once again to the fellowship. And the community of the saints shone down on us with its wonderful, rocking warmth and always—after the hugs and kisses and affirmation of this sister and that brother and the pastor, and all the ushers and stewards and stewardesses and fellow saints—we returned home smiling and renewed and redeemed.

My father, at church, would appear as an angel—a massive and handsome Gabriel in his satiny white choir robe, worn over his beautifully pressed "dress pants" and his white shirt, stiff with starch, and his tie—purchased downtown at the expensive men's store Cottrell's, where his good friend Tracy J. Smith was the first Negro salesman to get hired.

So Daddy's Sunday clothes were befitting a church trustee, church finance chairman, Sunday school teacher, senior choir member. In fact, nothing of consequence happened at that church that my father, while he was alive, didn't oversee or undertake or organize—and he wasn't even the preacher. If every church has a human pillar on whom the business and life of the church rocks and rests, at Cleaves Memorial Christian Methodist Episcopal Church that pillar was my father.

James Baldwin, in his first novel, *Go Tell It on the Mountain*, described this even better. "On Sunday mornings," Baldwin wrote, "the women all seemed patient, all the men seemed mighty."

This, in fact, is what I remembered most about church—that my father seemed mighty—and this is how I learned to love him. I loved him because he took me to the place where I was never loved better.

When I pushed opened the heavy, wooden front doors and ran back to my kindergarten Sunday school class, I was running for a certain heaven.

Our beloved teacher, "Miz Hall" as we called her, threw open her arms and shouted, "Look children, it is *Patricia!*"—announcing my name, rejoicing in it, as she did with the name of every child who entered her light. Then the big, rocking hug. "Aren't we glad to see *Patricia* this beautiful Sunday morning? Children, say, 'Good morning, Patricia, we are so glad to see you!'"

The other children looked up from their coloring sheets, grinning at Miz Hall, grinning at me, brown faces beaming, then chimed in unison: "Good morning, Pah-trit-cha—we are so glad to see you!" And so it went until we were all gathered around the low tables, each in a tiny chair, seated before our teacher, our Sunday angel.

Years later at Mrs. Hall's funeral, grown men—who'd been among her "little people," as she had called us—broke down in sobs as they passed her open casket. They understood that this was a woman who, besides loving children, greatly respected us. She taught us amazing stories about miracles and great battles and astounding people—folks whom we could emulate.

Then, after giving us graham crackers wrapped by her fragile hands in white paper napkins and cold juice in Dixie cups, she sent us on our way—assured that we were wonderful and could achieve anything. Through this, I suppose, I learned that other people should be valued.

This was the great sustaining message at our little church.

So to be bored with God things—or God's people—or to call church "boring" never would feel right to me. But how could I say that to a pretty, new sister-in-law with beautiful long hair?

-♦-

Would she understand? At age twelve, while sitting one Sunday on a pew with my clutch of church friends, I listened to the weekly sermon. Then when the preacher, a serene and handsome man named Rev. L. L. Barnes, made the altar call, I stood up.

I can't now explain why on that Sunday I did this.

I don't recall that it was a unique day, in any particular way.

I don't remember what I was wearing. I don't remember the worship songs or the sermon text or what exactly, on that day, moved me from my seat.

Maybe accepting the altar call said, in a public way, that God is real.

So that summer Sunday morning, I stepped out. Something pulled me off the pew. Maybe, in truth, it was the place itself, this place where I lived my childhood and learned every single thing that I knew about God and his Son and his Holy Spirit.

It was the comfort that I felt there, and the safety and affirmation that always surrounded me there. It was the adult Christians—good, kind, cheerful, helpful, hospitable, generous, joyous, down-to-earth, sanctified people. Phony and terrible people were probably members of our church too. But the people who loomed large, who still today will give me a great, rocking hug when I see them, weren't phony and terrible. They were real and wonderful.

That's what I wanted too: To be a Christian, real and wonderful. I longed to be like Jesus, to be good, kind, cheerful, helpful, hospitable, generous, joyous, down-to-earth, sanctified. Never then could I have predicted that parts of my life would later veer so far from this standard.

On that day, however, without first talking about it with my parents or my church friends, I stepped from the pew and walked toward the front, coasting up the red-carpeted aisle to the sounds of "Pass Me Not, O Gentle Savior."

Almost immediately, pandemonium broke out. The front-pew stewardesses descended on me in a wave. They were hugging me and rubbing my face and some were shouting, "Oh, praise the Lord! Praise you, Jesus!"

Eventually, my parents came forward, both looking surprised but pleased. They stood beside me, Mama on my left, Daddy on my right, along with Miz Hall and some of the others, all looking on with approval. Then the preacher descended from the pulpit, adding a word about the Lord moving in the hearts of even young people.

"Amen! Amen!" Everybody agreed.

The preacher then invited folks to give me "the right hand of fellowship." My clutch of friends and others stepped out to form a line down the aisle, everybody passing by and shaking my hand, some reaching for a hug.

After church, my mother looked at me and said, "I'm so proud of you!"

She was? Apparently, I had done something really important, even though then I didn't understand fully what I had done. Years would pass before I knew what it truly meant to "accept Jesus as your Lord and Savior." This was a phrase that I had heard all of my life. Only later would I learn that a relationship with Jesus could save me *and* turn me into a praying woman.

But on that Sunday, I was just a Negro girl who needed a home, and Christian people offered me theirs—our church. So I said yes.

Do prayer warriors start out on Sundays like this, giggling at friends while the Inspirational Choir sings "What a Fellowship"?

Maybe that's what Diana was missing. When she said church was "boring," perhaps she meant her church hadn't thrown out the lifeline.

⧊

Jesus. She hadn't met Jesus?

He was the Word. The Bible said this, and if I knew anything, I knew the Bible. Miz Hall saw to that. She and Mr. Bell, the Sunday school superintendent—and the first Negro salesman to work downtown at Denver's new Woolworth—drilled us on the Bible, singing songs about it, playing word games and Bible bingo and gospel musical chairs and every other manner of fun that colored Christian adults could conceive for mischievous, beloved children.

"So, look," Mr. Bell said, reading from the Gospel of John. "'And the Word was made flesh, and dwelt among us, (and we beheld his glory, the glory as of the only begotten of the Father,) full of grace and truth.'"

"And what's his name, children?" We always had the answer: *Jesus.* So easy to know. So easy to miss when I wasn't looking for him.

All along, indeed, I thought Diana was on the losing side, not loving church, not talking as I did every other minute about Bible things, about Jesus, about God, God, God.

I thought her father, with his scotch drinking and cigarette smoking and arguing and money-spending, money-lending ways, was on the losing side with her.

But more than that, for years I thought Dan was on the losing side too.

After all, *he* couldn't find the Gospel of John, not without a struggle. But like his sister, he loved from a place that I didn't understand. Like her, he loved despite flaws. Like her, he loved despite hurt. Like her, maybe he didn't know Jesus or all of his stories. But like his sister, he loved like Jesus. Without condition. Without limits. So really, they already knew an early lesson of prayer: Before you pray for folks, look for Jesus in them. Then love them, as Jesus loves.

Would Diana be praying for Dan? Wrong question.

The right one? Had I looked hard enough for Jesus in Dan that I could pray for my husband when he needed it so much? Looking not with eyes but with heart. In that way, the heart gets softened. And God must need

soft hearts to hear our prayers. Surely God must need us to look at each
other as he does, seeing not our flaws but seeing Jesus in us. Even in me.

So who could pray better?

We were in a storm, and Diana's sick brother—now deep in surgery—
was in the middle of it. But only one of us knew the story of Jesus walking
on the water, calming the wind, reaching out his hand to hold up a storm-
tossed Peter in the midst of his irrational fear.

No wonder the desperate Peter cried out: "Lord, save me!"

In my kindergarten Sunday school, I sat with my ankles crossed, following this story on the felt board. Miz Hall narrated, tacking the cutout
Jesus and Peter and the boat rocking to glory on the cutout-paper waves.

There was Peter, starting to sink, his face racked with fear, stretching
his shaking hands toward Jesus. "Lord, save me!" Miz Hall cried out.

But Jesus was so kind. Right away, he reached out his hand. He caught
the sinking Peter. Then he chastised him: "You of little faith," the cutout
Jesus said. "Why did you doubt?"

Sweet children, why? Why did he doubt? Miz Hall asked, her eyes searching ours. But, praise God, we knew the answer: Peter doubted because he
looked at the waves. Looked at the storm. Focused on upheaval. Not on
Jesus. That was the lesson. Peter looked at his troubles. Not at Jesus.

Then as soon as they got in the boat—I mean, the exact second—the
waves and the rocking just stopped. Then this happened: Peace. Be still.

It's a good Bible story. And I knew so many. For a while, in fact, I felt
superior to Diana, believing I had an advantage because I grew up on
those stories. I knew my way around the Bible, surely better than she.

But the truth is different. When it came to prayer, we were both begin-
ners, coming off different landscapes. And maybe *she* had the head start.

She knew how to give. She knew how to love. Such as I have to give,
take it. And she was on her way.

I gripped my Bible, ready to meet her—such as I had.

Neither of us was perfect.

And Jesus already knew every little thing about me. So he waited
on the water. I had to step out. Here was his hand.

It was bruised.

It was worn.

It was bloodstained.

Lord, save me. I gave him my hand. He held it in his, holding on tight.
A lifeline.

And so I held on. Nothing in the world would make me let go.

Have Faith but Be Precise

Elijah, for instance, human just like us, prayed
hard that it wouldn't rain, and it didn't—not a drop
for three and a half years. Then he prayed that
it would rain, and it did. The showers came and
everything started growing again. JAMES 5:17-18

I rode the elevator down to the first floor to find the hospital chapel.

Maybe others would be there. Reading the Bible together. Maybe singing. Or praying. Or maybe they'd just *be* there—warm bodies, ready with
sympathy. Or a hug. Or a bit of a smile. Or a portion of something that
Dan and I needed on this challenging day.

I found the room with no problem, right off a busy corridor, not far
from the main lobby.

The hallway was crowded with people rushing and leaving, going and
coming, hurrying and attending to the lives of those in the hospital. So
I was encouraged to see the sign by the door: "Zonta Chapel."

But the little chapel was empty.

It was always empty.

It was yawning with empty—the air stale, the spirit absent—as if no
human presence had ever entered the beautiful room.

And it was stunning. Polished wood pews, about a dozen bordering
a center aisle. A small, white marble altar spanned the front wall. Plush
carpet, a turquoise color, covered the floor. Its own little church. A fairy-
tale sanctuary, it seemed plucked from an enchanted forest and plopped
down in miniature in a massive city hospital.

But where was God? This little place was beautiful, but it felt absent,
as if God had never arrived, or maybe never was invited.

But I had to try to find him. So I walked deliberately to the first pew in the front and I sat down. I waited—for that sturdy, immovable, loving presence that just fills up some places of worship, even when they're empty. I had found it in New Jersey. At St. Bernard's, there it was—one step inside the door—that loving, assuring feeling. Outside, in contrast, the New Jersey heat and the braying cicadas and the drone of summer mosquitoes and the stir of Sunday life on the street in front of the church slowed our walk from parking lot to church. We dragged, more or less, into the Sunday service.

But inside everything suddenly changed. Cool air met us. God's breath. Or, okay, maybe it was just air-conditioning. But inside the humble cathedral, something cool and assuring wafted across our faces. I closed my eyes. Took a deep breath. Inhaled the peace.

Instantly, without a doubt, I knew: God is here. And people have prayed here. And prayers have been answered here. And the knowledge of that felt certain and good. So I leaned back in the pew and God just washed all over me. Some places of worship are like that. When you enter, God is already there.

Rick Warren, whose best-selling book, *The Purpose-Driven Life*, has challenged millions, warned against that feeling. God "wants you to sense his presence," Warren wrote, "but he's more concerned that you *trust* him than that you *feel* him. Faith, not feelings, pleases God."

I'm sure this is true, certain that Warren was correct when he said: "God is always present, even when you are unaware of him, and his presence is too profound to be measured by mere emotion."

But God forgive me. On this day, after sending my husband into the hands of sober surgeons, I wanted the mere emotion.

In this hospital chapel, I wanted to be washed by the presence of God.

I didn't know, as prayer warrior R. A. Torrey taught, that "when we least feel like praying, and when God is least real to us, that is the time we most need to pray."

But how do we do that?

"Simply be quiet and look up to God," Torrey wrote, "and ask God to fulfill His promise and send His Holy Spirit to lead us into His presence and to make Him real to us. Then wait and expect," Torrey added. "And He will come. He will take us into God's presence, and He will make God real to us."

In fact, some of Torrey's best prayer seasons happened when "as I first knelt to prayer I had no real sense of God." It was like talking "into empty space," he said.

Then looking up to God, he asked God to send his Holy Spirit, to lead him into God's presence, and to make God so real "that it almost seemed that if I opened my eyes I could see Him, in fact I did see Him with the eyes of my soul."

⌗

Well, I didn't see like that yet, and I couldn't see it here. In this chapel, I only heard silence. Saw absence. Felt emptiness. Maybe it was me. Surely others had offered life-giving prayers in this beautiful, little room, prayers fervent enough to snatch folks back from death itself. But I sensed none of that power.

So I picked up a Bible. I waited for that nice rush that comes from holding a worn, loved copy of the Scriptures. Bibles like that have their own heat. They've been prayed over, cried on, sung with, stroked and gripped and loved so hard they just emote—just by being touched—that human loam and steam and hope that faith gives off.

But this Gideon was cold and dry. Good intentions had delivered these Bibles here, I was sure. But the book was ice.

I knew my husband needed me to try. So I opened the dry cover anyway. It sighed with relief. The lovely Bible was so untouched, so unused, so unthumbed through, so lacking in the telltale sign that says "human hands have touched me," that its lack seemed criminal.

The same crime afflicted every Bible in the room, stacked pristinely at the end of my little pew.

People can pray anywhere, I suppose. Jesus taught "*when* you pray" not "*where* you pray." This chapel, in fact, was an earnest and lovely area. Good and honest people surely picked the carpet color, debated the wood stain, hired the artist who carved the decorative wood framing the door.

But on this morning it seemed the most forlorn space in the entire CU medical complex—not for what it was, but for what it was supposed to be but wasn't. Still, I said some words. I struggled to make them sound like a prayer, but my heart wasn't in it.

I grabbed my purse and left, not sure where to go but certain I didn't want to stay here. Maybe this was giving up. But it was time to move on.

⌗

Back in the main hallway, I headed for the Critical Care Tower, rushing to its sunlit lobby. Outside, the Colorado sunshine was showing off its best stuff, in fact. Big shafts of endless rays poured through glass windows near the elevators to the ICU.

So I turned, drawn by the promise of warmth and light, and found myself in the doorway of a bustling hospital cafeteria. The space looked fairly new, perhaps built when the newer-looking Critical Care Tower was added.

A sign out front said "Wall Street Deli." No, not a chapel. But it had life. Black-and-white checkerboard floor. Little café tables. Big glass windows. Sun pouring in. It looked cozy and welcoming. In fact, the deli was filling up with coffee drinkers, alert now and ready to plow into the day. They huddled at small tables, socializing. Others, wrinkled with fatigue after a long night, sat alone, looking glad to find a warm, quiet place to rest.

I could see an empty table in a far corner, next to windows.

So I settled there in a chair, putting down my purse and my Andrew Murray book and my NIV Bible, and suddenly I didn't feel a purpose. So I let the warm sun heat my back. I was thinking about Dan on the operating table. But I was pushing down the worry rising up. Maybe the sunshine helped.

Then as I looked up, I saw her.

The check-in nurse, Dianne, was sitting alone at a nearby table. Stirring a hot beverage, blowing on the steam, she had a book open, reading.

She didn't look tired. But she did look occupied, with that vibe that said *Taking a Break. Do Not Disturb.* So I held back. I'd worn that look in cafeterias during morning breaks myself.

But here she was, her table inches from mine.

A *praying* nurse. And at this moment, maybe the only other human being alive in this little deli. Or maybe the only person alive in this entire hospital or maybe in this entire world. Or maybe in God's entire universe.

Yes, I put a big spin on this. But in my view, she *was* the only being alive—certainly the only one who knew my husband's odds and, at the same time, also respected the power of prayer. And here she sat, stirring her tea, enjoying her book.

I had to talk to her. Didn't want to bother her. Knew she was on break. But she was steps away. That couldn't be a mistake.

I got up from my table.

Then I was standing in front of hers.

Then I was gripping the table edge, longing to cry out loud: "Pray, woman, pray!"

But that would be crazy. So I just stood there, willing her.

Right then, of course, she looked up. After a half second, she recognized me.

"Well, hi again," she said, being nice. Good smile.

A nurse's smile should be good, indeed. It should come from a place that knows about hurt. So it also knows about comfort and help and healing. It should rise from a tender, smart place that knows wholeness can come in a touch. Or even in a look, assuring and affirming and receiving—just as surely as hurt can come in a look that condemns.

I'd shot folks both of these looks over the years. Too many were condemning. Looks that indicted my daughters when they made choices I didn't understand. Looks that condemned my husband, vainly trying to set him straight. Looks that even berated my mother, who was often befuddled now because she just couldn't hear well. She hated wearing hearing aids. "Beg pardon?" she'd say so often, sounding embarrassed. But I wouldn't laugh with her at her old-fashioned phrase. Instead, I'd sigh heavily. I beseeched the ceiling with my eyes. Sometimes I rolled my eyes. So altogether my sighs and eyes and looks of annoyance added up to one loud thing: "I condemn."

But here I was today, begging for a smile myself. Now here it was. Dianne's look said, I see you. So how can I help? Want to talk?

I tried to talk, in fact, to say the usual stuff—*sorry to bother you, looks like you're busy.*

Instead tears sprang to my eyes, then cascaded freely—a wet, drenching flow in a busy hospital restaurant.

But Dianne is a nurse. She reached for my hand.

"Here, sit down," she said. She pushed away her book. Moved aside her tea. Reached again for both my hands, encircling them with her own.

I felt her kind, warm touch: Jesus. But what did she look like?

Not remarkable really. She looked my age, in fact, but maybe she was younger. She looked like the West, raised in Reno, living forever in Colorado. Her blond hair was graying without a worry, pulled loose in a ponytail. Once she was a hippie. Once she did drugs. She told me this later. She smuggled drugs into a prison once where a boyfriend, a guy she married briefly, was doing time.

It's her story. It's a sixties-era tale of drifting and alienation. Then one summer, on an aimless road trip with a girlfriend, she stopped at a Christian camp to visit the friend's sister. Before she left, she found Jesus.

"It was like meeting somebody who's always been waiting to see you." Her eyes looked blue and intense.

"It changed my life. People say that. But it happened. I was *changed.*"

Now she's a good nurse. She is forgiven. She knows how to love. On her best days, she knows this anyway.

"You're feeling anxious," she said now, her warm hands still holding mine.

"I'm sorry to bother you," I said through tears. "But I saw you sitting here . . ." The words stopped. I gulped back salty water. "And I know you're somebody who knows how to . . . *pray*."

I blurted the word—almost as if it was a prayer.

Dianne's intense eyes studied me half a second.

"You want me to pray with you?"

This beautiful question. She asked it perfectly, without that pious, saccharine sweetness that I myself often used. How many times had I lazily said, "Sure, honey, I'll pray for you"? I'd told folks this at church for years, knowing there was a good chance I might forget the request. For too long I'd done that.

But here was Dianne, offering prayer without pretense or affectation, without embarrassment and without reminding me that we were in a big urban hospital and that she was a hospital employee. She said it without thinking for a minute that she might not feel completely comfortable sitting here, in broad daylight and before everybody else, holding my hands while we prayed.

Instead, she held my hands. And the nurse Dianne, in her hospital nurse's uniform and before a room filled with people, closed her eyes tight and prayed like there was no tomorrow.

Prayed like she had been praying all night anyway.

Prayed like she knew who was listening.

Prayed like she knew a God who hears and answers prayers, especially prayers in hospital cafeterias, when one shift is coming in and another shift is going off and when a husband's odds are fifty-fifty.

She prayed like Daniel. Prayed like Paul and Silas; like David and Jacob; like Gideon and Nehemiah. She prayed like Mary and Martha; like Rachel and Ruth; like Lydia and Priscilla; like Shadrach, Meshach, and Abednego. She prayed like Jesus. She prayed to move mountains—not just because she believed, but because in this hospital, at this moment, she knew exactly what to pray for and how to ask.

"And, oh blessed Father, in Jesus' holy name, guide the hands of the surgeons and all of their assistants, recalling to their memory the knowledge that you've already given them to perform this surgery with skill and success.

"And, oh Lord, for your glory, give them all steady hands and skilled hands. . . ."

The sound of her soft voice was God's, God's Spirit praying back to

God, as Foster describes the mystery of prayer. In fact, Dianne told me later that she sometimes had prayed for a patient, asking things she couldn't possibly know to ask "except that the Holy Spirit was guiding me. Then I found out later I was asking for the precise thing that particular patient needed at that particular time."

It's not God who needs us to ask with precision, Dianne told me on another day. "He's God, so he already knows what people need." But when a prayer gets answered, precisely and right on time, "we know that God heard our precise prayer and that he answered."

⌘

For people who don't pray—who think the spiritual life is so much weird jumping around and superstitious mumbling and jumbling; who think God-fearing, God-believing people are intellectual weaklings whose trust in the unseen is laughable and silly, if not downright foolish—a fervent prayer must look childish and stupid and ludicrous.

Praying to God?

To unbelievers, it must look naive and impractical and hopeless. But to a nurse—who knows when doctors have done all they know, and who has seen what God does when believing people pray—the spiritual life is fresh hope and new air and, more than that, good medicine.

"I mean, the miracles I have seen," Dianne said.

In the burn unit, paramedics brought in a beautiful man, a Mexican immigrant, with second- and third-degree burns over 98 percent of his body. A ranch worker, he was engulfed in flames when a propane tank blew. The lovely man had run down the road, fanning the fire, screaming for mercy.

He was hospitalized for months. Didn't speak English. Dianne didn't speak Spanish. So they figured out how to sign. She comforted him. He received it. They became good friends. She prayed for him.

"It was during a time when I really wasn't walking with the Lord," Dianne said, her eyes looking pained. "But I believed that God would heal people. So I would ask God to staunch his pain before we changed dressings, that sort of thing."

Twice the man almost died. Her new friend was, indeed, horribly injured.

"But he actually ended up walking out of here."

He went back to his life. A miracle. Just one of many she witnessed.

Her favorite healing was her close friend's recovery from appendicitis. No rupture, but a septic inflammation caused the woman to fall into a coma. For thirty long days, the woman was near death. Doctors said that nothing else medically could be done.

Dianne told it like a registered nurse.

"She was in total body failure. Her heart was failing. Her kidneys were failing. Her liver was failing."

But Dianne and the family kept on praying.

"And one day," said Dianne, "she just woke up."

The woman was healed. For certain, she was healed.

She'd had a heart attack during the ordeal. "According to tests, she'd had a heart attack," Dianne said. "But after she woke up, they tested her again and her heart was completely healed. Her kidneys were healed. Her liver was healed."

The woman's daughter, who had a drinking problem and liver problems, "discovered *her* liver was healed."

Dianne, telling this story, started to laugh.

"I know it was a miracle. I know that God brought her out of this. I know that God heals."

I know this, she said. God will answer prayers for healing.

⊰⊱

Dianne prays evenly. No theatrics. No begging. Her requests are fervent but plain and clear. Perhaps she doesn't think she's worthy, so she isn't loud. But her voice is steady and confident and knowing.

And so for my husband, in the hospital cafeteria, she asked "for you, oh blessed Father, to block any complications that might arise from the procedure.

"And to prevent the fistula from rupturing during the repair . . ."

I listened to this, tightening my grip on Dianne's hands, surrendering to her words, asking as she prayed for God to hear them.

But a ruptured fistula?

I never imagined it. I didn't know such a thing was a risk. But I could tell she was asking God for a significant thing, and I felt grateful that she knew to ask because Dan needed all of this precise asking and he needed it *now*. He needed precise people to pray. Jesus must have wanted the same precision, the same fervor and purity and clarity.

In the Bible, there was Bartimaeus, standing *precisely* before Jesus.

"Rabbi, I want to see."

Jesus must have loved this answer. He'd been trading word games with Pharisees all the livelong day, rebuking disciples for petty questions—

who gets to sit next to you, Jesus, when you get into your Kingdom? He'd advised rich men trying to weasel their way into glory. And now? Here was a blind man with a simple need who knew how to ask.

"I want to see."

Maybe he'd been studying prayer. Reading Fosdick and Murray and Foster and Forsyth, Hallesby and Calvin and Mather and Mueller.

Oh, that George Mueller. He fed, clothed, and educated thousands of homeless street orphans who were starving and languishing in the dank of Bristol, England. This was the 1800s. Poverty ruled. But by prayer alone, Mueller brought in more than a million pounds sterling for schools and missions, Bibles and tracts, food, medicine, and clothing for the lovely cast-off children. This, in addition to other charity work.

One man praying. And Mueller's first great lesson? This is how Andrew Murray explained it: that if we come to God, in the way he has pointed out, "with definite petitions"—made known to us by the Spirit through the Word as being according to the will of God—"we may most confidently believe that whatsoever we ask it shall be done."

⊰⊱

"I want to see."

Now here was Dianne, praying with the same precision for my husband. But beyond preciseness, she prayed with faith. That's what God demands. That's why Jesus told Bartimaeus: Your faith has healed you.

Knowing this, Dianne followed his example.

"And so, blessed Father," she prayed, "we thank you in advance for every wonderful thing you are doing right now, and will do on this day, for Patricia's husband, Dan."

Where in the world does such faith come from? Yes, it is a gift. I knew that from the Bible.

But again old Andrew Murray, my spiritual leader on this day, taught in his twelfth chapter this simple lesson: "The power to believe *a promise* depends entirely, but only, on faith in *the promiser*."

Murray used italics like that all the time to make his big points. So I'd be an idiot to miss it. It's not the gift of faith that's so critical. It's the One who gives the gift. The promiser, almighty God himself, prepares for each person a gift of faith, personalized for each person's concerns, each person's problems, each person's individual circumstances. Then he says, Here, open the gift.

Here, it is enough faith for your situation.

Doesn't have to be much. Not any bigger than a mustard seed. A little bitty thing. Barely big enough to hold between your fingers without dropping it. That small. Only that much faith in me you'll need, God says, because I am so big. I am the Great I Am. So have faith in me. Yes—have a little faith.

Jesus himself said that same thing just a couple of days after Bartimaeus got his blindness healed. He was with Peter when he said it.

"Have faith in God," Jesus declared. He went on: "I tell you the truth, if anyone says to this mountain, 'Go, throw yourself into the sea,' and does not doubt in his heart but believes that what he says will happen, it will be done for him.

"Therefore, I tell you, whatever you ask for in prayer, believe that you have received it, and it will be yours."

I looked up at Dianne, a middle-aged, believing white woman holding on to me, a middle-aged believing black woman, and I surrendered to the gift. God had sent a soldiering angel, a servant with faith.

Yes, she was a white woman and I was a black woman. But none of that mattered. And, yes, people around us were starting to look at us now, thinking privately perhaps that she and I looked downright foolish, grasping each other's hands, speaking so confidently to some unseen, unknown higher power.

Indeed, we'd met only an hour or so before. But she was God's emissary. And this lieutenant could pray. And let us thank God every time for a praying warrior.

My face was puffy from crying. Dianne's tea had gone cold.

Didn't matter. We were warm as buns.

She said, "Amen!" I echoed her. "Amen. Amen!"

Every request that God had brought to Dianne's mind had been spoken. Indeed, we'd heard the question: What do you want me to do?

Dianne had prayed a checklist, and she'd prayed it by faith.

I now stood in agreement with her. Two praying saints, united in faith. Double power.

And then we looked at each other soberly. Praying people also know something else. That God is sovereign. So, yes, we had obeyed by praying precisely and by asking in faith. But now the matter was in God's hands.

That's how it goes.

God has the final say.

Love Each Other

And whatsoever we ask, we receive of him, because
we keep his commandments, and do those things that
are pleasing in his sight. 1 JOHN 3:22

Now the waiting room. I'm a Christian so I wasn't supposed to grumble.
But the third-floor waiting area for surgical intensive care—and also the
burn unit—was a neglected and jumbled mess. Puzzles and magazines and
board games, half-played decks of cards, abandoned magazines. The disar-
ray of waiting, scattered helter-skelter in a small room with mushroom-
shaped purple chairs, consumed the space and the air.

It wasn't a place to pray.

So like the others there, I found an empty purple chair and slumped
down to wait. Soon enough, I'd look like the others, curled up inside a
winter coat or a blanket loaned by a nurse, struggling to sleep, attempting
to wait. I checked the beeper the nurse had given me, longing to hear it
buzz. But I knew that in surgical ICU, no news was probably good news.

The TV in a corner was tuned to a game show. *The Price Is Right* or
Wheel or *Squares* or something like that. But nobody was watching. So
I dared to walk over and turn off the set, silence the drone. A man and
woman who slouched together in chairs against one wall both glanced up.
But they didn't protest. Neither did a woman curled into a chair facing
mine. So I figured turning off the TV noise was okay. Then I pulled my
big, fluffy house slippers from my tote bag. I took off my snow boots and
put on the slippers.

The woman sitting across from me looked up.

71

"Those look comfortable," she said, gesturing to my feet.

"Yes, they are," I said. I gave her a real smile, acknowledging her comment. I understood her need to be cordial. It can make you feel better.

I tucked my snow boots under my chair, settling my purse and other plunder around me. I could be cordial, but I was tired now. All I desired—no, all that I craved—was to close my eyes and rest. Maybe I'd even sleep.

Wasn't that okay?

I crossed my feet in front of the chair, wriggling my toes inside the fluffy slippers. I didn't need a single other thing. I just adjusted my feet, savoring the kind fluff. I leaned back slowly, gratefully into the chair, taking a deep breath. I was ready. Just close my eyes and forget everything.

"You have somebody in ICU?"

The woman's voice. I took a deeper breath. I opened my eyes.

The lady was uncurling herself, shifting toward me, adjusting her purple chair. *Please go away.* My thought didn't feel like a prayer. But here she was. So I sized her up as people do: Middle-aged. Slept-in clothing. Tired sweatshirt, company logo across the front. A weary face. Brown hair going gray. Weary brown eyes. A tired woman. Tired jeans. Scuffy sneakers. Everything faded.

Her sad eyes were faded too. She sighed loudly, making it plain she needed compassion, that hard and vital caring that Jesus had for folks who needed it most. But I pushed Jesus away. I wasn't up for it now.

Sure, being friendly and good and available was the Christian thing to do. Compassion doesn't mean convenience. Like the night my younger daughter, Alana, was set to watch a movie about Mozart, *Amadeus*, for a college music course. She wanted somebody to sit with her, just for company, to watch the Blockbuster video. "We'll have movie night!" she joked. So I sat down to watch. But it was late and soon I folded.

In truth, I was nursing a worry that night, and I hadn't been smart enough to give the little problem to God.

"I think I'll go to bed," I told her, giving up. She looked at me, rejected, thinking I had failed her. In truth, at that moment, I had.

Even Jesus faced that. "Can't you keep watch just one hour?" he pleaded with his sleepy disciples. Sure, they said. But late hours overcome folks. Peter, James, and John gave up, snoring like zombies on Jesus' last night while he prayed, knowing his own crucifixion awaited him. Still they slept, snoring like cattle. So he asked again:

"Are you *still* sleeping and resting?"

But didn't he really mean this: Can you love me?

Here in this hospital, a sorrowful woman maybe wasn't asking for love. But she looked like she was asking, *Can you love me?* In her faded, rumpled, mismatched clothes, with those weary eyes, that sorrowful face, she looked desperate, indeed. She also looked needy. Worse, she looked inconvenient. Well-dressed folks in matching clothes can look inconvenient too. But this woman screamed at me, just by her looks, that she was begging—inconveniently—for love.

Or at least she needed Christian kindness.

And I was sitting there, big as day, a Christian cross slung around my neck. Who else but me? And here *she* was, reaching with small talk, asking about the ICU.

"My husband," I said. "He's having brain surgery today." Cordial tone but not feeling cordial anymore. I backtracked, correcting myself.

"Well, it's vascular surgery, on some veins," I said, pointing toward the back of my head. "But it's around his brain," I added.

The woman's sad eyes widened.

"Will he be okay?" Her concern looked genuine.

"Well, I've been praying all night for him," I said, and the woman nodded.

"That's all you can do sometimes is pray."

Yes, I nodded, agreeing.

Okay, was this all?

Did God mean for me to make small talk with a woman I didn't know? I just wanted to take a break. Go inside myself. Maybe even meditate on *him*.

But here she was, faded sweatshirt and tired eyes, looking beseechingly over at me. So I gave in. I asked the next question.

"What about you? Is somebody in your family in ICU?"

And with that, the woman took a deep breath and started to tear up, her eyes glistening.

"My son," she said. "He's in the burn unit."

Lord Jesus, I thought. What do I say now?

"An accident or something?" I managed. But as I spoke my own words of concern I had an odd feeling. Had God put this woman here before me? I wasn't sure. But here was a woman in need. So she was an opportunity, a chance for me to receive her in need. Was that so God, in turn, could receive me?

Or as Andrew Murray would say: "My prayer will depend on my life." That is, "If I do what God says, God will do what I say."

And, of course, glory to God, I did know what God said to do: Love one another. A hundred zillion times in the Bible. "This is my command," Jesus said so simply and so plainly. "Love each other."

This order to love was so absolute—and absolutely so hard for me. Love is surrender. It's giving control to God, who's in control of everything anyway. But I tend to hang on. Forgetting myself long enough to help others tripped me up every time. But I knew it was a key to my rich, abundant life—not to mention a key to answered prayer.

The prayer books all said this.

"To forget oneself," Murray said, "to live for God and His kingdom among men, is the way to learn to pray without ceasing."

Murray, of course, wouldn't let it go.

"It is the forgetting of self and yielding ourselves to live for God and His honor that enlarges the heart, that teaches us to regard everything in the light of God and His will, and that instinctively recognizes in everything around us the need of God's help and blessing, and opportunity for His being glorified."

Glorifying God by forgetting about myself. Good grief. That seemed inarguable, but I groaned under the challenge. The poet W. H. Auden put it this way: "We must love one another or die."

But nothing was harder. Some days it seemed easier to go ahead and die than to love a hard person.

Nothing was tougher than love, nothing harder than the selfless surrender that love asks, not just for strangers but also for people we know. It's tough, indeed, to surrender everything when the heart just doesn't feel like it.

But I did a tough and surrendering thing. I leaned toward this woman. Then, oh well, I stood up.

Didn't feel like it. Didn't like doing it. Didn't want to try. Of course, Satan worked like the devil to push me back down. My little purple chair felt so important suddenly—more essential, amazingly comfortable, more relaxing than any chair I'd ever enjoyed in my life.

My feet, too, now finally warm and cozy in fluffy slippers, and the sun, streaming through the window behind me, toasting the air around me, ordered me: Don't move!

Show love to *her*?

But there she sat, sad and weary and sighing, uncurling before me and needing my love. I had to do something, even if I wasn't good at showing the love she needed.

Holy Spirit, help me.

I didn't pray like that back then. I didn't know that the Spirit helps us in our weakness, for "we do not know what we ought to pray for, but the Spirit himself intercedes for us with groans that words cannot express."

Oh, if I'd known—if I'd asked God to fill me up with his mighty Holy Spirit—then, I would have simply whispered, "Holy Spirit, help me."

Then, even without speaking such words, the Spirit of God would already have started to move. I think now that's how it would be. The love of God would just saturate me—not by power, not by might, but by God's Spirit—and this Spirit would remake me into what I couldn't make myself. A lover. Keeping *that* commandment would lead me, indeed, to answered prayer. Here was confirmation:

> And we will receive from him whatever we ask because we obey him and do the things that please him. And this is his command- ment: We must believe in the name of his Son, Jesus Christ, and love one another, just as he commanded us.

Yes, God demands reciprocity.

That's what R. A. Torrey said: "He demands that we listen to His Word before he listens to our prayers."

Even better: "If we have a sharp ear for God's commandments, then God will have a sharp ear for our petitions. If we do the things that God bids us to do, then God will do the things that we ask Him to do."

I had underlined the words in my Torrey book with yellow marker, then again with my black Bic pen.

And my husband needed answered prayer, so I stood up.

By God's Spirit, I stood up.

Didn't want to.

Didn't feel like it.

Didn't know how to do it. God knows, I didn't know how.

But I unsettled myself. I took the three small steps over to the empty chair beside the weary woman. I sat down and took her hand. A big, big thing for me. Touching a rumpled stranger.

She pulled a linty ball of tissue from a pocket and wiped her eyes.

Then she told me her long story—of course, it would be long. Loving other folks never is short work. Love didn't care at all that I didn't know this woman.

But God knew her, of course. And clearly God had placed her right

smack in front of me. I was assigned to listen to her, talk to her, show
kindness and compassion, not to mention give her the gift of my time.

And the best way to spell love? Rick Warren was clear: "T-I-M-E."

So there I sat, next to a woman who was ramping up to tell me her *long*
story, who wouldn't pull her hand from mine. She just let it rest there, a
persistent, yearning, pleading weight of weary flesh, longing for me to do
the loving thing and just stroke away.

So I forced myself. But I held back, just letting one of my thumbs do
the good work, stroking the roof of her longing hand. By this, I thought,
maybe I could display love, maybe convey care. So there I was. Thumb
stroke. Thumb stroke. And, like this, with my uneasy thumb stroking her
hand, the woman told me her endless story.

Her son was a drug addict.

Meth, I think she said. Or maybe she said heroin. Or crack. Whatever drug she described, it was terrible and its effects were awful.
The details are lost but for one stunning fact. Her son had tried to
kill himself.

"How?"

Oh, why did I ask this?

"He swallowed Drano," the mother said.

I gasped. My thumb froze.

She said this like she was talking about the weather.

"Yes, it's unbelievable," she said, responding to my horror.

Swallowed Drano?

I finally gripped her weary hand.

"His mouth and esophagus and stomach and intestines and everything
were totally burned raw . . ."

I shut my eyes against her voice. I couldn't listen anymore. I didn't
want to think about this, or even to know about such horrible despera-
tion. This injury was its own horror movie, not something I should
encounter in my good and professional life. Swallowing drain cleaner?

I didn't want to know, to imagine, to share the depths of hurt and
anger—and spiritual emptiness—that would compel a child of God
to buy a bottle of caustic drain cleaner, open it, and then drink it.

What could create so much pain? So much despair?

I looked around the ICU waiting room, and suddenly I despaired myself
of every puzzle-splattered, purple-chaired messy inch of it. This was the
headquarters for the hurt of the world, and suddenly I felt a great and
unbearable burden for this place and everyone in it.

This, as Susan Sontag described, was "the kingdom of the sick." And the lives of those sent here seemed sometimes so unbearably awful. Here in ICU, the misery seemed appalling.

But almost worse than the horrible afflictions, the accidents and the traumas, was seeing that so many families here seemed not to be quite together.

Many seemed topsy-turvy. I could see it in the bored stare of sullen teenagers, huddled inside their oversized, hooded coats, grunting and rolling their eyes when a mother or father dared to ask them a question.

I saw it in the tense politeness between a husband and wife. Their grown child was here, attached to life support. But almost worse was the parents' dying marriage, obvious by their stiff, awkward way with each other. Barely talking. Shoulders not touching. People look like that when they won't surrender, fearful of giving God their pride.

I knew that pride. It was self-centered, arrogant. Pride made it easy to be offended by any off remark. Prideful people keep up our guard, loathe to do what's easy—surrender to love, to turn once again to each other, to fall in love deeply again.

And love is so easy, Jesus said. An easy yoke, a light burden, and all of that. But we mess it up. Running around like gods, trying to control things and other people. And we get all weighted down.

Surely God didn't allow sickness to come just to dysfunctional families. But here we all were. One rumpled, burdened story after another, dragging off the third-floor elevator, slumping down into the purple mushroom chairs, struggling with our deficit of love and our pride. Broken marriages. Divorcing parents. Unwed mothers. Tattooed boyfriends. Insolent teens. Wild, disobedient children jumping like inconsolable delinquents on the purple mushroom chairs, their young mothers covering their eyes, desperate for sleep.

Maybe the stress of illness and trauma disclosed the cracks in everybody's armor. Maybe otherwise okay people, under stress, were realizing that we weren't God. We were out of control. Maybe the surprise of that was doing us in.

The awful truth was that our loud tattoos or chic hairstyles or hip fashions or rebellious attitudes or even our sober, prideful living couldn't save us. God was in control. Now, in fact, somebody was sick or injured, and we couldn't have done a single thing to prevent it. We were shocked, and it showed.

God help us.

Did people have to get sick before they prayed that?

I had to ask, because soon my family would gather in this ICU waiting room too. Then all of *our* secrets—our lack of loving and our wrong loving—would be obvious for the rest of the ICU kingdom to see.

In our family, the cracked armor showed first in our looks. For a black family, that too often means skin color. With us, it was one dark-skinned daughter and one light-skinned daughter. Beautiful little girls, but different.

Joi was tall and chocolate brown like *her* father, while Alana was fair and milky cream like *her* father. So right off the bat, there was that outward suggestion: This woman has had two husbands. Or to be more truthful: This woman has *slept* with two men.

That made me a cousin to the woman at the well, the Samaritan harlot, the one Jesus asked for a drink of water. She challenged him.

"You're a Jew and I'm a Samaritan. How can you ask me for a drink?"

But he trumped her. I have *living* water, he said, and she was greedy, so she wanted some.

Jesus: "Go get your husband."

Now the Samaritan woman doesn't skip a beat.

"I don't have a husband."

Jesus doesn't skip a beat either.

"In fact, you've had five husbands and you aren't even married to the man you're living with now."

The truth always comes from Jesus' mouth.

My own truth looked sort of like this. I'd had two husbands and now my two grown daughters—one so dark, one so light—gave away my early divorce just by the way they looked.

Even friends mentioned it, confessing that my family looked "kind of different" the very first time they saw us.

"I don't know, I couldn't figure it out," one friend said. She looked embarrassed. "Dan was so light and Joi was so dark and then here comes Alana, and she's light like Dan, but you're a different color than either girl."

What she didn't know was the rest of the story. I *had* slept with two men, and here were their daughters—one light, one dark. But I had slept with these men *before* I was married to either of them. My dear mother will cringe at this. I don't want to hurt her, but in fact, I already did when I made that phone call.

"I'm pregnant."

I wasn't married. But I was having sex. Why write that here? Because in the Christian church, we don't tell the truth about our secret selves. We are saved, most of us. But some of us act so holy we forget what we were like before saying yes to Jesus. Saying yes to his remarkable power. To his cleansing, transforming, clarifying grace. So we make church life look closed to everyone but holy people. Then we wonder why people stay away.

I mention sex because my children were challenged by the sins of my youth, as children often are, even if the parents are forgiven. In my family, my children struggled with the oddity of looking so different, the result of my own lust, my indelicacy, not theirs.

"Now what race are you?" folks asked Alana. "Are you mixed?" She hated the questions. "Why don't I look like you, Mommy?" she asked when she got old enough to worry.

"'Cause we have light-skinned people in our family and you got those genes." A true answer, and that's how things in America get explained. The real truth was this: Love and lust crossed the color line in America, and our progeny give away the secrets. I had added to the mix with more than one marriage. More than one man. More than one husband. Sex before marriage, which puts stress on matrimony. An unchaste woman may even marry the wrong man because they've had sex; sex before marriage confuses everything.

Moreover, with us, the perplexing twist of skin color remained. I'd had two husbands who didn't look alike. I had two children who didn't look alike. I had a blended family. But the work of merging differences was full-time work.

And I was in the middle—not quite dark, not quite light, not quite tall, not close enough in looks to either of my daughters to show our biological connection. Even with my husband, Dan, standing right next to me, neither of my children looked quite like mine, despite the fact that I had carried them in my womb for nine extraordinary months and then given them birth.

But stand us together in a room—or in a church pew or at an airport ticket counter or in a grocery-store line—and we looked odd. Not quite together.

⊰⊱

But God is merciful.

The Father, as Murray said, waits to hear every prayer of faith.

I was twenty-three when I left my first husband, soon after college.

Mercifully, my parents didn't balk. They just said come on home. So I went. I was jobless, despite a new college degree. I was broke, despite my parent-paid education. I was a prodigal daughter returning for atonement and renewal in my parents' good home.

They did the remarkable thing. They never once said, "We told you so." They just put up a crib in my old bedroom. They bought baby food and diapers. They ordered nursery books and toys.

Then my daddy, a tall brown man with strong arms and confident ways, spoke in his clear voice the words that would forever change my mortal life: "You need to open your Bible."

He didn't elaborate. There was no fussing or lecturing. On that morning, Daddy just left me alone in the living room, not provoking, not berating, not going on about bad choices and wrong living. Daddy just left me alone with a choice. In all the years that I was his daughter, this was my father's best and biggest moment.

He made a small gesture. He spoke a few words.

So I lifted the big Bible from my parents' coffee table. I opened it, surprised at first by the sheer weight of it. It felt as weighty, indeed, as Moses' stone tablets, as Ezekiel's heavy wheel, as Jesus' own remarkable cross. It was just so filled up with the wisdom of God that I was humbled by it, suddenly aware that years had gone by since I'd lifted a Bible of any size, even to dust off the cover.

I was surprised to find that the words of my recovery had been underlined by my father—years and years before—with his black ink pen. "There is therefore now no condemnation to them which are in Christ Jesus."

Daddy's fountain pen, always his favorite thing to write with, tended to smudge. But in and around the smudges, I saw my daddy's past, linked with my mother's dreams for me, all these things tied together and underscored in black ink years ago by my father's hopeful hand. "And we know that all things work together for good to them that love God."

Further down—same page—was a verse I'd read so proudly in Sunday school for our teacher Mr. Bell so many long years ago, Romans 8:31.

"This verse starts with a question," Mr. Bell had said. "And what's the question, children?" Mr. Bell promised a prize, a candy bar. Answer the question and you get a Milky Way, maybe a Kit Kat. So I raised my hand high. Call on me! I have it. I have it.

We were so naive. So carefree as children. Just trying to get our mitts on the chocolate candy. So we shouted our answer, reading from our tiny children's Bibles: "If God be for us, who can be against us?"

But Mr. Bell wanted more.

"I can't hear you."

We said it again, laughing, even louder.

"If God be for us, who can be against us?"

But Mr. Bell wanted us to be sure, so he taunted us again.

"I CAN'T HEAR YOU!"

So we gave him the answer, loud enough to blow out the windows and lift the ceiling in our renovated, hand-me-down Methodist church building. But we also shouted it loud enough to never, ever forget.

Or maybe we forgot for a while, but now it was time to go back to that lesson, holding on to it, like a lifeline.

And what is the lesson, beautiful children?

We were shouting now, screaming at the top of our little lungs:

"IF GOD BE FOR US, WHO CAN BE AGAINST US?"

But first, before God is for us, comes this: Love each other.

Tell the Hard Truth

If I have the gift of prophecy and can fathom
all mysteries and all knowledge, and if I have
a faith that can move mountains, but have not
love, I am nothing. 1 CORINTHIANS 13:2

Now here was Mama—the first to arrive at the hospital.

I loved her. But I didn't understand her. God was for us, but Satan was
against us and we'd grown so far apart. Maybe it was age. She was eighty-
four. I was fifty-one. My father had been dead now almost twenty years.
And Satan had blown up the difference.

These days I thought my mother was moody, distant with me, and self-
absorbed—a widow who'd never gotten beyond my father's death.

She thought I was moody, distant with her, and self-absorbed—a work-
aholic who was too busy with my job and my children and my husband
and my life to notice how hers had been changed by her big, big loss.

I was right. She was right.

So I knew she'd arrive soon, ready to take up her vigil for Dan, intent
to worry about him, but not offering any spiritual comfort in the form of
a prayer or loving assurance, and offering no loving interest whatsoever
in me. But why did that surprise me? What loving interest did I offer her?

As Torrey said, it's obedient love—the evidence of a *"living* faith"—
that sparks the prayers that God will answer.

Or Murray: "My prayer will depend on my life."

In recent years, I hadn't obediently loved my mother in her life. I'd
dutifully attended to her cares and needs as best I could. But duty isn't
love. At this point, we were little more than polite strangers. So we both

were in pain, and it showed. Anybody in the ICU waiting room would see it.

She walked slowly off the third-floor elevator wearing purple velour, carrying a bag of orange-juice cartons, a package of peanut-butter crackers, and the day's newspapers.

"How's Dan?" she asked. She sat down slowly in a chair and put down her plunder. That's what she called whatever stash of supplies she was carrying on any day—plunder—and she was always carrying something. Always had a plastic grocery bag when she walked through my front door. "Here's some underwear I saw on sale," she'd say, handing me yet something else for my granddaughter, not seeming to know that often it was the wrong size or something my grandchild already had or didn't need.

Then the next day: "I just picked up some canned fruit. I know Dan likes it."

Then the next day: "Can Alana use this notebook paper?"

It never ended.

"Just picked up a gallon of milk."

"Thought I'd get a couple loaves of bread."

"Here's a bag of salad. I know you two like salad."

A bag of this. Of that. Of the other. Never did she walk into my house or get into my car without a plastic grocery bag, and often, it seemed, it was something we already had or didn't really need. Rarely, it seemed, was it joyfully given. Instead, she'd pull herself through my front door, looking a bit sorrowful, and offer up her bag of plunder for the day.

"Here's something," she'd say, laying it down wearily on the kitchen counter, as if just lifting it to the counter and dropping it from her hand were the hardest things she'd ever done in life.

It was as if my once-vibrant mother—who at one time seemed to run through her days, who taught gym for twenty-odd years in Denver public schools, racing after children on school playgrounds, kicking and hitting balls as hard and as far as any carefree, athletic kid—had gone from effervescent joy to bag lady.

It made me crazy.

"Why do you buy this stuff?" I asked, my voice short and cutting.

I couldn't see that these were love offerings. As self-absorbed as I was, I grumbled about not having room in my kitchen cabinets for another row of canned fruit, another loaf of soft bread, salty snacks, or gallon jug of sugary juice that nobody ever drank.

In truth, I didn't have enough room in my heart for an aging, perplexing woman who happened to be my mother. I was dismayed, indeed, by my mother. Where had she gone?

Surely she was pondering the same things: I am dismayed by my daughter. Where did she go? She used to be malleable and fun. She used to love my little gifts. Now she acts so annoyed.

My annoyance already was percolating as I watched her, dragging off the elevator, weighed down by that day's plastic bag. She opened it.

"I picked up some peanut-butter crackers and some Fritos and things."

She handed me the bag. "How's Dan?" she asked again.

We hadn't touched, of course. Hadn't hugged. Hadn't greeted each other with a warm, enveloping embrace like families do in Hollywood movies or TV.

I knew real families touched like this sometimes. I'd seen them at church or in the airport. Real families with real people in them, reaching so warmly for each other and hugging for a long time—even closing their eyes while they hugged to shut out the world for those luxuriant moments while they made contact.

I didn't know this kind of contact, not from my mother. Someplace deep inside me I missed it and ached for it with hurt, painful longing. She certainly longed for the same thing.

But we grew up in the fifties. Did anybody *ever* hug their children back then?

Mary Pipher says adults of my era carry a deep longing to be touched. We *weren't* caressed and stroked and loved that way as children, she said.

But maybe Mama wasn't either. Maybe Mama's family had never hugged her with total abandon, closing their eyes during the hug because the love and longing were so great. Maybe that's why she'd never hugged a longing daughter.

Instead, she handed me plastic bags.

I bemoaned the sight of them. God forgive me. And God help me.

I needed God's help, indeed, to fix my understanding. I had it all wrong about Mama. I thought my relationship with her was all about me. That was my biggest problem, so I didn't understand.

Loving other people, it turns out, is all about *them*. Then in serving and loving the other person—after making that person's cares my priority—the reward from that eventually comes back to me.

That means hanging on. Praying without ceasing.

But I was so mixed up about this. I hadn't figured out that I needed to love Mama, not because she was perfect but because she *wasn't*.

Love one another as I have loved you. Jesus meant that for real, it turns out. And what a Savior. He showed us how to do it: Love imperfect people because I have loved even you.

⚜

I needed a Savior, indeed, to do elder care. On my own, I kept on getting it wrong. I tried to love Mama for who she was. But she wasn't herself anymore. Her former self had been stolen by a thief: the tumble of years, lost memories, the ironies of powerful medicine.

I was trying to love the shadow of my mother. That is how it felt many days—like I was putting my arm around a fading picture, but it kept shifting. The picture kept going soft and disappearing, right before my eyes.

So Mama's blood-pressure pills and things did a fair job. But they also took the wind right out of her. So I spent countless hours chasing down doctors, juggling medicines, struggling to get things moderated, regulated, coordinated—struggling to get the answers she needed.

She had gone from vibrant and sassy to lethargic and cast down, and she moved so slow. I mean, Mama's pace some days felt downright glacial. So first I needed to slow down, which always felt artificial and odd.

I was struggling to gear down to her elder's stride, to finally stop rushing and just sit with Mama. To just "be with" her, not really going anywhere or moving—just being and being still.

I failed at this. And the more I failed, the more guilt I felt. But she felt bad too. I could tell. She started apologizing.

"Don't worry about me. Don't wait for me. You two go on. I'll be okay," she'd say to Dan and me.

And she was okay, for her beautiful age. But I wasn't okay with it. I was always off-kilter with Mama, knowing I was impatient, feeling guilty about my impatience, looking and feeling perpetually in a bind—not understanding what Jesus meant when he said it: "Love one another, even as I have loved you."

Instead, Mama and I made our small talk about Dan's surgery:

Yes, he seemed a little nervous.

No, he didn't seem in pain.

Yes, the doctors will call us along the way.

It's been two hours since surgery began and he has miles to go before he can return—before the final stitch.

We were trying to talk, that is, through awkward attempts at conversation.

But it was all surface. We were mother and daughter, indeed—forever linked by her womb. But beyond that, there were many acres of emotional void.

At least that's how it felt, like she didn't know me at all. I will tell the truth: I resented that. I was still egotistical and mistaken, still believing these matters with Mama were all about *me*.

I like what T. D. Jakes said one night on TV: "You're worried that nobody really knows you?" he asked. "Well, *God* knows all about you. He knew you before you were a piece of tissue in your mother's womb. He knew you before your fingers unwebbed. Before your toes were formed, He knew you . . . He knew you. He knew you!"

So God knew me before everything. Understanding that should have been enough.

But I was greedy. I wanted knowing love from my mother. I wanted to feel her love, just as I knew that I sometimes felt God's. Without that feeling, the negatives filled the void. Resentment. Anger and frustration. And more resentment.

For a Christian woman, thinking such things about one's mother skirts the edge of what's okay. For an African American Christian woman, however, thinking such things hurled me to the brink, to the very lip of hell, threatening to push me right in. I recognized with a groaning heart that the emptiness between my mother and me was a sin against God, and that on the issue of parents, God was exceedingly clear: "Honor thy father and thy mother: that thy days may be long upon the land which the Lord thy God giveth thee."

True, I wanted to live a long *and* good life. But if it depended on honoring my mother, I was playing roulette with my own longevity *and* quality, because honoring means deep reverence. I looked up *honor* in the big dictionary on my desk: Honor means feeling big and noble traits like admiration and respect, love and awe, high regard and esteem. More than feeling, honor also means expressing those things. So I was aware of how far away from honoring my mother I was.

And now, to complicate things, she was steadily growing more distant, more critical, and she was losing her hearing—but, of course, refusing to wear her hearing aids.

"Beg pardon?" she said whenever I tried to talk to her—to tell her what I was facing at work, what I endured as a commuter, what I longed to accomplish in my life, what I was dreaming and praying for, not to mention when I asked how she was feeling—but she wouldn't even look at me many times.

"Beg pardon?" she'd say again, looking half-interested. I wanted to scream. Please listen to me, Mama! But wasn't she saying the same thing? Just look at me, Patricia. I'm not my old self. This is me *now*. But I wouldn't look. We closed a door.

And I knew it hadn't always been like this.

I have proof—photographs—of the two of us, laughing together, me enjoying her caustic wit, she making fun of my supersensitive ways and me being okay with that. At least I think I was okay with it.

Then the laughing dried up. Then it just stopped.

Well, it stopped with me. Other people still seemed to love my mother and laugh with her. "She's something else!" I heard at least once a week from her neighbors, from salespeople, from a flight attendant when she got off a plane after visiting my sister in Atlanta. "She kept us laughing the whole way."

I'd hear these things and I'd think, *My mother? Why doesn't she laugh with me?*

God bless me. I couldn't see.

To make it worse, my mother was getting older with every passing day. But so was I. Our time to fix this was growing shorter. What did I need to change to fix this? How could I find a better way?

That's a prayer, of course. It's not just a question. If I'd known that, I would have prayed it.

Heavenly Father, I would have prayed, *these feelings against my mother are first a sin against you, a sin against your own forgiveness of me, against your own example of love for me, and against your own model of grace.*

Therefore, I'd have just prayed, *in Jesus' matchless name, and by his precious blood, and by your Holy Spirit, replace these illogical feelings of resentment and anger—stirred up only by our enemy—with the indwelling of your Holy Spirit.*

In Jesus' loving name, I would have prayed, *usher in your Spirit to help me—as you promised your Spirit would do—to become the loving daughter to my mother that I can't seem to be by myself.*

And that's a good prayer.

And I would have prayed it just like that, if I'd known anything at all then about praying.

Instead, I tuned my ear to my mother's comments, already setting my shoulders against whatever she would say next. Her comments and questions always went right through me. Today would be no different.

"Where's Joi and Alana?" she was asking me now.

I took a big, deep, long breath.

"Remember, Mama, Joi's in Chicago at a conference," I answered. My oldest daughter, Joi, was a bookstore owner then. She'd left town the past weekend for meetings and a book conference. She wouldn't return until the weekend. Even then, she'd be busy because she had to tackle her struggling business and she also was a single mother. Her life didn't fit neatly into a box.

I was learning to be okay with all of that.

But acceptance of my younger daughter Alana's choices was coming much slower. So questions about Alana left me prickly and argumentative.

"She's with a friend, the girl who has sickle cell," I said, explaining why Alana, too, wasn't keeping vigil here at the hospital with me.

"Her daddy's having surgery and she's hanging out with some friend?" Mama asked. She mumbled, "I don't understand it."

I took another deep breath.

I explained that the friend had a sickle-cell crisis a couple of days before. Alana had driven the girl to another hospital, in fact, and had been staying with her there because the girl didn't have family in Colorado. But Alana and I had talked on the phone, I said. She would be here as soon as she could.

But Mama set her mouth.

She'd grown up when families were ruled by order and duty, by good manners and assumed expectations. In contrast, I'd failed my family by not expecting enough. And here was yet another example of my compromised standards: allowing Alana to run off with "some girl" who none of us even knew when Alana's own father was sick unto death himself.

Mama loved and treasured my daughters. But her questions about them sounded instead like disappointment in me as their mother. At least that's how I heard them. So I stayed defensive. Our generation gap was stretched to the limit.

As proof, Alana wasn't here.

From my mother to my daughters and back again, it didn't seem as if I could get anything quite right. That was the truth, and prayer warriors are bound to tell it. Hard or not, we tell the truth.

Try Again to Love

Whoever claims to live in him must walk
as Jesus did. 1 JOHN 2:6

So more truth. Our beloved Alana's life then *was* unorthodox.

How does a Christian mother explain how a daughter has left the church, dabbled in New Age religions, and at that moment, had joined Louis Farrakhan's black religious group, the Nation of Islam?

"The Black Muslims?" Mama had asked.

"Yes," I had answered, breathing deep again.

"How did she get into that?"

The question sounded like condemnation. I didn't approve either. But I half-understood how it had happened. During college in the sixties, I had high-fived Malcolm X's speeches, fluffing out my Afro, raising my fists in rebellion and defiance. At night I sat in dorm rooms and off-campus apartments and student unions listening to Black Muslim tapes, mesmerized with friends, fluffing my Afro higher still. Malcolm's voice was our music. Bold with fire and flair, he castigated "white exploitation" and "black indifference," then exhorted black folks to fight back. He brought us to our knees. Then to our feet. Power to the people and all of that, indeed.

But then I found Jesus. And the revolutionary Jesus had lifted me higher, made me big enough to stop seeing race in every other little thing, to know that salvation was in my heart, not in my hairstyle.

I could see right through the Nation of Islam's seemingly self-glorifying, ego-centered cult. And now my own baby girl and her array of disenfranchised friends were members of this very group, drawn to it like drowning men to a lifeboat. I'd been powerless to stop it.

Or maybe parents don't see what they don't want to know. So I denied that at age twenty, she was on a journey, and it already had taken her worlds from home—light-years from the church where she was raised. But I wanted her back. To come back to her *real* home. To return to church, that is. To be my little baby girl again. To sit next to me in the pew at early service and clap her pretty hands to the gospel music and smile at me while we both shouted "Amen!"

Indeed, we went to church every Sunday when she was growing up. Alana rode in the backseat, next to her sister—wearing her pleated skirts and matching tights, her turtleneck sweaters, her Sunday clothes. Hair in a ponytail, matching ribbons coming undone. Then she joined us in the pew, repeated the liturgy, sang in the children's choir, served on the children's usher board. As a family we showed for the Sunday sermons, the Saturday fish fries, the Easter pageants, and the Christmas sing-a-longs. But back home after church, it didn't carry over.

"We never talked about church, not after we got back home," Alana said now.

So church was something we did, not something we lived.

In truth, church was a place to see other black people, most of them—like us—transplants to Colorado's suburbs. Like us, they drove from their new tract houses out by the malls to the old family church back in town. Church was beautiful most times, in fact. Music was great. Sunday school was congenial and insightful. Then back to the parking lot. Hug people. Drive home. Next Sunday, get up early and do it all over again. I assumed this was right. My family was safe.

But Alana wanted more.

Maybe she'd read George MacLeod, or pondered his blazing manifesto:

> I simply argue that the cross be raised again
> > at the center of the market place
> > as well as on the steeple of the church,
> I am recovering the claim that
> > Jesus was not crucified in a cathedral
> > between two candles:
> But on a cross between two thieves;
> > on a town garbage heap;
> > At a crossroad of politics so cosmopolitan

that they had to write His title
in Hebrew and in Latin and in Greek . . .
And at the kind of place where cynics talk smut,
and thieves curse and soldiers gamble.
Because that is where He died,
and that is what He died about.
And that is where Christ's men ought to be,
and what church people ought to be about.

But maybe our church wasn't enough like that for Alana. She was searching. And she was young. And I was still on a fence.

So she fell for a New Age movement promoted by rappers, her generation's seers. They had a New Age premise that the movement's followers were themselves gods, but only if they were black. Black people alone were gods, this group claimed. So Alana fell for the idea, called herself a "queen" and sat in her room for hours, studying the movement's propaganda. She called it "building."

I called it Satan.

Then I condemned her.

"How in heaven," I begged her, "can you fall for that ridiculous cult nonsense?"

She sat cross-legged on her bed, laptop open, eyes glued to the group's Web site, reading—over and over—its premises, its rules, its manifesto.

"You actually believe this stuff?" I mumbled, reading over her shoulder. "You're too smart for this. You're a *college* student. You earned four digits on the SATs!"

"So?"

"So, it's a cult, and it's not even an interesting cult."

"Well, you're running around talking about praise the Lord and worshipping some white God!" Alana closed her laptop, looking up at me.

"Jesus was *not* white," I said, my voice rising. Then I calmed myself. "But even if he were, so what? Even if he were *green*, so what? That's not the point."

"Then what's the point, that Jesus was the *Son* of God? Of *God*! You actually believe that?"

"And you actually believe that folks in this New Age cult are gods?"

"*Black* gods," she shouted. "And it's not a New Age cult."

"Those folks have brainwashed you," I shouted back, angry again.

"And the Bible hasn't brainwashed you?"

"The Bible is the Word of God!"

"The Bible was used by slave owners to justify slavery! To keep black people down!"

"Alana, why do you believe that garbage?"

"Why do you believe the garbage *you* believe?"

She was well schooled in her questions. I wanted her back, but she wouldn't budge. And this wasn't even a real discussion. We were fighting to score points, maybe even to hurt each other.

❈

Of course, I kept praying, begging God to grant us relief, to take us back to the way it was when she was five and six and seven and she'd crawl into my lap and take my face in her hands and tell me she loved me. And I would tell her the same. And I actually thought it would always be that way.

Her children arise and call her blessed and all of that.

But my child had cursed me. She had screamed that she hated me.

At one point, she whacked off her curly, long hair—in some New Age ceremony with her girlfriends—leaving barely an inch of it on her head, which she now covered in elaborate head cloths made from African fabric.

She left a high-ticket university in New York City after an expensive, roller-coaster year. Then, after a long, hot, argumentative summer, she started taking classes at the Denver campus of the University of Colorado. She started one semester, started and ended another. Then she stopped going.

"I don't know what I'm doing," she told me one day, and I felt helpless to guide her. A daughter on a journey needs a mother who has already mastered the road. But I was still struggling myself. Still praying my prayers but not reaping the changes I kept begging for. I wanted an instant fix—*sha-zaam*! Alana returned to church. The happy ending in a triumphant Christian movie.

But Alana wouldn't hear a word about Jesus. She refused to go to church. She wouldn't return to those places and people who I believed could help and love her most.

She drifted from the New Age movement and after a while took up with the Black Muslims, referring to Louis Farrakhan and Elijah Muhammad as "honorable" whenever she spoke their name.

I rebuked them and called them Satan.

She cried.

I cried.

I prayed.

I beseeched God to save her from the lies of cult religion and to bring
her back to the truth of Christ, my "cult," as she called it. She kept wrap-
ping her head in mud cloth, refusing to eat pork, ridiculing the other food
on our table, and going to the scruffy Nation of Islam mosque in Denver's
inner city on the northeast side.

So I went with her one Sunday afternoon. I had to see it for myself.
Dan refused, saying he didn't see the point.

But I insisted on going. I had to see for myself where our daughter was
spending her time. Maybe I didn't believe that God already knew.

So there we were, at a weary storefront in the rundown Dahlia Square
shopping center in northeast Denver. I pulled the Nissan into a parking
space on crumbling asphalt. Young black men in dark suits, white shirts,
and bow ties competed to open my car door. A sign above the door said
"Muhammad Mosque No. 51." I couldn't believe I was here.

"*Salaam alaykum*, my sisters. Can we assist you, my sisters?"

The young men, their voices softened to whispers, approached the
Nissan regally, as if it were a royal carriage, not an aging used car. Two
of them, arms outstretched, split off from the group. Each then headed for
either side of the car, reaching for the door handles.

On my side, the young man bowed at the waist, stretching out his arm
in a gesture of welcome. I clicked open the car lock. I looked at him. Somebody's baby boy. Maybe seventeen or eighteen. At the most, twenty. His
smooth skin was one shade past cream. His eyes were green, piercing, clear,
and tired. Green eyes in a young black man. I knew he had seen a lot.

His collar and cuffs, frayed and wrinkled, hunched out of his ill-fitting
suit jacket. Maybe he washed this shirt every night, ironed it as best he
could every morning. He was remaking himself, like the other young men,
as an urban gentleman. Fatherless at home perhaps, and alienated from his
mother's and grandmother's church for some reason, he'd found his way to
the Nation. It would be his training ground now. And finally, after growing up on funk and rap that defiled females, he could, as his grandmamma
had wanted, treat women with respect.

"My sister," he whispered, the voice velvet, holding the door gallantly.
The other young man, just as gallant and velvet, held the passenger door
for Alana. He bowed to her, polite and deferring. He stood by the door,
reaching for Alana's hand to help her up, but lowering his eyes.

"My sister."

Alana melted into the greeting, scarves and necklaces floating all about her, elaborate turban poised like a crown on her head, arms extended as if she were, indeed, an African queen.

It felt as if we were in a stage production with everybody wearing costume clothes and overacting.

Just then, in fact, the half-dozen or so men standing guard at the storefront stepped back almost in unison, making way with drama as Alana and I walked the few paces to the weary building.

Then one of them reached for the heavily barred glass door and opened it, ushering us inside.

I took a deep breath. I didn't want to be here. But my daughter was here and I had to see for myself what was drawing her. Me, inside a mosque. *Lord Jesus, help me.* I couldn't believe it.

Inside the front door, we stood in a narthex just big enough to turn around in. Photos of Elijah Muhammad and Louis Farrakhan covered the walls. I closed my eyes for a second. I did not want to see this. It looked like a church lobby set up by somebody who'd confused Jesus with Louis Farrakhan. To my mind, indeed, the wrong pictures were hanging on the walls. But everything was neat and painfully tended.

I noticed a doorway just left of the little lobby and turned to go there. But a young woman stopped me with her hand. That was the men's entrance, she explained. I stepped back from it. As if on cue, some of the young men standing outside entered the building and turned left with ceremony through the door on the left, closing it behind them.

This same young woman, dressed head to toe in a billowy white skirt and blouse, directed us through a doorway on my right. Now we were in a separate closet-sized space, the *women's* entrance, draped with a sort of curtain. The woman raised her hands and smiled as it became suddenly clear that in here we would be *frisked.* For *weapons.*

I looked, disbelieving, at Alana.

This was *not* happening.

This was as far from our upscale Shorter Community A.M.E. Church as I could imagine.

"They frisk people?" I whispered to Alana.

She gave me a look: *Please* don't make a scene here.

Then the young woman in charge of frisking females turned to me, apologizing. "Thank you, my sister. I'm sorry for the inconvenience. This is for everyone's protection."

She ran her hands over my clothing, gently enough. Did the same to Alana. I allowed this but I was numb. I couldn't believe I was in this place, and on a Sunday afternoon. This was our after-church time, family gathered around a long table, finishing Sunday dinner, diving with joy into the sweet potato pie. That was the picture I had always wanted. Instead, Alana led me from the frisking closet into another room, a modest gathering space staged for a talk. A podium stood up front. A few dozen metal folding chairs were set up in two small sections, one for men and one for women.

So I sat down.

I turned to my daughter. Our eyes locked.

"What?" she whispered.

I just shook my head. I couldn't find words.

All I could think of was the phrase "false gods." But this wasn't the time to bring *that* up.

Or to bring up my complete dismay that my precious younger child, who had been baptized in water in the name of Jesus—and who had a lifetime of Sundays in one of the city's most respected black Christian churches—had rejected all of that and landed here.

It was so run-down, this place, and a lot of the people looked like throwaways too. In truth, they looked like people Jesus would hang with. One young black girl sat in a wheelchair, body twisted, voice trapped by palsy. Alana hugged her. Everybody wore worn clothing, every garment sized too big or too small. Scuffed shoes scraped the worn floor. And Farrakhan smiled from framed pictures. My numbness grew deeper, my dismay smothering. But the bigger surprise was how at home and comfortable Alana seemed here.

She got respect here, certainly. Clearly, people liked her. She got attention and understanding and time. She got love. Not that she didn't get that at our home church.

But here—what was it?—she wasn't born into this religion. She had picked it for herself. She had followed her peers here. One, a pretty Latina married to a young black man—who together had two children, plus the young woman's older ten-year-old son—had proselytized to Alana about the loving acceptance she'd found in the Nation. The young woman's husband was a convert too.

Now instead of staying in her parents' all-black Christian church, my daughter also had migrated to a place that looked to her more like a kind of heaven. It was younger, more diverse, nontraditional.

But the message wasn't much better than the New Age group she'd dallied in. The Nation preached superiority over white people and Jews, so the theology was all wrong. I argued that as we drove back home.

"The Nation just tells the truth," Alana answered. She sat demurely in the Nissan's passenger seat.

I looked over at her, dressed in her modest clothing, looking more composed, to tell the truth, than she had since her adolescence began. Indeed, modest clothing is good, but it can cloak lies.

"Preaching hate is never the truth," I finally said.

Alana was quiet for the rest of the trip to our house. But when we got home, she reached over and gave me a hug.

"Thanks anyway, Mom, for going to the mosque with me."

In the house, Dan was in the kitchen, stirring up salmon croquettes, one of his favorite meals. Our Sunday dinner.

"How was it?" he asked. But he could read the answer on my face.

How was it?

Did he have to ask?

That was a few short months before.

Now, here we were, in the hospital. Alana was still in the Nation, and Dan couldn't stand up, let alone fry salmon croquettes.

So my companions were my mother, who never touched me, and a woman whose son had swallowed Drano.

"I tried to love him the best way I knew how," the burned boy's mother was saying.

I nodded. "Children challenge parents, don't they?" I said.

"And parents challenge children," she added.

We were up walking now, stretching our legs in the corridor fronting the waiting room. We weren't suddenly fast friends. But you look for sympathy in a waiting room. I had tried to give it. She tried to give it back.

I offered to pray with her. She agreed. We stood by a window, looking over an interior courtyard, and held hands.

What to pray for?

Peace? Calm? Good medicine? Yes, we prayed for those things. Of course, we did. But there was more to ask.

"Help us," I tried to pray, holding the other mother's hand, "to love."

That seemed to be the key. To love better. Love more. Love with sincerity. Love enough to listen. To show respect. To give our loved ones our time. To follow the big, hard commandment: that we love one another.

John the apostle explained one reason why: "Dear friends, if we don't feel guilty, we can come to God with bold confidence. And we will receive from him whatever we ask because we obey him and do the things that please him."

Answered prayer is conditional, that is. And I had heard *that* sermon, indeed. But what, Rabbi, is the greatest commandment?

No mystery here.

Love God with all your heart. Then love your neighbor as yourself.

All the Law and the Prophets hang on these two commandments, Jesus added, and he never equivocated.

At Shorter A.M.E. Church, I heard these words repeated in the liturgy every Sunday—in the Decalogue, lifting up the Ten Commandments of Moses but ending with Christ's answer to his skeptics. In short, love God and love everybody else.

I was ready to try, even before I learned that obeying this commandment to love is one condition of answered prayer.

Mother Teresa gives her warning, however: "We cannot give to the outside what we don't have on the inside."

Love, indeed, on this day seemed outside my understanding, the hardest thing to master, an impossible skill to perfect. So how to grow into love? The Catholic saint and Torrey and Foster and Murray and the other prayer warriors across time all agreed: First, love Jesus. Love him for his sacrifice. Love him for his grace. Love him because he first loved me. Then, filled with that love, give some of that love away.

But could I do it? I wasn't sure. But I had tried.

Over the summer, I had welcomed Alana's friends from the Nation into my home. The young Latina and her boys slept overnight once when she was between apartments. I made waffles the next morning. The woman who frisked us stayed a different night. Something about a problem with her husband. I didn't ask, just turned down clean sheets in a spare bedroom and fluffed the pillows.

"You can rest here," I told her.

To thank me, she brought me flowers in a small glass vase.

I set the flowers on the kitchen table, watched the lavender petals dance in the sunlight. Then what would Jesus do? Make breakfast and eat together. So I did this. I tried to show Christian love. I didn't understand what was happening in my family. But Paul said love never fails. So sleep well and have some breakfast. Maybe, as the song said, I would understand it better by and by.

⎯⧉⎯

Now, standing in a hospital lobby, I tried to obey again. *Heavenly Father,* I prayed, *equip me to love a stranger as Jesus would. Help me to love a mother as Jesus would. Enable me to love a daughter as Jesus would. Show me how to love a husband as Jesus would.*

Not just to meet your condition for answered prayer, but because love never fails. You promised that. And learning to love is why we're here.

Rick Warren said it well: "The point of life is learning to love—God and people."

But the Bible said it perhaps best. "Anyone who does not love does not know God, for God is love."

Indeed, I needed God to hear my prayers now and to answer. So I would love. God demanded it, so God would help me.

Yes, I had work to do. But God would help us all.

I'm sure he already had.

Persist

Keep on praying.
1 THESSALONIANS 5:17

Bzzzt! The pager buzzed suddenly. I almost dropped it, trying to respond.

"They're calling from surgery."

The burned boy's mother looked at me with hope, tired eyes daring to shine. She hugged me. I thanked her, racing back to my tote bag, digging for my phone. Then, with great care, I punched in the phone number I'd been given.

A surgeon answered. It was almost 2 P.M. Dan had been in surgery for four hours.

"Mrs. Raybon?"

My heart pounded.

"Yes! That's me," I answered.

"Just wanted to check in, let you know everything's going fine."

I exhaled. Praise God.

"Okay," I said. But I wanted to hear . . . more? Indeed, I wanted to forget that our little medical drama wasn't one of countless millions unfolding around the world that day. But this doctor had a calm, warm, assuring voice. I closed my eyes to hear it. I pressed the cell phone to my ear to catch every nuance, every clue, every word.

"We've arrived at the location where we will make our repair," he went on.

"Yes, okay," I said.

I waited for more. I had hoped for greater . . . progress?

"So you haven't started the operation?" I asked then, surprised, opening my eyes.

The doctor responded, still calm and easy.

"It just takes awhile to get to the location where we start our repairs."

My heart sank. But now I understood. Our little surgery was precise surgery, indeed. So our medical team was moving precisely—that is, they were moving slowly. They had to.

"So how are you doing?" the doctor asked. "You holding on okay?"

A compassionate man.

"Actually, I've been praying," I said. "Praying with good people all morning."

The doctor's voice brightened.

"That's good!" he said. "That's *real* good. It helps!"

His reaction surprised me. I still expected professional folks to be naysayers about prayer. But here was a doctor, a brain surgeon at that, saying that prayer counted for good in his meticulous work.

"I figure that's my job today," I told him. "I pray. You operate."

He laughed.

"Yes. Well, four, five more hours," he said. "We'll page when we're finished. But right now your husband is doing fine. We're taking good care of him."

Years later, when I culled enough courage to read the operation report, I would see why this doctor welcomed my prayers. The brain is mighty and fragile territory. Dan's condition was critical, precarious, always potentially *that* close to catastrophe.

Medical details can swamp ordinary people. In a crisis, one of Dan's doctors told me later, most adults comprehend at a seventh- or eighth-grade level. Even very well-educated, tuned-in adults won't always handle complicated medical details in a crisis. "So we're trained to use simple phrases and concepts to explain what's going on," he said.

Simple, in Dan's case, wasn't hard to understand. He was in critical shape. With his surgery, the potential for disaster was always real.

So I focused instead on the doctor's encouragement. The medical team was taking good care of him. That meant so much. I could return to my purple chair in the waiting room and sit down with hope next to my mother.

Mama dug in her bag and handed me a peanut-butter package.

"You hungry?" she asked.

I shook my head no. I told her about the doctor's call, about the doctor's delight that I'd been praying.

Mama smiled, but we didn't have our Hollywood movie moment: her grabbing me and me grabbing her with grateful, loving hugs, then breaking into a spontaneous prayer of thanksgiving and hope.

None of that, in fact, was happening in our waiting room. It was filled with people now. The TV was on again, droning too loud, tuned to an afternoon soap. Cranky children whined. Adults snored. Some stared, eyes blank, into aging magazines. Everybody was waiting.

I decided to call Dan's sister, Diana, with an update. She was still in the Newark airport, waiting for her plane to Denver. She sounded relieved by the progress report.

Next I called Joi in Chicago at her business meeting and left a message.

I called Alana, who answered, promising to get to the hospital as soon as she could. I left a message with my friend Denise, who had said she'd come sit with me too. I called my sister in Atlanta.

I called the benefits office at the University of Colorado in Boulder, confirming that Dan's medical insurance was current.

I called the church office, requesting that one of the ministers call me back.

I checked our messages at home.

Beep. Beep. Beep.

Staying busy on the phone took the edge off any lingering nerves.

Mama watched me make the calls.

She asked me again if I wanted something to eat.

"No thank you, Mama," I said.

At eighty-four, she still looked at least ten years younger—a plus in modern eyes, to look like you haven't lived the years that you've earned. But looks aside, she was still eighty-four and that is a long time. A good long time.

But Mama's years truly were good. She had a college degree. A marriage of forty years. Her two daughters were both college educated too. She'd taught for years in public schools and volunteered as many years in hospitals after retiring. She'd helped my father buy two homes, buried him well, then lived alone almost twenty more years up to this point. She still went swimming three days a week. Still drove a car. And here she was, still asking if I wanted peanut-butter crackers.

Moreover, she did this usually without making it look too hard. That's how she did many things. Just name it and do it.

That's how she taught me to pray, in fact. Mama, indeed, taught me to pray.

But it doesn't add up because Mama wasn't a praying woman.

Instead, she was practical, waking us for church on Sunday mornings, calling from the kitchen, always starting with my sister's name: "Lauretta and Patricia!" We would groan under our breath, knowing it was time to crawl out from under the insulating covers and get moving.

Still, we never complained, not loud enough to be heard anyway. And we didn't need a second calling. Not for church. Sunday mornings Mama hollered our names and we jumped from our twin beds. Bare feet searched for the throw rugs beside each bed. But no laying in. Down the hall in the bathroom, we washed off sleep. We were *so* tempted to goof off. Instead, we slid into our crinolines, our matching dresses, the dime-store velveteen ribbons, lacy white socks, black patent leather slip-on shoes—each piece laid out on the foot of our bed by our mother the night before.

Mama kept a place for every single item. I can still see my mother's linen closet in that first house on Gaylord Street: every towel, washcloth, tea towel, sheet, and pillowcase scrubbed clean and starched and ironed, folded perfectly and stacked by size, color, and season.

With her, everything had its special position, even, as my husband would say now, her emotions. So if she is sad, I can tell. But she probably won't talk about it. "I cry when I'm by myself," she says. To her, that's the orderly way, and order is right. Moving her emotions outside of that space would seem to her like a heresy.

For her, indeed, life doesn't work without order. So on a recent morning when it was snowing outside, she told me on the phone, "I'm going to fix my oatmeal now." Then she explained, "When it snows, I have oatmeal." That means if it's *not* snowing, she *doesn't* have oatmeal. She laughed then, knowing I could hardly keep up with such logic.

We are so different.

Mother and daughter, yes, but day and night, hot and cold, down and up, here and there. Hardly are we on the same page.

"You hungry? Want some caramel corn?" she asked now, and it had no deeper meaning. I was looking for the metaphor, the myth, a Joseph Campbell story. She was only asking: Are you hungry or not? The practicality of Mama. Nary a spiritual bone in her body.

That's why it's such a surprise that I learned to pray from my mother. In church, this wasn't her role.

In church, Mama sat in the same place for fifty years: same pew, five rows from the back, left-hand side, next to old friends who had been known to talk, sometimes not too softly, during the sermon.

They covered their mouth, joking sometimes about a pastor's remarks, especially any plea from the pulpit for money. Mama would describe "that no-good preacher" without blinking an eye. Mama would dust the family Bible and rearrange it carefully on her living-room coffee table. But I don't *ever* remember seeing my mother, in a quiet moment, open the Bible to read it. I don't remember her talking about Jesus or calling on the Lord's name or crying in church or shouting from her pew, filled up with the Holy Ghost.

I never saw Mama wave her hands in the air in submission or in worship or in sheer awe of the God of the ages. This was in a church where, every Sunday of my childhood, at least one beautiful saint was slain out cold in the Spirit—as in flat-out unconscious. Other folks whirled in the aisles like tops. "Thank you, Jesus! THANK YOU, JESUS!"

Meanwhile, one of the women preachers, notorious for her full emotions, lost her hat, her handkerchief, and her *shoes* whenever the Spirit moved through that congregation, filling her up. Then, for good measure, this woman sometimes fell like a rock to the floor, limbs stiff like a board, totally knocked out by the Holy Ghost.

All around her, the woman's pocketbook, hat, handkerchief, church bulletin, and shoes skittered across the floor like leaves after a sudden springtime storm. Meanwhile, the choir leaned back into their song, hitting impossibly high notes, releasing with joy their praise and every pent-up emotion.

And Mama? Never said a word. Even now, after all that church, I felt a shock if my mother repeated the church-folk refrain: "God is good. All the time, God is good." From her mouth, it sounded sincere enough. But it still sounded shocking, because church talk wasn't her style.

But now I was seeing that my mama, who sometimes complained to us that Daddy wanted to go to church "every time the church door opens," was the one who first taught me to pray.

That means she taught me to believe. And to listen. Listening "to the silent thunder of the Lord of hosts," said Richard Foster, is how believers begin to pray, especially when they want to pray for others.

Without this listening, said Foster, our praying "is vain repetition." So listening to the Lord is "the first thing, the second thing, and the third thing" necessary, he said, especially when praying for somebody else. For confirmation, Foster then quoted the renowned Søren Kierkegaard, who observed: "A man prayed, and at first he thought that prayer was talking.

But he became more and more quiet until in the end he realized that prayer is listening."

To my knowledge, my mother, who loved to read John Grisham novels and stories and such, never had read a book by Kierkegaard or Foster. But when she took my small hands and pressed them together, leaned her face toward mine and instructed, "Say your grace, precious," she taught me the one thing that, for the rest of my days, would sustain me.

At the end of each evening, when Mama knelt with me by my bed and taught me to repeat after her, "I pray the Lord my soul to keep," she was telling me that God is—and that this God is *listening*.

Maybe even better, she was saying that every prayer of faith gets an answer. So every night, kneel down and do it again.

Never fail. Bedtime on Gaylord Street, Mama kneeling at the bedside. Night after sleepy night. *Stop that foolishness. Say your prayers.* The right thing to do. Orderly and good and right. Not much love in it, to tell the truth. But she *was* teaching. Maybe better, she was faithful.

So I *had* to love her.

She taught me that prayer wasn't a choice and it would keep me. Going to college and earning degrees taught me many things. But my mama taught me that prayer is a way.

Years later, in a stark hospital room, with my husband inching toward death, that lesson was a life preserver thrown in from my past. So I clung to it. I pressed my face into the folds of his bedsheets and I breathed in this lesson's promises. Prayer is the way, indeed. Or as Frederick D. Haynes III put it: "If our prayers are to mean anything to God, they must mean everything to us."

But was I naive? Perhaps.

But more than that, I was a dying man's wife. So it was praying time. Believing time. Working time. And, yes, I had prayed half the night. But this was a new day. And Dan still had hours and hours to go.

So *walk with me, Jesus.*

Didn't we sing that in church, back then? I couldn't remember. Maybe it was a Motown song? *Walk with me, Henry?*

The mind plays tricks and mine was weary now. I just knew my prayer work wasn't over. Real prayer is persistent, indeed. I remembered that.

Midsummer, I had read that whole discourse on prayer in the eleventh chapter of Luke, where Jesus taught the Lord's Prayer, as most people still call it.

After teaching that prayer, he told his disciples a beautiful parable—

the one where the friend is knocking at midnight, asking for a loaf of bread to feed a hungry traveler. But the sleepy man rebuffs his friend. Go away! Get lost! He is incensed. My doors are locked! My family's in bed. And you want *bread*?

But look at this, Jesus says. Even though this angry man won't get up out of friendship, he'll get up because his friend at the door is *persistent*. He'll give his friend the bread because *he won't go away*.

Then Jesus, who taught like none other, spoke the deep and big words, perhaps his greatest lesson on prayer: Ask and it will be given to you. Seek and you will find. Knock and the door will be opened to you.

The Living Bible makes it plain, just lays it out there: "Keep on asking and you will keep on getting; keep on looking and you will keep on finding; knock and the door will be opened."

Keep on knocking because, as Jesus said, persistence will bring us finally to the prayer that matters most. He put it this way: "If you sinful people know how to give good gifts to your children, how much more will your heavenly Father give the Holy Spirit to those who ask him."

It isn't a question. It's a statement.

That is, the prayer that the Holy Spirit inspires, as Torrey said, is the prayer that God can answer. My mama taught the same thing in her own way. But God himself would finish the teaching if I kept at it. So Holy Spirit, come—then, help me pray without going away. Without fainting or giving out. Or giving up.

Again and again—the same prayer, until I get it right.

Heal this man. Heal our marriage. No, banish my resentments. Deepen my love. Raise up beloved daughters. Bind our weary hearts. Teach me to trust.

Keep on knocking? I was at the door.

And my mama was a faithful teacher.

So open the door, blessed Jesus. I'm knocking.

Still knocking, sharpening my prayer saw.

Still knocking. Louder and louder and *louder*.

Son of David! Let us in.

It's Hard

But the greatest of these is love.
1 CORINTHIANS 13:13

By six o'clock, the night sky had turned the waiting-room windows to black. Winter takes daylight too soon.

Families had abandoned the third floor to find dinner. A few restaurants and fast-food places were cooking nearby. The hospital deli was open too. But I couldn't eat. Dan was still in the operating room, and the pager hadn't buzzed with the final word.

Mama was napping. So I turned off the TV once more, not willing to hear the day's news, whatever dismal goings-on had happened. Then the elevator opened and Alana, my younger daughter, emerged. I was thrilled to see her.

We hugged.

"How's Dad?" she asked.

I didn't care tonight that she wore the flowing garb of the Nation of Islam, her shorn hair covered in a long scarf, her face scrubbed of makeup. She always got stares.

Tonight, however, it didn't matter to me, not the clothes anyway.

After a lifetime of getting stared at because I was "colored," then "Negro," then "black," now we got stares because Alana was dressed like a Muslim, hair covered in scarves and her body covered with long, heavy tops and long skirts. But tonight I wouldn't let that matter. I was just glad she was here, earnest and aware and passionate about her life and the lives of others. My prayers for her salvation in Christ continued daily. But God's orders, in the meantime, were to trust him always and to show her love right now.

I hugged her again.

"Dad's still in surgery," I said.

She looked surprised.

"Didn't he go in this morning?"

"Long procedure," I said.

"Yeah, but all day?"

I shrugged, but I understood.

"They gave me a pager, but it hasn't gone off. It should soon."

I looked at my watch. I was getting impatient too. Oh, my beloved husband. What an ordeal.

Alana sat down next to her grandmother, nudged her awake, and hugged her. The two of them did that these days—the hugging, the warm greetings, and this was all good, as the young people said. And I was glad for it.

In fact, being glad, even when things felt bad, was new for me. But now I worked at being glad every day, one blessed day at a time. I would do like the apostle Paul. He was in prison when he wrote that joyful letter to the church folk at Philippi. And what did he tell them? Rejoice! In the Lord, *always* rejoice.

Well. Yes, my daughter had left the church. But as a Black Muslim, ironically, she had adopted Christian ways: kindness, respect for elders, a helpful attitude, a clean lifestyle.

As a teenager in the church, sadly, she'd pushed every limit. Talking back. Tight clothes. Heavy makeup. Running with friends to nightclubs and smoking and drinking and maybe even doing drugs. Staying out late. Talking back even more.

Now she was Mother Teresa. Out of the church, yes, but Mother Teresa. She even dressed kind of like a Mother Teresa, or a close match anyway. She looked beautiful.

But I still didn't understand what was happening. When I prayed, God still spoke to my spirit with one answer: Love her. Trust me. And have some peace. Stop turning yourself inside and out, trying to run *my* business.

So I looked at the good—her new Christian attitude, even while she renounced Jesus as the Son of God—and I thanked God for the attitude change. One thing at a time.

But it was hard.

There are points in life, indeed, when a person feels forsaken, when nothing in one's life makes any sense. Her rejection of church doctrine and church life and Jesus as Savior of the church was now that wounded point.

So in response, I moved from despair to honesty.

I talked to God, confessing.

I *had* been a lousy Christian mother—not all of the time, of course. But on a certain level, yes, it was true. I was a lousy Christian mother. I was casual with the faith. That is, I acted holy in church and hellish at home, bullying my girls, ignoring my husband and dismissing his concerns, holding back love, condemning, belittling, impatient.

The girls said I was mean.

They were right.

But their adolescence had scared me: boyfriends and parties, drugs and sex, or the threat of boyfriends and parties, drugs and sex. My girls turned sullen. Or maybe I turned sullen first and they followed suit.

But moody was the rule of the day. Grunts replaced talk. Anger ran high, week after contentious and angry week. And there was also dirty laundry and slammed doors and tied-up telephones and lies and yelling. And crying. And "other kids' parents let them go, so why can't I?"

And it got worse.

There was a quiet, hard coldness that settled around our house. Strangers living with strangers. Every hour a strain. Any word a fight. My girls, as children, knew how to laugh and act silly and have fun. But during those years, they weren't having fun anymore. Not with me, anyway.

They said I was controlling. I was unfair. I wouldn't listen. I was demanding. Oh, and I was mean.

All those things were true. I turned into a screaming crazy lady who then felt guilty every night about each day's outbursts. It shouldn't have happened like that.

My daughters and I are smart women. We are nice people. Other people say this about us, so it must be true. Other people even love us. But we didn't show love to each other then, not on enough days. We disappointed each other. We took each other for granted.

And one day I finally heard the worst words a parent can hear from a child.

"I HATE YOU!"

My girls screamed the words, slapping my face with them.

Right away, I knew what that meant: I hate that we don't talk easy like we used to. I hate that I'm trying to pull away and you won't let me, so I have to say stupid, hateful things to force you to *let me go*. I hate that we're Christians who never pray together at home, never have one moment of devotion as a family in our home, never hear one word about the Bible inside our home unless it's a threat. Thou *shalt* honor your mother and your father and all of that. But what about the mother and father? Aren't they supposed to honor and love the kids? But you don't honor and love me. So since you don't, I will hate you.

I will hate that you call yourself a Christian but you don't act like one. You don't love like one. You don't parent like one. Or live like one. You live with false piety and pride, like you're so darn holy—only she didn't say "darn." She cursed at me, indeed, forcing me to hear what she wanted me to know: I hate your piety, Mother, and your pride. I hate that you don't shut up sometimes and just listen. So I hate that your lack of respect and understanding pushed me into rebellion. In fact, I hate rebellion. I hate wearing these tight clothes and short skirts and black mascara and orange lipstick. I hate smoking these stupid cigarettes and drinking bad-tasting drinks and driving fast with my friends. But I don't know how to stop this car.

If Alana was saying those things, I could hear them, but I didn't know how to stop the car either.

So she'd stopped it herself, found a structured religion that forced her, by mandate, to take off the heavy makeup; take off the tight, short clothes; put down the cigarettes and bad drinks; clean up her living; and stop the rebellion.

Not just because I had prayed, although I had prayed like a mad woman—on my face, stretched out on the floor in the dark, in the middle of many long nights, pleading to God.

But I had been praying without a vision and without understanding.

So I began to pray to get back our old life. But real prayer isn't about "maintaining our own Christian life," Andrew Murray wrote in his precise, polite way.

So with all of my dramatic dropping on my face, sorrowfully praying—no, pleading and begging—that God would save my beloved daughter from partying and drinking and cigarettes and all the other craziness, I was, in fact, *praying for the wrong thing*.

That *other* work, whatever it was that God had entrusted me to do, is what I should have been praying and longing for *first*. Indeed, seek first the Kingdom and all the other things will be added.

Isn't that *other* work what Christ prayed so desperately for on his last night? That we would do great works in his name and bear much fruit and all of *that*? I knew the Scripture, instantly knew where to find it: John 15:16. You didn't choose me, Jesus said. "I chose you. I appointed you to go and produce lasting fruit, so that the Father will give you whatever you ask for, using my name."

I'd read that verse countless times in my fifty-one years, slept through it in boring sermons, glossed over it in Bible-study readings. But now with my daughter shouting with her life, and with that same daughter reinventing her life because I hadn't properly lived the life God had entrusted to me, this verse finally was burning through.

So look: Jesus himself had appointed me to go, to truly throw down my mediocre, safe, bourgeois, self-absorbed ways and instead produce fruit that would last so that the Father would give me, in Jesus' mighty name, *whatever I asked for*. Jesus, praying on his last night, made sure a big "if" was attached. *If* I produced the fruit entrusted to me—the "other" work—*if* I produced that other work, then the Father would hear me and answer me whatever I asked. Then came verse 17: "Love each other."

Jesus knew it was hard.

Doing our work and loving other imperfect people at the same time— while they tried to love an imperfect me—it was downright hard. It seemed almost impossible on most days.

I thought of Mama and Daddy, who didn't love with big hands-on affection. That's just the truth of it. But they were saturated in *other* work. Mama—a Sunday school teacher, even Sunday school superintendent, then Girl Scout leader, PTA mother, club woman, fund-raiser, committee woman in half a dozen ladies' clubs with their countless luncheons and banquets and marathons, all to help hurting and less-advantaged people.

Then Daddy too—a church trustee, church steward, church everything. Driving to church on subzero Colorado mornings to stoke the furnace and coax the heat, so saints could worship in dignity and warmth. Then, during summer, repairing the noisy cooler, painting the faded walls, tearing up the worn linoleum in the fellowship hall to install the shiny and new. Then on Sunday mornings, the little church would feel open and welcome and clean and right to all who walked through the doors, those doors freshly painted sometimes by my daddy alone.

I went with him one night, begging to go, just liking to be around to watch him work. This wasn't his day job. But he loved his church. So we stood together outside in the dark, lit by a single bulb hanging out front, while Daddy rolled the last line of paint on the wooden church doors.

Then when we got home, the phone rang again—a committee calling about yet the next assignment.

So Daddy and Mama were chosen, appointed by God, and they were faithful. They did their other work. They weren't perfect. Neither was the world, putting up every barrier to stop progress for a colored man and his wife. But still they did their other work.

But it was hard.

I thought of my husband, Dan, generous and affectionate at his best, but sarcastic and hurtful and insensitive at his worst. Probably we're all like this. Maybe that's why we work so hard serving others but forget to love at home. We get out of balance.

With Dan, it meant staying too long at work. Helping anybody who asked. So I condemned again.

"You gave that student *two hundred dollars? To pay a bill?* What about *our* bills?"

But he kept at it. Then he rushed from work to his choir practice, then to that church board meeting, then to this church panel, dropping everything to answer any call.

But when I asked for his help, he looked at me wearily. Annoyed. His other work was the better work, he seemed to say. But it became a god. And none of it, in truth, was done for the only reason that matters: to glorify God.

With me, on the other hand, I just never found my other work. Between commuting to jobs, ferrying kids, shoveling food into pots and pans and calling it dinner, then commuting back to jobs, I never discovered my other work. Whatever God entrusted to me lay neglected. But the problem was my neglect in spending time with God.

Nothing matters more, Oswald Chambers argued. "Prayer does not equip us for greater works—prayer *is* the greater work." Our prayer time, and the relationship with God that ensues, is everything, he declared. That is our *first* work, he said: spending time with God. That relationship corrects everything else. Instead, I lay awake at night, wishing. I longed for a day when Dan and I would stop, get off the treadmill, just sit down face-to-face, and agree on a family mission—throwing out the other demands that crowded out what mattered most: our time with God.

But we kept our pace, paying homage to Carl Jung's thesis that "hurry is not *of* the devil; it *is* the devil." So our household was out of balance, the lives in it out of sync with the words of Jesus on his final night. I command you: Love each other.

But, sweet Jesus, what is love?

Well, I had read that thirteenth chapter of 1 Corinthians. Love is patient. Love is kind. It's not rude. *Blah, blah, blah.*

Oh Lord. Help me say it.

Love doesn't boast. Sometimes I got the order of it mixed up, never really memorizing it to the letter. If I tried harder, maybe I could get the order right.

Love is patient.

Love is kind.

Love is not jealous—or boastful or proud.

Love is not rude.

Hey, Dan, were you listening to this? Did you read the apostle's epistle? Did I?

Had I considered all the things that Paul was writing to the folks at Corinth? That love does not demand its own way. That love is not irritable—and, hey, Patricia—it keeps no record of when it has been wronged.

So love is never glad about injustice but rejoices whenever the truth wins out. Love never gives up, never loses faith, is always hopeful, always endures in every circumstance.

Love never fails. But it's hard.

No wonder so many prayers don't get answered.

And yet? The promises of God remain. He "hears the prayers of the righteous."

So my task was clear. I had to love *and* act right. And yet? Right now it was hard.

So Ask! Then Get Moving

Jesus told him, "Stand up, pick up your
sleeping mat, and walk!" JOHN 5:8

Sometimes a light blasts on.

Mine came in the form of a nurse, striding with purpose off the third-floor elevator. I turned to her anxiously. But she wasn't from Dan's medical team, so she wasn't looking for me. But she did notice us.

"Long day?" she asked in passing, just being friendly.

I nodded and she paused. Then she walked over.

"It's kind of hard to rest in here," I said. I gestured around me at the waiting room, now a riot of discarded newspapers, magazines, unfinished puzzles, and games on almost every surface.

"Try the *fourth* floor," the nurse said. "It's nicer up there. Quieter. Not so messy. Lots of people don't know about it. It's really a nicer waiting area."

She was right. Just one floor up, the waiting room was quieter, cleaner, orderly, and almost empty. Just one other family group sat in one corner. No clutter. No chaos. It looked as if it hadn't been occupied all day.

I walked into the space and inhaled a deep, long breath. Quiet and peace—just one floor higher.

I called my friend Denise to tell her where to find us, called Joi to give her an update, then left a message for Dan's sister, Diana, on her cell phone.

Then Mama and I, with Alana, resettled in our newfound space—

not really sitting together, but together in the room. It felt good, a reasonable way to be while waiting for news about Dan.

That's where Denise found us: "All of you were just sitting there, in your own space, but not really together. That's the main thing I could see: introspection," she said later.

"Was it that bad?" I asked.

"Well . . . you were sitting by the window, alone," Denise said. She was right. Outside, the early black night didn't offer a view. But I was looking out anyway—alone, indeed. Mama was slumped in her chair, weary from the day. Alana, in another corner, was holding a Bible, looking inward, reflecting perhaps on a Nation of Islam review.

Each in our own thoughts, we had retreated, not admitting that we were still waiting, waiting, waiting for some word on Dan. We were waiting, each in our own strength, indeed. Our waiting, as wearying as we were making it, had drawn us not together but apart.

So Denise, a modern woman of God and an extrovert by nature, instinctively sought to bring us together.

"Let's pray," she said, gesturing to the three of us. I was drawn by the look of her, glowing like sunshine and good health in a bright green fleece jacket that felt, when I touched it, like a warm and holy blanket. She pulled us into a circle where we'd have to touch and agree. The three of us consented, but we weren't jumping up and down about it.

We didn't understand what my friend was asking. We didn't realize that she had needed the entire day to get ready for this visit. We'd forgotten that in a hospital just two blocks away, she'd watched her father die after a stroke less than a year before. Then a few fast months later, her mother's heart attack came without a real warning. Then her mother was gone too.

When parents die, it is a massive, unspeakable loss. But for Denise, the loss was cataclysmic. She was adopted as a baby, just seven months old, by her loving parents. Losing them forced her to grieve for the only parents she knew—and for the parents she'd never known.

She'd already prayed all day, in fact, to find the composure to walk into a hospital—for the first time since her mother had passed away—and not fall apart.

But here she was, breezing off the elevator with her big smile and hugs all around.

We fell into her arms.

"Okay, I'm here!" she said, even if we didn't fully know what that meant.

"Took me all day to get here," she added, laughing. "But I'm here now. Tell me what you need."

Denise looked at us, isolated in our introspective reflections. So she tugged us toward her instead.

"I don't know what you were doing before I came, but I'm here now. So let's pray."

She was like Jesus, telling the paralytic man to just get up. "Pick up your mat and walk," Jesus told him. Go home. Get moving.

I loved that Denise was my friend that way.

Not many knew how our friendship came to be, how, at a moment of courage and honesty, I asked God to send me a friend—a real friend, somebody I could talk to about anything. Somebody to laugh with, joke with, cry with, pray with.

It was a good prayer—a real good prayer—asked *years* before I even thought about taking time to study the principles of prayer.

God was merciful, indeed. He answered it.

You have not because you ask not, James said, and even when you ask, you ask amiss, for your own pleasure. But back then, there I was, asking anyway. Still, it was a hard prayer because I was a grown woman.

Back then at forty, I should have had a nice, tight set of friends: like-minded adult women with whom I told secrets, laughed, joked, cried, and prayed. Those circles grow out of shared passion.

Instead, I shared the drudgery of car pools and committee work in social clubs and job tasks at work.

I was impassionate, however, about most of it. The sin of "impassion"? Did that show up anywhere in my study books?

In fact, in the Andrew Murray book, over in chapter 9, there it was: "It must be our prayer that the Lord would so fill all His people with the spirit of devotion, that not one may be found standing idle in the vineyard."

The Bible, of course, said the same thing: "Whatever you do, work at it with all your heart, as working for the Lord, not for men."

A devoted and passionate life, filled with passionate, devoted work in God's vineyard, not in my own, was a good goal, indeed.

I think I had that, years ago, before both my marriages, or between marriages maybe. So long ago, I could barely remember that I was devoted and passionate, helping out in the youth department at my parents' church. Once I organized a rambunctious crew of children and teens to put on a play for Easter. I found the script in a box in my parents' basement, so the play was old-fashioned in a way. But it had a sound moral theme and funny lines. The kids lapped it up. The play was a hit. Everybody rejoiced. The audience beamed. The youth soaked up the accolades and appreciation. Nobody had put on a play like that at my mother's church for years, not since the days when Mr. Bell and Miz Hall and Miss Fontenot and my mother and the other young parents staged *A Christmas Carol* and, once in a fit of grand design, a fully loaded version of *Snow White and the Seven Dwarfs*.

I played Snow White. Apparently nobody in our black church thought that this was very odd.

❈

God help me. Passion and devotion. Where does it all go?

Mine went the way of laundry and traffic jams and diapers and Girl Scout cookie sales and countless trips to the orthodontist and thousands of hours at jobs that were okay but weren't ever really wonderful. Then came a thousand other demands, always more obligation over devotion. So resentment choked my path. Somewhere along the way, passion died.

I did my duty and got things done.

But now, I was . . . angry? I was angry at myself, yes, for not bailing off this trajectory when I had a chance, when I was younger and knew something was wrong. But I thought I was supposed to put up with the wrong and keep working at it. Staying with wrong jobs. Going to dead-end meetings. Wearing shoes that hurt.

My sister did just the opposite. After teaching second grade her first year out of college, she left the suburban neighborhood, weary of doubting parents who scrutinized her classroom. Every day the "parent monitors" showed up—not to help, but to oversee, unable to believe a "colored" teacher truly knew what she was doing.

She knew.

But after just one year, she left anyway. She went to Atlanta, entered graduate school, completed a Ph.D., and ended up serving God as a psychologist at a school for emotionally disabled children who love her and who love that she loves them and the work she is doing.

A coworker once asked Lauretta, then in her midfifties, if she was going to retire soon.

"Retire?" She looked at him, surprised. "I *love* what I do. Why would I retire?"

This is the "finding your bliss" reflection, I suppose. But Joseph Campbell *was* right. Dying to your current life to come to another life is necessary, not just practically but spiritually. "All you have to do is die spiritually and be reborn to a larger way of living."

But do we know the way?

I am the way, Jesus said. So go home this other way, he told the people he had healed. Don't go back that old way. Go *my* way.

But taking this step is "miraculous," Campbell added. "If you do follow your bliss you put yourself on a kind of track that has been there all the while, waiting for you, and the life that you ought to be living is the one you are living. When you can see that, you begin to meet people who are in the field of your bliss, and they open the doors to you."

Campbell went on: "I say, follow your bliss and don't be afraid and doors will open where you didn't know they were going to be."

And sometimes a friend is standing on the other side.

But first there's the door: Jesus.

So ring the bell. That's how Jesus put it.

"Ask and it will be given to you; seek and you will find; knock and the door will be opened to you. For everyone who asks receives; he who seeks finds; and to him who knocks, the door will be opened."

James reinforced the idea.

"Ye have not because ye ask not." But even if you ask, you ask amiss, James said, because you ask for your own pleasures.

Somewhere in the midst of this was my life *and* the answer to my life's prayers.

The pager buzzed.

"I'm on the *fourth* floor," I told the doctor. "I moved up a floor."

Soon the elevator door opened and out walked Dr. Breeze. Thin and fit and focused. Not a single gesture lost on the man. A healer.

He walked over to the four of us. It was almost seven o'clock. This had been a long, long day.

Dr. Breeze looked accomplished. He also looked pleased.

He told us doctor things: He and his team had isolated the malformed vein and repaired it. Along the way, they had also encountered three "aneurysmal dilations," which they had also repaired.

I listened. I nodded. I didn't understand, not really. But I seized on the doctor's main point: Dan was alive. He was doing well. He came through the operation in strong shape.

Lord Jesus. Dan was alive.

I looked at Denise. She was grinning from ear to ear. I hugged her.

I looked at Alana. She was crying. I hugged her.

I looked at Mama. She was thanking God, using that phrase she had learned. "God is good," she said over and over. So why not? I hugged Mama.

I looked at Dr. Breeze. He didn't seem to smile much, but I hugged him anyway. Then there it was: He smiled. He said thank you.

Dan would be on a ventilator for a while, Dr. Breeze said. They wanted to make sure his breathing was stable.

Dr. Breeze explained why the operation took so long, detailing how he and his colleagues spent hours planning their strategy. Again, he used that phrase: "real expensive real estate." That's where they did the operation.

Dan's problem, located right next to the brain stem, was that pricey real estate, Dr. Breeze stressed, and the work was intricate and had to be precise. But for now, he said, he was feeling pretty good about how far they'd come and how well they'd done with the challenge.

Dan would be in intensive care for the next few days. His condition was critical, but that could improve soon. They would watch him carefully. The nurse would come get us when Dan was back in his room. Then we'd see.

⚜

Okay, this was good news. Getting a new life is a godly gift. It compares to nothing.

But then came that odd moment, after answered prayer, when the urgency kind of evaporates. Praying people know this moment. You just prayed for a job you needed, the house you wanted, a sick child to be healed, a husband to survive surgery.

Then the prayer is answered.

There is rejoicing. But then comes the recognition that this prayer is only one request of countless thousands that you will pray in a lifetime. Other needs are sure to follow this one. Other crises, unseen now, are down the road.

So, yes, I had prayed for Dan and I had asked that he would survive the intricate neurovascular surgery and that he would go on to walk again and come back home again.

But at this moment, just after the doctor said the first hurdle had been jumped, I felt an odd . . . letdown?

Jerry Sittser, in his book *Why God Doesn't Answer Your Prayer*, explained that he'd figured out why: "We pray not to get something but to know someone." That someone, of course, is God.

Sittser went on: "That God answers our specific requests is wonderful, just like vacation time is to us, however much we enjoy our jobs. But it is all secondary. It is enough simply to know God because a relationship with him is what we desire most."

Dan's healing was crucial to me. This is truth. But to tell the whole truth, a crucial part of that truth was this: I didn't want to be a widow. I wanted my husband back in my home, sleeping next to me in our bed, walking with me around the one-mile park in our neighborhood, driving with me to church, going to our Saturday afternoon movie, laughing with me, loving me—all the things we'd once done and now maybe could do again.

With God's help, we could do these things.

So, said Dr. Breeze, here he is. I have given your husband back to you. With good recovery, the things you want should happen.

But suddenly I instinctively knew that these things—while wonderful and so soon delivered to me—weren't the core of it. Something even greater than a healed husband was at the core of my longing to pray.

Eugene Peterson in *Answering God* gets at the center of this. "Prayers are not tools for doing or getting, but for being and becoming."

When Jesus healed people, he always exhorted them, after the healing itself was accomplished, to *go*. Get up and get moving. Change your course, my brother. Take the higher way, my sister.

Then you'll look at the mountain from a different vantage point. It will look different. First, it will probably look smaller. If you're standing up with me, you might not even notice it anymore. Maybe you'll see other mountains that need your attention more.

For Jesus, moving after an encounter with him *was* everything.

You've received my touch, he said. Now go do something vital with your life. But how? He was clear about the first step: Get moving.

But moving is hard.

The problem is not knowing what the move will bring, if anything. Like the time Denise's husband announced he wanted to move their family clear across the country, from New Jersey to Colorado, and she wasn't ready, didn't feel eager to start anew. She didn't want to leave. So she asked their pastor how to make peace with her husband's plan to relocate.

The beautiful pastor looked at her, not blinking.

"Go home and pack a box," he gently said. "See how *that* feels."

Get moving.

She did that and the move—made, in some respects, in protest—turned out to be the best move ever for her family. She couldn't see the result before it happened. She just had to trust that moving would be the right thing. Indeed, we met the same week she arrived—both desperate for friendship. And the friendship still thrives, just gets deeper.

For me, indeed, moving at God's heeding only felt right if the move was supposed to bless me, rather than glorify God. I was still confused about that then. I thought any effort I made was connected to whatever I desired of God.

I didn't understand that prayer for Dan's success in surgery could have a larger purpose, for God's glory. So, for example, the surgeons might learn something while treating Dan that could help somebody else, or maybe even help millions of other people.

So I had prayed the past twenty-four hours for my husband to be healed, for God's glory—but I didn't begin to imagine what that "glorification" could be.

In truth, I said the words "for your glory" with my mouth, more than with my heart, saying them with the hope that they'd supernaturally get the results I wanted: my husband's recovery and healing.

Moving my heart to say those words, however, was like turning a massive ocean liner. So I thought that I was praying for my husband's recovery, and, thanks be to God, we'd crossed the first of what could be many medical hurdles.

Immediately, however, God was pressing me for more. I could feel it in my unrest.

Denise might have felt it too. She grabbed Alana's hand and asked my daughter to take a walk with her, giving me space.

Mama went back to her chair.

I walked to the window, looking out at the inky sky, feeling aware that others in the hospital hadn't received good news tonight. Others were hearing, after this day of surgeries and treatments, devastating reports. I'd seen them in the third-floor waiting room, families huddled with a doctor, then suddenly collapsing into sobs and sorrow.

A hospital is a place of healing, but it also can be a kingdom of despair and pain and great loss.

What separates the two?

Why did I risk feeling for one crazy second as if I really must be a *good* person because our medical report wasn't one of the *bad* ones?

⚜

God knows me like a book. I can go from piety to arrogance without skipping a beat. And there it was. I was feeling not so much gratitude to God but rather a self-satisfied pride—it was pride, indeed—that *I* had taken time to study prayer. Then *I* had prayed when the need arose so suddenly, and now look! My husband was on the road to recovery, so look at *me*.

Look what *I'd* done.

I will confess this foolishness and the folly of it because none of this prayer business was about me, not even remotely about me.

Prayer business is *all* about God.

So, oh God, help me to rise above myself, to move out of the way, and then to move up, to a bigger vision and a bigger life, to glorify you.

Oh God, indeed, help me to move.

Now isn't *that* a prayer?

Thank God

Devote yourselves to prayer with an alert
mind and a thankful heart. COLOSSIANS 4:2

A nurse found us, announcing that Dan was finally back in his intensive-care room. He could see visitors, but family only—one person at a time—and only for five minutes.

Mama said she didn't want to bother him. Alana, looking tentative, said she'd wait. I was tentative too. But I took one flight of stairs down to the third floor, buzzed for admittance into intensive care, and walked the linoleum corridor to Dan.

My legs carried me. But my heart was trembling. I needed to see Dan for myself, that is—and with my own eyes. But my eyes were terrified of what they would find. Alive, yes, but I expected my husband to be a shadow of himself, a man buried in white blankets and huge bandages, staring at the ceiling with black, haunted eyes.

But Dan looked right at me with clear brown eyes when I walked in, shocking me actually. I didn't expect such clear and *present* eyes. I had expected he'd be half-dead in sleep or at least groggy. But Dan was aware and alert. His eyes were big as bowls. And they were shining, not the bloodshot eyes I expected, eyes dark and weary from the ordeal of the day.

But here he was, alive with openness and open with being alive. His eyes were wide and clear as a baby's. Swathed in white sheets, Dan looked, in fact, as innocent as a newborn.

Most notably, his face—so gray-looking and sick early that morning—

now had a rosy, shining glow. He looked as if he had a new tan, as if he'd been away on some cool vacation. He looked plain great, in fact, in contrast to what he'd been through all day. It didn't make sense. But I was overjoyed.

I didn't understand that he'd spent the day in the arms of Jesus, totally surrendered. No wonder he looked fabulous.

I grinned big at him. "Hi, sugar," I said, showing a big smile, red lipstick, happy eyes, trying to look surrendered myself. "Surgery is over. All done!"

With the ventilator, of course, Dan couldn't talk. But his eyes followed me into the room. Big, bright, shining eyes. And his chest, rising and falling with the insistent ventilator. That's what he was: eyes and breathing.

I'd seen ventilators on television and in movies. But this was my first up-close encounter with the big, noisy machine. Right away, I didn't know whether to love or hate it. Yes, it carried life-sustaining oxygen to Dan. But it stood between us like a sentry, blocking our connection. Plus it was noisy.

So with every *whoosh* and *click*, it gave Dan a new breath of life. But it lifted up his chest unnaturally high, letting it down unnaturally low. Each breath looked like heavy lifting, like it demanded unusual effort from my husband. Nothing easy about these breaths at all. So while the breathing was good medically, it looked hard and hardly normal.

In fact, only the ventilator made my husband look as critically sick as the doctors said he was. This was intensive care, and we still had hurdles to go. And yet he looked *good*. I held back tears, walking over to Dan's bedside.

I kissed his eyelids and his eyebrows, the only unhindered places I could find. Otherwise, his entire head—neck to forehead, ear to ear—was wrapped in white bandages, like a fat turban. The ventilator noisily occupied his mouth.

But his eyes. Shining like big lights. His eyes were dancing!

I squeezed Dan's hand on my side of the bed.

"We got good news, sugar!" I said.

Dan opened and closed his eyes once, responding with a yes. Yes! Eyes open and shut once.

"You came through the operation with flying colors!" I grinned at him again.

Eyes open and shut again. Yes. Yes!

"Dr. Breeze feels good about everything. They fixed everything."

Dan wanted to say something. He reached for his mouth, wanting to talk, but the big ventilator wouldn't allow that, of course.

For a moment, he waved his arms around, as if trying to grab the ventilator tube. Then it struck me: *He was moving.* His hands and arms had *life.*

This morning, before the operation, the paralysis had reached as far as his armpits. In fact, he'd said he felt nothing below that point, nothing in his arms and hands, nor could he move his arms or hands. This morning, they lay beside his body—lifeless deadweights.

But now he was waving one arm, then the other, struggling to reach me or the nurse.

We both tried to calm him.

He was trying to tell us something. Clearly, not talking was frustrating. Dan was a natural extrovert. Normally he woke up talking a mile a minute. And with him, nobody was a stranger. Any cabdriver, cashier, store clerk, doctor, lawyer, teacher, tailor, little kid, old person, you name it— could be a new friend for Dan.

Not to talk, in fact, was just unnatural for him. So, yes, the ventilator was helping him breathe. But it would feel to Dan like a mouth gag. Then I had a thought. "Do you want a pencil and paper, to write?"

Dan opened and closed his eyes.

"That means *yes?*"

Dan opened and closed his eyes again.

I turned to the nurse. But she was already leaving the room, returning a minute later with a clipboard, holding a white sheet of paper and a long yellow pencil.

"Let's try this," she said.

I placed the pencil in Dan's hand, and he tried to grasp it with shaky fingers.

Then I placed his hand on the clipboard and, shaking, he started to write slowly—kindergarten letters, big and ungainly and nearly uncontrolled, all over the page.

I was sure he had questions about the operation, wanting to know more details. So I followed his hand with my eyes, determined to make out the letters on the page.

G OD IS GOoD.

I said the words out loud. "GOD IS GOOD."

Dan opened and closed his eyes.

"God is good? Is that what you're saying?"

Dan opened and closed his eyes. Yes, I could hear him. I understood.

The door moved. It was Alana. She eased quietly into the room.

The nurse looked up, surprised.

"This is our daughter," I said. "This is Alana."

The nurse's kind eyes took in Alana's scarf and clothing for half a second but didn't show judgment, and for that I was grateful. Whatever Alana was wearing tonight seemed trivial compared to Dan's long day in surgery. So the smiling nurse was cordial and she wasn't petty. Praise God for folks who aren't petty.

"Your dad's doing good," she said to Alana, who walked slowly to Dan's bedside. Alana kissed her father's eyes and his nose.

"Hi, Dad," she said. A prodigal daughter's voice, almost unbearably sweet.

Dan stretched a hand toward her. Instantly his eyes started to water.

"Don't cry, Dad," Alana said, sweet voiced, reaching for her father.

The nurse and I agreed in unison. "No, no, no. Don't cry." Crying while hooked up to a ventilator didn't look to me like a good idea at all. So, together, we all calmed him. The nurse resumed her work, checking Dan's IVs, monitoring the other machines humming around us. This space was now a small symphony of lights, beeps, whooshes, clicks, and ticking noises—all of it focused on the vital signs of my husband's life.

I showed Alana the clipboard, and Alana asked Dan if he wanted to write some more. He opened and closed his eyes.

With shaky fingers, he wrote again.

GR ANM A

"Grandma?"

That's what he called my mother.

He opened and closed his eyes.

"Grandma's here," I said. "In the waiting room."

"Everybody's here," I told him, not bothering Dan with too many details like the fact that Joi was still in Chicago at her business meeting and couldn't get back until Sunday, another two days.

"And Joi is praying for you, sugar," I said. "You know she is."

Eyes opened and closed once.

Indeed, to Dan, his family's whereabouts seemed to matter. I think he wanted to know: Did my family rally for me? Was everybody supporting me?

Or maybe he was checking the status. Is everybody okay?

"Everybody's fine," I said, still smiling. "And Denise is in the waiting room. I sent e-mails *everywhere*," I told him. "People all over the country prayed for you all day."

I named people Dan had worked with for years. I named church friends. I named pastors. I named neighbors.

Dan opened and closed his eyes. Still looking. Eyes still bright. Alana was holding her father's hand.

Then we both noticed that the ventilator tube was starting to sound slushy.

"Can we clean his mouth?" Alana asked the nurse.

"I'll get something," the nurse said.

When she returned, she showed us how to swab Dan's mouth. The device looked like a little turkey baster, we all agreed, laughing, trying to lighten the moment.

So I tried first, without good success, to clear away Dan's mucus and saliva. Every time I tried, he moved his head away from me. I was either hurting him or not helping. But Alana felt sure she could handle it better.

"Let me try, Mom."

Soon, indeed, she'd figured out the trick of clearing Dan's mouth, which made him look and sound more comfortable. He opened and closed his eyes slowly, saying thank you, showing his gratitude.

In fact, Dan's blood pressure, which had been higher than normal when we first entered the room, now actually registered normal—128 over 79.

"You're helping him," the nurse said, not rushing us away.

"Can we stay with him tonight?" Alana wanted to know.

"Well . . . how about one of you?" the nurse said.

Suddenly it became clear that the one person would be Alana. Dan clearly was responding to her attention. In contrast, to be honest, he wasn't responding to mine.

"I feel like I should stay and help . . ." I started to say. But Alana was already talking to the nurse about swabbing Dan's mouth with an antibacterial gel to keep his skin from drying out.

"I'll go check on Grandma," I told Dan. "I'll be right back."

Dan opened and closed his eyes once. I turned, picked up my purse, and left the room.

The kingdom of the sick is a foreign place.

Every mystery that is the body and the mind—and the connection between the two—is laid bare in this kingdom, and there is no mercy in the baring. In my other, regular life, the life where sickness didn't reside, I could pretend that everything around me was okay. In the kingdom of the sick, in the hospital—in the intensive-care unit—that pretense didn't hold.

Dan and I were husband and wife. Both of us were grateful for his survival thus far. But Dan and I still were estranged. That was the real truth, and the evidence of it filled up his hospital room. His matter-of-fact response to seeing me—in contrast to his warm, emotional response to seeing Alana—was impossible to miss.

His obvious gratitude to her attentions and his unremarkable reaction to mine were more reminders of where we stood. Still together, as such, but standing far apart.

Lord Jesus, so far apart.

❦

Upstairs on four, Denise rushed to meet me at the elevator.

I gave her the report. Dan looks great. He's moving his arms! He's writing notes. He's writing: "God is good."

"'God is good'? That's amazing." Denise looked at me.

"So what's the matter?" Denise, like any wonderful friend, is discerning.

I shook my head. Nothing's the matter.

She didn't say anything, then put her arms around my shoulders, held me for a while.

"You've had a long day too."

Stepping back, still holding me by the shoulders, she looked into my eyes.

"You're a good wife."

Denise is married too—twenty-plus years, like me. She knows the odd patterns of marriage, the up-and-down emotions of it, how the good rhythms can suddenly get dashed by a single bad moment. She knows marriage has its seasons, sometimes just sailing along for weeks and months on end, miraculously smooth, as if riding on a glassy ocean. Then, suddenly, out of nowhere the boat upends.

So Denise didn't need any explanation this night in the hospital. She just kept saying, "You're a good wife."

Dan, in turn, was a good husband. We'd just been through a lot of years. But God knew there was so much arguing, too much belittling and second-guessing and accusation.

When a man and woman are not bearing fruit for God, not impassioned about glorifying God together, too distracted by their own wants and needs and hurts and oversights, they pick at each other. That's how we lived. For years. And now here we were, with a second chance.

I didn't know how to start over. All I could do now was thank God. *Thank you, God, for my husband's life. Thank you, blessed Jesus, indeed.*

I picked up my tote bag and found a pen and my prayer notebook.

"Thank you, God," I wrote, adding a colon mark at the end. I made my list.

"For good doctors. For skilled doctors." For sure, Dr. Breeze had skills, as the kids said.

And thank you, God: "For hospital insurance." What did folks do without it?

"For the right diagnosis." The MRI team and the angiogram team— all the audacious and caring medical folks had performed a miracle.

These were the big things. Of course, I would thank God for such blessings. After all, how many people in the world could even dream about such remarkable medical care—and here it was, right down the street at our local hospital?

How many people in the world died every day from ailments that couldn't get fixed because they couldn't find a doctor, let alone a hospital or the right medicine?

Just look at the facts. I saw them in my newspaper: Africa had more than 11 million AIDS orphans. I also heard that figure on the news on my car radio, and the number was too big to stick. It slid right in and out of my ears. Eleven *million*?

I didn't know how to think about such numbers. The news was groaning with this data: 30 million to 40 million children suffering every year from measles, of all things, nearly a million children dying from measles complications every year, half of them in Africa.

Wild numbers.

This made measles the "leading vaccine-preventable childhood killer in the world," said my TV news anchor. That translates to "more than 1,200 children dying every day of measles in Africa," the newscaster said, or "fifty-one children dying every hour of measles in Africa, one child dying every minute of measles in Africa."

A sweet mother's child every minute. Dead. Gone forever from the face of the earth.

And still more: "Approximately 2.2 million will die from complications associated with diarrhea this year, mostly among children under the age of five, according to UNICEF, the United Nations Children's Fund."

The pretty announcer read the numbers from her teleprompter. She was smiling while she talked. "This number is equivalent to one child dying every fifteen seconds, or twenty jumbo jets crashing every day."

She wet shiny lips. Malnutrition, foul water, and poor sanitation will be to blame for most of the cases, she added.

But it didn't stop: "An estimated 6 million people are blind from trachoma, and the population at risk from this disease is approximately 500 million. Providing adequate quantities of water could reduce the median infection rate by 25 percent."

Then another day: "Some 200 million people in the world are infected with the tropical disease known as schistosomiasis, of whom 20 million suffer severe consequences. The disease is still found in seventy-four countries of the world."

So thank you, God? *Thank you, God. God, thank you.*

I couldn't say it enough.

I had taken for granted the material and technological things that most people in the world—millions in the world, right at that instant—would never enjoy.

Dan understood this before I did.

"God is good," he wrote in scratchy and feeble handwriting, saying with his first three words beyond the operating room what we both had forgotten for too long.

We had forgotten, indeed, that to thank God is to look with new eyes on everything else.

Dan had new eyes. Illness had taken him down into hell, then right up to heaven, and now he was back, already praising and praying: Thank you, God.

And I was worried that my marriage might be in trouble?

Thank you, God, that I have a marriage—that I have a husband, and that I have more material and emotional and scientific wealth at my disposal than most people in the world will ever know in their entire life.

Even the night before, I'd used my personal computer—in the quiet comfort of my own home—to instantly notify scores of people about Dan's emergency, urging them to join me in prayer. What a quaint scene, and I'd thought this was praying.

No wonder I felt a letdown.

Had I thanked God yet for clean water? Had I thanked God for safe streets? Did I thank God that I had a nearly 100 percent chance of driving home tonight in safety and comfort and material integrity in a used but very nice car, with four brand-new tires and a tank full of gas?

This didn't even count the spiritual blessings—forgiveness and grace, joy and peace, assurance and hope—all stirred up by the half dozen or so Bibles lying so casually around our wildly comfortable house. This was in a world where people were dying to bring translated copies of the Bible to Word-starved people.

The mind goes everywhere when it's tired. But I knew my big, big thoughts and my big, big questions were on target. Maybe they were too big for tonight, for the wife of a recovering but critically ill man. But they were right on time.

Would I use such blessings to help anybody besides myself and my family and our little material and emotional concerns? Would I even ask such questions if I hadn't first stopped to thank God?

Or as Henri Nouwen, the saintly priest, put it in his book *With Open Hands*: "To pray means to stop expecting from God the same small-mindedness which you discover in yourself."

God, indeed, had been so patient.

Dan would be okay. I suddenly knew that. I received this assurance with gratitude, without doubt, and with the awareness that Dan was healed *before* he went to surgery. By faith, he was healed. By Jesus' stripes, he was healed, with faithful people receiving the gift in prayer. This was wonderful. A wonder, indeed.

But what would we do next, and how? *Oh my Jesus, how would we live?*

This was God's question, not just mine. But I only heard it because I had thanked him. And God already knew:

I couldn't *ever* thank God enough.

Forgive

> But when you are praying, first forgive anyone
> you are holding a grudge against, so that your
> Father in heaven will forgive your sins, too.
> MARK 11:25

In the ladies' restroom, I turned on the water and gold ran from the faucet. Clean water. Lord Jesus, thank you. Good, clean water. I splashed it on my face, anointing myself, pouring on Jesus, washing away the day.

Thank you, God.

I looked at my reflection in the mirror.

After seeing the hand of God, what would I be? And who would I be? These were the right questions, especially after looking in mirrors for years and never asking. For fifty years, I had seen a decent picture: Driving under the speed limit. Going to church on Sundays. Sending thank-you notes. Buying birthday gifts. Taking food to funerals. Have a nice day.

A good person. That's what I saw in the mirrors.

But God, it turns out, wanted me to be *transformed*. Born again, for real. For years, instead, I thought rebirth meant shouting amen in church and feeling the Spirit. In fact, it meant being renewed by the Spirit. Being revived, made new with fresh sight by God to have the character of Christ. And why? For one reason alone: to glorify God.

That meant a lot of work. I knew what the Bible said. I'd read Paul's letter to the Galatians—well, at least the fifth chapter. I knew the fruit that God wanted to grow in me: love, joy, peace, patience, kindness, goodness, faithfulness, gentleness, and self-control.

Did I reflect *any* of that fruit? Would anybody looking for the face and heart of Jesus—that incomparable glow of Christ, that golden radiance of goodness and mighty power—see that transformed picture in me?

In truth, I truly longed for such change. But I knew that real renewal came only through trials. I mean, I had read Peter's letter to the early church, those young Christians in Asia Minor: "Dear friends, do not be surprised at the painful trial you are suffering, as though something strange were happening to you."

Trials. Was that the marching order for Christians?

And here was Paul again, preaching to the Christians in Rome: "We also rejoice in our sufferings, because we know that suffering produces perseverance; perseverance, character; and character, hope. And hope does not disappoint us."

James laid down the same hard argument: "When troubles come your way, consider it an opportunity for great joy. For you know that when your faith is tested, your endurance has a chance to grow."

This was hard gospel. The gospel of trials. Endure—and you get to be better?

I wanted to perfect my wobbly character, yes. But life kept interrupting. I wanted a large character, but here came life. Not spectacular life. Mundane life. Like the Sunday I was ushering—wearing my sharp black skirt and white blouse—and a woman in a pew asked for a bulletin. But the service was just starting. I looked at her. I sighed. Couldn't the woman see? It was time for me to take my position "on the floor." So I brushed her off. I pointed to the back of the church.

"There's a stack back there," I told her, rushing away.

Halfway through the service, I saw her struggle out of her pew and hobble to the back of the church for a bulletin.

Then it hit me. This woman could *barely walk.* She was my age, but she had arthritis, or something like arthritis. Her legs were misshapen. She didn't walk, she hobbled. She leaned on two canes, in fact, one in each hand, struggling as she moved.

Could she forgive me for still being wrong?

⊰⊱

Now here was my sister-in-law. Diana was walking off the elevator after a long flight from her home back East. She wasn't struggling, but she looked stressed. She gave me a quick, good hug. She searched my face up and down, trying to find answers to her urgent question: Is my brother okay?

"He looks good, Diana," I said. "*And* the doctor sounds optimistic," I added.

"I want to see him." Diana pulled off her coat, dropping her purse in a chair. "Where is he?"

Well. Here it was: life interrupting again. A problem. Not a spectacular problem. A mundane problem. So I told her yes, Dan was back in his room. He looks good.

"But—how can I say it—he's emotional."

"Okay," Diana said. "I want to see him."

"He's on a ventilator," I said. "He can't talk. He can't express himself, Diana. And he's really emotional."

Diana looked at me, arms crossed. But even mad, she's always so pretty. Her navy blue jogging suit was stylish and new. So were her pink and white sneakers. She, too, was dressed to cheer her blessed loved one. And now I was saying *no*?

Maybe I wasn't explaining things right. Dan had just been through his own hell: His head opened up, rogue veins cut away, his head stitched up again. It was good medicine. But this kind of thing doesn't happen every day. And I couldn't explain it like that to Diana.

She was intelligent, sensitive, reasonable, *and* beautiful. But I believed if she walked into ICU, surprising Dan, he might crash, overwhelmed.

"He's not expecting you. And he's tied up in his ventilator tube, so he can't . . . speak."

I still wasn't explaining it right. And Diana wanted to see her brother *now*.

"Can you wait until morning?" I begged with my eyes.

But Diana was incredulous.

"I didn't come this far *not* to see him." She was getting angry, surprising me. We'd never really had an argument.

"Of course. You'll see him," I said, "as soon as they remove the tube. Then he can talk to you." Diana crossed her arms, telling me no. So I begged. "Please, Diana, trust me on this."

We were family. And I wasn't pulling rank as "the wife." In truth, I always walked carefully around Diana, trying to be a "good" sister-in-law. I wasn't her best friend. But I could be family, faithful and warm. I tried to be, anyway. She always did the same. And I loved her for trying.

But now we were facing off. It felt awkward.

"I'm not going home without seeing him," Diana said.

"I understand. I'm glad you're here. I want him to see you. But I need you to wait till morning," I said. "They're taking the tube out then."

"Well, I'm not leaving the hospital," Diana said.

"I'm not either!" I said, trying to show that I understood. "Alana's with him now, trying to keep his tube cleaned out. Nobody's going home."

Denise watched this exchange, looking back and forth, from Diana to me and back again.

"I'll find some blankets," Denise said, walking away to find a nurse.

⊰❖⊱

Mundane life just gut-kicks character. At those moments when I want to be grand, expansive, noble, deep, generous, beautiful—life shows up.

The last thing I wanted now was to argue with my husband's only sister, his only living close relative. We'd had a victory tonight. Dan was alive! And we were arguing? This should be our moment of highest praise.

Besides, we shared a love for the same person. But our love suddenly felt like competition, with both of us clamoring to hold the prize, to win at life.

But wait. Richard Foster said life is precisely where the deep disciplines and the character lessons are learned. In fact, God intends the spiritual rigors to get practiced on ordinary days, Foster said, by "ordinary human beings: people who have jobs, who care for children, who wash dishes and mow lawns."

Spiritual discipline is "best exercised in the midst of our relationships with our husband or wife, our brothers and sisters, our friends and neighbors," Foster said.

The amazing saint Mother Teresa said the same thing. Don't look so far to give love, she said. "Love begins at home." She saw too many people running to Calcutta, wanting to love the poor. That's easy, she wrote, "to love people far away." But "you will find Calcutta all over the world if you have eyes to see."

She was clear about this.

"The streets of Calcutta lead to every man's door."

The saintly mother was talking about giving love to aging parents, of course, or to disabled relatives or to one's own innocent little child—love at home. If love was *there*, "love and peace and compassion in our own homes first"—then peace would thrive "in the world," she said.

But to Mother Teresa, love also meant listening. Seek first to under-

stand the other person's view, not the other way around, she said—
and she wasn't the first to say it.

On this day, I wasn't hearing Diana's view. She had lost both her parents, her mother gone too soon, her father gone too hard. So she wanted
to see Dan *now*. She feared what I couldn't hear: What if he took a turn
for the worse? God forbid. But what if he downright died? That happens
and she knew that.

But I wouldn't budge. I still thought I was in control.

That problem kept coming up at this hospital. Indeed, I thought my
purpose here was to focus on Dan, on his recovery, his well-being—and
to control and manage all of that. But life kept interrupting.

The next morning, after Dan's ventilator tube was removed and he
could talk for himself—and, man, was he talking; he wouldn't *stop* talking: "God is real! God is so good!" After he burst into tears at seeing
Diana, the euphoria started to wane and the lessons started to arrive.

Then, of course, the tension began to rise.

I started it.

"I just feel like you're squeezing me out," I told Dan the third morning
after surgery. Diana had returned to New Jersey, promising to return to
Denver whenever Dan was released from intensive care and admitted to
rehab upstairs. Mama hadn't come to visit yet that day. Alana was at her
part-time job. Joi was back in town, but at her bookstore.

Just Dan and I, husband and wife, talking. And my timing is bad, or
at least it was then. Worse, I still thought everything was all about me.

Me. Me. Me.

But Dan still couldn't walk. He had regained feeling in his legs and feet,
not 100 percent, but a little more every day. So he could at least feel his
body. But he couldn't control it. The damage in his spinal cord had been
so acute that he still couldn't bear his own weight. His spinal nerves had
been traumatized, and they were coming back slowly. So obviously he
couldn't stand. He couldn't control bladder or bowel, so he still wore the
catheter.

Meantime, Dr. Breeze and the others were optimistic that he would
regain all his functions over time. But how quickly was anybody's guess.
Since the onset was acute, the recovery could be quick, too, Dr. Breeze
said.

But the truth was nobody knew how quickly, or how much, if at all, Dan
would recover. Well, God knew. But the rest of us could only guess. We
could only pray. But Dan's spirits were up and his face was shining. That's

how he looked to the psychologist assigned to Dan's case. She was young and capable, even though she wore a frown, almost perpetually.

She asked the expected questions, frowning: "How are you feeling?"

"I'm feeling great," Dan told her. Couldn't walk. But feeling great and not worried about a thing.

"Not worried about anything? Concerned about walking?"

Dan thought the question was funny.

"Let me say it this way," he told the frowning young woman. "God is *good*. And if I walk out of here or roll out in a wheelchair or crawl out of here, I know what I can count on: God will see me through."

His eyes would start to water about this time. He'd bite his lips, holding back tears. Then between grateful sobs he would whisper: "Hallelujah!"

Then he would start to laugh again, and the poor psychologist would look dismayed. She wrote on her clipboard. She asked Dan where in the world he got so much faith.

"I told her it's a gift from God," Dan said to me later. "Then she wanted to know more about my religious feelings and I ended up counseling *her*," Dan said, laughing.

"I told her I don't need a shrink. But, honey, let me talk to you about *Jesus!*"

Dan laughed some more when he told me this. The sun was shining in his room. His status had been downgraded from critical to serious. His nurses promised to help him sit up in a chair for a few minutes, once in the morning and again in the afternoon.

But what was wrong?

❖

For a black woman, that's one loaded question. What was wrong? Where do you start? At my age, there was too much to think about, let alone explain.

Many things, in fact, I'd already forgiven. I'd gotten over the race stuff—the Jim Crow limits, the "whites only" signs and their counterparts: "Colored entrance in the rear."

I'd forgiven the places that said *no:* hotels and food places and amusement parks and restrooms. I couldn't even count all the places that had told my own family no.

My good friend Marsha remembers a drive-in theater in Baltimore that turned away her father's car, filled up one summer night with *his* family:

his wife and their adorable three daughters. It was as if their car, by parking next to a white person's, would bring down the status of the sorry drive-in theater.

"Why do I remember this?" she asked me.

"I know what you mean," I told her.

We were eating breakfast in a suburban breakfast place near Denver, enjoying our eggs, drinking hot tea, ignoring the cool indifference of our rude, young waitress. The young woman was white and pretty and looked uncomfortable. Well, yes. We're still learning in America.

So on this morning, maybe she thought she was *supposed* to be insolent and cold. Or maybe she was too young to know what we had already seen. She couldn't understand how my friend and I had moved so far beyond those hurtful years that the waitress and her curt talk didn't even raise our eyebrows. When we paid for our meal and got back in the car, in fact, we didn't even mention her. We'd been hurt too many times.

But the scars. They linger in wounded people.

So I doubted myself as an African American woman. I wasn't *truly* lovable, was I? Do black women anywhere have a clean answer to this question? Are women—of any color—ever convinced that they are lovable?

To my husband, that's what I still wanted to ask: Dan, can even a black man love a black woman? I couldn't ask it that way, of course. So I sat in my husband's hospital room and said: "You're squeezing me out." I said this to my husband, a man still fresh from surgery, still wearing bandages.

Dan, lying in his hospital bed, looked at me across the sheets.

"What are you talking about? *What?*" He gestured with hands held open. He couldn't believe what I had started.

His blood-pressure monitor beeped. We both ignored it. But my words had pushed his buttons.

"I don't want to bring this up," I persisted, "but you act like you don't even want me to touch you. You only let Alana help you."

Dan looked stunned, shocked at my accusations and my self-doubt.

"Why are you starting this?" he asked, a frown creasing his forehead. "Look at me." He gestured again. "I can't even walk and you want to start *this?*"

Yes, here we were. A battered marriage doesn't necessarily get *better* when it faces crisis; it can get worse. And so we argued.

"Whenever I try to do something for you, you push me away."

"I can't believe this," he said.

"Well, it makes me feel bad."

"*You* feel bad?" He struggled to sit up in bed. "*You* feel bad?"

"I'm just trying to explain. I try to fix your covers and you tell me to leave you alone. Alana fixes your covers and you let her fluff them and fuss over you."

Dan rolled his eyes. "Are you finished?"

He shook his head. He couldn't believe that I didn't see: that his joy at Alana's concern for him didn't neutralize his love for me. I just couldn't see that then. Always, I was still thinking only of me.

I started to cry silently. Dan said nothing.

"I'm just trying to be a good wife," I finally said. I wiped my eyes with one of Dan's hospital-issued tissues. "But you act like you don't even want me in the room."

A black woman cries for love.

❧

I didn't get enough hands-on love growing up, like so many people. Who, indeed, ever gets enough love? But only one thing fixes that. I had to forgive. But not in a statement: "I forgive."

In fact, I'd already spent years forgiving *racial* pain. I'd written a book, for goodness sake, about that kind of forgiveness: My *First White Friend: Confessions on Race, Love and Forgiveness.* A heavy theme, indeed. I'd gone on TV to talk about all of it, given talks in fancy ballrooms, in churches, in school auditoriums. I was the queen of racial forgiveness.

But I wanted my husband to love me. Perfectly.

But only perfect love casts out the fear of being unlovable. Only Jesus could fix this. Was this right? I went back to my books on forgiveness. Big stack of them.

I'd read them all. Underlined everything. Yellow. Yellow. Yellow.

But sometimes you have to read something again—even the queen of forgiveness can learn something new. So soon the bottom line just jumped off a page.

Forgiveness wasn't about me and the other person. Forgiveness was about me and God. Even King David said that. When he lusted after Bathsheba—sleeping with her, another man's wife, then sending that man to the front line to be killed—he still realized his sin was first against God.

Psalm 51. Yellow. Yellow. Yellow.

David saw his sin, knowing his first fault: "Against you, you only, have I sinned and done what is evil in your sight."

He was talking to God almighty. He put it like this: "Create in me a pure heart, O God. . . . Do not cast me from your presence or take your Holy Spirit from me." Then: "Restore to me the joy of your salvation and grant me a willing spirit, to sustain me."

The whole scenario wasn't about sinning with Bathsheba, then sending her husband to face his death. Instead David first had to go home to make peace with God.

In my household, my husband and I had our share of work to do, years of hurts to repair. I kept picking at that, trying to move us forward. But God understood what I didn't: that God was my first love. Not Dan.

What a crazy thing. I never imagined this. God first, then Dan. Without loving God most, without giving myself first to God, I couldn't love well or forgive right—not the wounding white people or the wounded black people. Not my good but distant parents. Not my husband's miscues. Not even myself. I couldn't love any of us, or forgive any of us, without loving God first.

My prayer life depended on this.

"And when you stand praying, if you hold anything against anyone, forgive him, so that your Father in heaven may forgive you your sins."

But would Jesus help me?

We forgive, said Lewis Smedes, for our own sake first, "for our own spirits, alone, and get the first benefits of forgiving."

Indeed, scholar Smedes argued, we forgive by "rediscovering the humanity" in the other person. So I ask: How did God originally make these wounding people, before they got so broken by life? What did God intend us to be?

I knew my husband's story: too many N words aimed his way, too many "whites only" signs, too many closed doors, too much no. A black man, even a light-skinned black man, gets knocked down too many times.

I knew my mother's story: Growing up down South. Losing her beloved daddy, him dead too soon when she was just thirteen. From then on, life never seemed fair to her. And somebody always was dying. All her siblings. Her blessed mother. Her beloved husband. One funeral after another.

I knew, indeed, my father's story: Growing up down South. Left with relatives by his mother who wanted to make a better life up North. So a mother's love never warmed him as a child.

I knew my own story: Born to these hurting people and always waiting. And always wondering, *Where is the love?*

I knew my sister-in-law's story: Her beloved mother dead too soon. Her beloved father gone. Her beloved brother now living on mercy.

I *didn't* know the young, white waitress, but I knew the agony of being immature and unsure of oneself. If those were her problems, I knew her well, indeed. I had been immature and unsure countless times myself.

For my own sake, as Lewis Smedes said, it was time to forgive, to make peace with the unfairness in all of their lives. To see instead the beauty of their resilience, to rediscover the humanity of each of these folks, myself included. It was time to move on, forgiving and forgiven.

And look.

The door of the Lord—suddenly open.

Glorify God

"... because the work of the Son brings glory
to the Father." JOHN 14:13

At church on Sunday, folks were still praying fervently for Dan. Praying
with power, indeed. I could feel their prayers, knew they were reading my
long e-mails, my daily reports. Some of the e-mails were long, because
I attached even longer prayers.

But did I pray too long? Are our best prayers short, as Martin Luther
said? I didn't know yet. But I kept praying and sending prayers into
cyberspace, messaging by faith, not knowing who would hit the Delete
button and bemoan my pleas. To some the messages would be junk e-mail.
And to others? Some saints seemed to love every word, joining with me
to pray. Like this:

Dear heavenly Father,

We thank you and we praise you this morning—first for who you are.
You are our best friend, our provider, our helper, our protector, our
keeper, our strong tower, indeed, our leaning tower, our sovereign Lord,
and certainly you are our healer. Oh God, thank you for your amazing love
for us—so much love you are ever waiting to commune with us and to hear
and to answer our prayers, just as you so mercifully and so lovingly heard
and answered our prayers for Dan—and continue to hear and to answer
our prayers, offered, indeed, in faith. Only you, oh sovereign and holy and

147

merciful and loving God, are in charge of Dan's situation, and we thank you for everything you did this week on his behalf.

Thank you for guiding the angiogram people, especially Dr. Goodbee and Dr. Rubenstein, and giving them the discernment and the persistence to safely and accurately locate the fistula at the base of Dan's brain.

Thank you for the excellence, skill, and discernment of every medical person attending Dan this week, today, and at all times—especially Dr. Breeze and all the operating room attendants, all the anesthesiologists and other operating room staff, and Dan's ICU nurses, Jennifer, Tammy, Heather, and any other nurses and attendants, and the respiratory therapists—particularly as they make decisions about his treatment this week, and as they carry out any treatment to him today, and any day, as he recovers.

Dear God, bless mightily these healing and devoted medical people. They are your angels of mercy and love, and for them, we are eternally grateful.

We are praying together for the complete, miraculous, and total restoration of every function in Dan's body, in particular every function affected by the fistula malformation—his leg function, his bodily functions, and restoration of any loss of sensation in his legs and arms, hands and feet—and the restoring to strength of his legs, in particular. Thank you, God, for hearing and answering this healing prayer. Hallelujah!

We are praying for the reversal of any and all inflammation and swelling in and around Dan's spine.

As a result of all of these things, we continue to pray for the cessation of any and all pain that Dan may experience connected to his surgery or any treatment or his recovery.

Also, we ask, dear God, that you touch Dan right now with your total and perfect peace and give him total assurance in you and also in your faithfulness, in your trustworthiness, and especially in your perfect love—Hallelujah!—for him, as he begins his recovery.

Indeed, heavenly Father, in the perfect name of Jesus, we ask that you quickly heal the surgical area—every detail of it—and keep Dan free of infection, any fever, any complications, both in the surgical area and anywhere in his body.

We ask that you totally restrain any negative aftereffect of the surgery in general, and in particular to the type of surgery that he had. Prevent and stop any postsurgical complications or remissions. You know all of these risks and we thank you, in advance, for letting Dan be a witness to your glory by lifting him above any of these aftereffects and quickly returning him to perfect and beautiful strength and health.

Oh God, we visualize the healing taking place in the surgical area near his brain; the reduction of any swelling; the healing of all of the blood vessel pathways involved; Dan's blood pressure being stable; and all functions of his legs and feet, and his hands and arms, and every other function of his body, being normal and whole and healthy. Hallelujah!

Lord, we thank you and we praise you for sending such skilled and discerning and kind medical people to Dan's assistance, and for keeping such skilled and kind and discerning people and any other assistants all around him as he recovers.

Recovery, Lord! Oh God, we thank you for recovering us all, for redeeming us by the sacrificial and loving gift of the life of your perfect Son and Savior and our Friend, Jesus.

Thank you, oh loving God, for ushering your Holy Spirit into every space that Dan entered this week, and for giving all the prayer warriors the will and the discernment and the clarity and the focus to pray effectively on Dan's behalf. Thank you for inviting your Holy Spirit to tarry—tarry and remain everywhere with Dan—and to tarry with all of us as we stand in the gap for Dan over the coming days. Hallelujah. Thank you, dear Father.

Thank you, oh God, for sending your angels to stand guard over Dan in every space he entered and occupied during this crisis, and thank you, God, for being his protector and his healer. What a privilege to testify to your perfect power and love.

Lord, right now, we continue to pray for complete restoration for every person in the surgical intensive-care unit on the third floor at the University of Colorado Health Sciences Center, especially for the lady whose son swallowed Drano and whose esophagus needs your miraculous healing, but whose spirit and mind need your miraculous healing even more. Oh God, bless this young man's faithful and praying mother, and the family in the fourth-floor waiting room, whose loved one had a transplant situation that needs your intervention and your healing. Thank you, Lord God, for hearing and accepting this prayer for every one of them.

Lord, we are grateful that you indeed care about our bodies and about our health, and God I pray right now for the perfect health of every person reading this prayer and saying it with me. Heavenly Father, help us not to seek healing for the sake of healing, but to seek good health so we can go out and help somebody else.

Oh God, we are comforted and assured in this prayer for your great faithfulness, your wonderful trustworthiness, and especially by your love made visible in Jesus from whom flows your healing power, especially right now for Dan. Hallelujah!

Lord, by the blood of Jesus, we hold captive every negative thought around Dan's recovery, especially any well-intentioned but ineffective, wrong-centered, or wrong-minded prayers by any of us for Dan, and especially any fears or any evidences of faithlessness in you by any of us. Help us, dear Lord.

Lord, at the same time, we loose in heaven—by the same power and authority that raised Jesus from the dead—every positive and heavenly power to heal Dan completely.

Oh God, we see it! We visualize it. We believe it, and like Bartimaeus in the good Gospel of Mark, we receive Dan's healing on his behalf, and in Jesus' mighty and precious name, by faith, itself a marvelous gift from you.

Oh God, send your Holy Spirit, right now, to empower and correct and refine our prayers on Dan's behalf, and to engage and empower Dan's own faith, even for himself, all of it truly and only for YOUR glory!

Lord, right now, I thank you for the positive and steadfast help of our daughter, Alana, assisting Dan with his breathing tube and suction tube, swabbing his dry mouth with cool water, and mostly for staying by his bedside. Oh God, thank you for children who love us enough to help us in times of need.

Lord, assist me today in contacting Joi in Chicago, and thank you for granting our darling and hardworking daughter your traveling mercies and love and assistance as she and Nia travel back to Denver tomorrow.

Lord, right now, I also thank you for the powerful prayers of praying friends who continue to pray for Dan right now, friends who don't stop praying because they know what Paul the apostle meant when he said "pray without ceasing." Thank you, dear God, for all the unceasing prayer warriors all over the country who love you and are obedient to your urging to continue to pray for Dan.

Thank you, in particular, for prayers and help shared on the phone Friday by our church family and the prayer warriors at churches in so many other places. God, bless them all.

Thank you for the warmth, the love, the laughter, and the help of our dear sister, Denise Materre.

Oh God, thank you for the hope and the optimism of so many, the steadfast hope of every loyal friend, and for the hope and bright optimism and joy of my sister, Lauretta, in Atlanta and all my cousins in North Carolina.

Thank you for bringing Dan's sister, Diana, safely from New Jersey and thank you for the love and the good cheer she brought to his bedside. Thank you, God, indeed, for family and friends.

And dear Father, thank you especially for the encouraging messages by e-mail from these precious people who love you and have faith in you, and bless them all for their love and their faithfulness and their faith in you. Thank you, God, for these loving family and friends! Thank you for the calming love extended to Dan by my mother, Nannie.

Oh God, we thank you for hearing—and for answering—all the healing expressions for Dan by so many, all of their prayer obedience for your glory!

For myself, Lord, thank you for providing some hours of rest this morning and for sending such helping friends to encourage and assist. Especially, dear God, I thank you for sending to me strangers in the hospital, who I now know are my friends: the nurse Dianne in the cafeteria and the lady in the waiting room, to stand with me as prayer partners. Hallelujah.

I ask you to continue to calm my heart and to send your Holy Spirit to assure me and to remind me of your faithfulness, your trustworthiness, and your perfect love—and the knowledge that you are in charge, so I don't have to try to be. Hallelujah.

Thank you, mighty God, for being bigger than any of our human problems, because you are our Creator. With Dan, we are resting now in your love, and we thank you in advance for your excellent care of every detail of his recovery. We celebrate you, Lord. We magnify you, Lord God, in this matter. We praise you. We are feasting now on your perfect love for Dan, but also for each of us. We are all saying hallelujah! Hallelujah! Hallelujah!

Dear Lord, with my praying friends, we each now breathe in the Holy Spirit, glad to be assured that we are praying with power. Hallelujah.

In Jesus' blessed and mighty name, we submit this prayer for Dan and for ourselves to you, and we thank you and we praise you for hearing it now and for answering it. We have received his healing and his recovery and his total and perfect restoration by faith. It is all for your glory, Lord, and we are excited to be instructed by your Holy Spirit as to how you will use it in just that way—for your glory!

Amen. Amen. Amen.

Confess

> Confess your sins to each other and pray for
> each other so that you can live together whole
> and healed. The prayer of a person living right
> with God is something powerful to be reckoned
> with. JAMES 5:16

So I confess now. I have to. After everything else, I can't go further until I tell the whole and final truth. So I confess it. I confess. With my own mouth, I confess: I aborted two babies. My own baby angels. Sweet little things, so sweet I believe they just melted into heaven, falling like rose petals into the Father's big hands.

Oh God.

I see them everywhere, saw the boy just the other morning at the Sunday service, coming around the altar at prayer time. So tall and assured, and so handsome. A bit serious looking for a child of seventeen. But he takes after his mother. Just like you, people would say, if they knew. Sensitive and studious. Kind of quiet for a boy so tall and sound. But a good boy. A beautiful boy. Just like his tiny sister. And sweet, like his big sisters. And so very, very beautiful. My own little angels.

So I'll know them in heaven.

Some people want to see Jesus first. But I want to see my babies. I think Jesus will understand, knowing by the sheer numbers how many mamas will be looking for their little lambs.

I was besotted with guilt. Then, when I looked at the numbers—some 1.3 million legal abortions in the United States alone in 2000 (the most recent figures) or almost 40 million little babies targeted and eliminated outright in the United States since *Roe v. Wade* in 1973, and an even bigger number, some 46 million abortions performed legally and illegally worldwide *every year*—I was paralyzed by the horror. *God in heaven, look what we are doing.*

No, Patricia. Look what you have done.

Mother Teresa, crying, said the same thing: "We must not be surprised when we hear of murders, of killings, of wars, of hatred. If a mother can kill her own child, what is left for us to kill each other."

I have never spoken about this. Couldn't get it out of my mouth. Could only tell God, and only in secret prayer. So I whispered. *How, Father God, can you forgive this?* Then I would dream of it: Forty-six million babies a year, given up, murdered by their own mothers. And God, could you wash *this* clean as snow?

I can wash this, the Lord answers. That's the point. To you it is unforgivable. But have you forgotten the Cross? It was for sin. That's why I hung there. The work of forgiving you was finished there. It is accomplished. Washed clean, one person at a time. Do you believe me?

I wanted to believe. I went to Sunday school all those years. I studied the lessons. But now I believe there's more that I must do. Indeed, I know the Bible. *Flip. Flip. Flip.* There's the page. There's the verse: "Confess your sins to *each other* and pray for *each other* so that you may be healed."

But how do you say to somebody: I had an abortion. Then, I had another.

Listen to me. I couldn't speak it.

So the horror just wouldn't go away. Abortion grief. That's what it is called. "Some days," one woman wrote about her own abortion grief, "I wanted to rip my skin off, hating myself so much, missing the children I would never see on this earth—because of what I had done. I killed my own children. And now I am dying too."

Other days I begged God, over and over again, to forgive me. *Please, God, forgive me.* And some days, I could almost see the healing. It was so, so close. But I couldn't quite grab it. I never could understand until now that the forgiveness and the healing promised by God weren't for the sake of forgiveness and healing alone. We confess and get healed in order to help somebody else.

Rick Warren said, "We are saved to serve, not to sit around and wait for heaven."

So I confess.

God, help me. I confess.

I aborted two babies.

God's little angels. God's little people, shaped by his own hands for his work in the world, but I ended it. Because of my fear, I ended it before their work could get started. God help me. The wages of sin, and the ways of unsaved men and women, are death indeed.

I had told myself that an abortion would end my problems, not complicate them by bringing an innocent life into my own upheaval. I swallowed Satan's lie, that is, then spit it out again, saying it with my own mouth.

"Why bring an innocent baby into the mess of our life?"

I yelled this at my first husband. And with such words, I slapped God in the face, throwing back his promise to always and forever take care of me and all of my needs.

No, I told God, you cannot achieve this. I must lean on my own understanding and end this thing now.

My first husband didn't see it that way. So what if the birth control failed, he asked. So what if the marriage is failing too? I was twenty-three. I just wanted out. Please don't kill this child, he begged me. I will raise him. I will pay for your care, even if you don't want to stay with me. But I wouldn't listen. I just flew to New York City, found a clinic in the phone book, took a cab, and got up on the gurney. They put me to sleep. It was over in minutes. I ignored the sobbing around me, the other girls lined up on their own gurneys like widgets in a factory line. The young white girl lying next to me had the most deformed face I had ever seen—*and* she wouldn't stop talking. Through a cleft palate that amazingly had never been repaired, she went on nonstop about her lousy boyfriend, her lousy parents, this lousy pregnancy. I just want it over, she said, looking at me, then she reached for my hand. So I reached over and I opened my hand, taking hers. It was cold. She was trembling.

I don't believe I'm here, I kept saying to myself. How did *I* get *here?*

Here was so far from my parents' upbringing, light-years from the sunshine of Cleaves Memorial C.M.E. Church and Mr. Bell's Sunday school class and Miz Hall's cozy, welcoming kindergarten and her green felt board, lined up with the cutout figures of Jesus and the blessed disciples.

How does a Christian woman stray so far, make so many mistakes?

She makes them in fear.

I couldn't face my daddy, tell him I was pregnant again. I couldn't bear to see the look of disgust on his face. So, yes, I was afraid, terrified that he would think less of me than he already did for getting pregnant before marriage in the first place.

But I had loved being held by that boy. Nobody else held me, and then there he was, with long hugs and deep kisses, and soon enough I was pregnant. Then came the quick marriage, signing the license, finding an apartment, promising my parents that I wouldn't drop out of college. I kept that promise. I finished school. But the marriage was a catastrophe. He struck me with his hands. *I've got to leave,* I told myself, *take my baby out of this disaster and go back home to Denver.* But there it was.

I was pregnant again. I couldn't believe it.

I looked with horror at the test strip, not wanting to believe it could be true. *Oh God, don't let this be true.* I bought another test kit, ran it again. But nothing had changed. I found a doctor who confirmed the test. Yes, he said, you are absolutely pregnant. But how? I'm on the pill. Stop taking it now, the doctor said. You are pregnant. I was crying.

The second time, the second marriage, I cried again. Cowards shed tears like rain.

My girls, one from each marriage, were getting older—one fourteen, one five.

Dan and I were working hard, scuffling to keep up, overwhelmed with our bills, our fights, our jobs, our run-down house—our life. Plus, I was sick all the time, one "female" problem after another. Fibroids were the worst. I'd had three surgeries already, my abdomen split open each time and things taken out. Then the slow recoveries, the night sweats, the ungodly pain. Then suddenly my periods stopped and the pain kept me doubled over half the time. I felt bloated, tired, nauseous.

What was wrong with me?

Another doctor said: You're pregnant. He seemed happy. He said it like this: "You're pregnant!" Eyes shining. But my heart dropped. Pregnant? How in the name of Jesus would we take care of another baby?

I can't do this, I told my doctor.

He was looking at me. He didn't try to argue. He agreed I was a medical risk. He approved a medical abortion, but another doctor would do it. I don't do this procedure, he said, looking away.

So another gurney. A fancy doctor's office this time.

It was over in minutes. No general anesthesia this time. Just the awful machine, the noise, the suction, the pain, the sin, the grief, the guilt. The loss.

Forty million babies.

I drove from the doctor's office. Dan met me at our front door.

I fell at his feet, sobbing.

What have I done? *Oh God.* What have I done?

The psalmist said it already. Against you only, oh Lord, have I sinned.

For years I didn't know how God could forgive this.

Now I know. He can forgive because he is God. Only God could forgive this.

He knows how we are made.

He forgives. Then he adds something: Now go help somebody else.

On the Project Rachel Web site, a place where mourning mothers can go to better understand our grief, it says to write a letter to your aborted babies. So I am writing.

Dear Babies:

This is Mama. You will know my voice, I think, even though we were together for such a short time. I did a bad thing. I didn't trust God.

I didn't understand that God would have made everything okay. I was like Peter on the felt board in Miz Hall's Sunday school class. Peter looked at the waves, not at Jesus. And when he looked at the waves, he started to sink—down, down, down.

That's how I felt, like I was sinking down.

When the doctors said you were growing inside of me, that's how I felt, so I didn't love myself enough to know how to love you. I was afraid. Oh babies, I had made so many, many mistakes. And I was afraid.

So I let fear convince me that more babies would just make things worse.

Instead, look what I did.

I robbed us. First, I robbed you—taking your own lives. Your own mama! I didn't think I was strong enough. So I robbed myself of all the joy you would've brought me too. Brought all of us, your sisters, your family, and for each of you, your daddy. I thought we'd have more prob-lems. That we didn't have enough money. That we didn't have enough time. That we didn't have enough love. But I just didn't know then that God is bigger. And God would make everything all right. I didn't know. I was like Peter, looking at the waves.

I know you are in heaven, waiting for us—waiting for me.

I know you've been waiting, looking every day, wondering when I would get there. Oh babies, I'm trying to get there—to be better, to live right, to be right, to learn what God wants me to learn, so I can make it to you.

Fast

"This kind goeth not out but by prayer
and fasting." MATTHEW 17:21

It was time for a fast.

But a fast isn't a cleanup or a quick wash. Instead, a fast focuses solely on God. That's where all the good things happen, where all the beauty begins and where it ends. "Ministry to God must come before ministry to people," Elizabeth Alves said. So every believer's first assignment is to commune with God, she said. To praise him. To worship him. To be still with him. To be washed by him. To sit with him and listen. To heed him. Only then should we even try to minister to people—"letting that over-flow pour into their lives."

So I would fast.

I was overdue, indeed.

But in truth, I had another reason to try. Dan faced one more big hurdle, a follow-up angiogram the next morning to make sure his surgery had repaired everything in the right way.

I knew the risks: Dan could have a stroke. That's what the doctors said. The stroke could kill him. I hated hearing these things, but the truth is true, and the doctors had to tell it.

Dan said he wasn't worried. I am resting with the Lord, he said. I am, too, I told him. So I signed the papers.

In fact, everything had changed. The only thing that made sense now was to put everything in God's hands. But I asked the e-mail people and the relatives—and the neighbors and the ministers and the missionaries and everybody else I could think of—to pray for the "angio" doctor.

Dr. Goodbee was his name. A good name, my sister-in-law said. She let it roll off her tongue. Goodbee. Goodbee. Goodbee. She did the same with Dr. Breeze. Breeze. Breeze.

"They're like names from Dr. Seuss," she said, laughing.

"I know. Aren't their names adorable?" I agreed, laughing myself. Then we laughed about other things, settling into comfortable smiles, enjoying a simple saved moment together.

"So thank God," I wrote to the praying friends. "Thank God for good doctors with funny names. Thank God for forgiveness. Thank him for health. And thank God for God. Help me to focus on him."

Then I turned off the computer and I went alone to my bedroom.

And there was the queen-sized bed. It was as big as a bus in our empty room, a space for two where I now slept alone. Well, the bed wasn't *that* big. But it looked empty, one-sided, and vacant on Dan's side. This was just his sixth night gone, more nights than we'd ever spent apart, but not so many nights, in truth. For all our fussing and arguing over the years, I was still used to his presence, the weight of him next to me as he slept, the citrus smell of the soapy showers he took before closing his eyes, the worn softness of the cotton T-shirts and pajama bottoms he liked to sleep in.

I never imagined he wouldn't be lying there, in his T-shirt and pajamas, clean and snoring and next to me.

I thought of widows and widowers, and the newly divorced and others alone, people whose bed once was filled up but now was unbearable and empty. Only God almighty could fill such a void.

I sat on the side of the bed, letting the light from the lamp on my nightstand fill the room while I closed my eyes, waiting for God, waiting for sleep.

❖

In the morning, after a cup of hot tea, I drove the half-hour trip to the hospital. Dan's angiogram was scheduled for 9 A.M., so I went up to his room in ICU to see him beforehand. He was finishing breakfast.

"What'd you eat this morning?" he asked. When I said tea, he wagged a finger at me.

"Not enough," he said. "You have to eat, keep up your energy."

I agreed, although I didn't mention the fast. Didn't feel like talking about it. But it turns out that's exactly what the Bible teaches: Keep your mouth shut when you fast. Don't draw the attention. "You dress in burlap and cover yourselves with ashes," Isaiah thundered away in his fifty-eighth chapter. "Is this what you call fasting? Do you really think this will please the Lord?"

Jesus said the exact same thing in his Sermon on the Mount.

When you fast, don't make it obvious "as the hypocrites do," trying to look pale and disheveled so people will admire them for fasting. "I tell you the truth, that is the only reward they will ever get."

Instead, when you fast, comb your hair and wash your face, Jesus said. Then no one will even suspect you are fasting, "except your Father, who knows what you do in private. And your Father, who sees everything, will reward you."

I wanted that reward, whatever it would be. So I kept my mouth shut as Dan greeted his orderly. The burly, smiling young man helped a nurse maneuver Dan into a wheelchair.

Then down to radiology, a small waiting area crowded and busy today. Sighing and coughing and impatient people were lined up on chairs. The orderly signed Dan in, gave him a thumbs-up and a final pat on the arm.

"I'll see you when you're finished. And don't ride back with just anybody."

Dan shot a thumbs-up back, grateful for the man's kindness. Then too soon, it was time for his test. We looked at each other.

"God is bigger," he told me. He looked sober, but he gave me a smile. Then he was wheeled away.

I eyed an empty chair, trying not to bother people or step on anybody's feet as I made my way to my seat. Then I opened my Foster book *Celebration of Discipline* to his chapter on fasting. In truth, I thought fasting meant denying myself food, in a sort of sacrifice.

But Richard Foster was saying something different in this chapter. He ticked off the different methods of fasting—political hunger strikes, food fasts for health reasons, that kind of thing. But biblical fasting, Foster said, "always centers on spiritual purposes."

So fasting isn't to get God to do what we want, Foster wrote. Instead, "fasting must forever center on God." He stressed that God focus. Then Foster quoted John Wesley, who said that the intention of fasting should "be this, and this alone, to glorify our Father which is in heaven."

Well, I could do that. I had to.

In fact, I'd take his advice to start with a twenty-four-hour fast, "lunch to lunch," which means missing two meals, a dinner and a breakfast. Water only. Well, I could do that too. I'd already had a head start, in fact. With only tea for breakfast, I was on my way. In a world where most people still go to bed hungry—because they've been nearly starving most of their life—my little twenty-four-hour fast would be, so to speak, a piece of cake.

If I could glorify God and focus on God by taking my mind off food for twenty-four hours, it would be easy. I was more than willing.

So I settled into my chair, arranging my prayer notebook and my Foster book and my Bic pens in my lap, ready to invest in an hour of quiet meditation, fully resigned to missing lunch and dinner.

Then a shadow filled the doorway to radiology.

A somber, harried couple and their three young children were squeezing in the doorway. They tumbled altogether into the crowded waiting area, looking for seats, squawking at each other, each of them talking louder than the next.

"Watch the lady!" the father yelled, holding a drooling toddler, as the two older children stumbled over feet, mine included, trying to beat each other to one of the empty chairs still left in the room—including a chair next to mine.

The mother was grabbing her forearm, holding it away from her pushing, noisy children.

The oldest boy, about eleven, dived into the chair.

"You cheated!" his sister yelled. She looked about eight, no longer a baby, but trying still to act big. So she kicked at her brother's shoes with her own big, scruffy sneakers. Hand-me-downs, for sure, it seemed. No small child needed shoes as oversized as hers.

"I'm telling!" the big boy shrieked.

"Stop bothering the lady!" the father shrieked back.

Then he turned to his wife, who was dropping into a chair across from mine.

"You forgot to sign in!" he yelled across the aisle to his wife.

"Okay, I'm not deaf!" she yelled back, pulling herself up. "My arm's broke, not my ears!" She turned toward the desk, going up to sign in.

Like the children and the father, the mother was far too large for her age, much too big for our thin-loving times. A fat woman with a fleshy husband and three fleshy children, everybody breathing loudly and grunting and spoiling the peace. That's how I saw it, and I felt an actual disgust at their oversized, slovenly disorder. Instantly I sensed my feeling and it was . . . superiority? I am thinner—and quiet. They are not. So I am better?

That's the equation, isn't it?

Other people were doing the same math. I could see them. All around the room, folks were pulling back from the noisy family, looking wary, revealing by their looks their true feelings and a prayer: *Please God, don't let these fat, loud people sit next to me.*

The Fat Family—that's who they were now. Or maybe even the Dirty Fat Family. Why not go all the way? Just look at the children. Their pudgy faces were grimy, their heads uncombed, their clothing tired and stained and ill-fitting, worn too many times without washing, handed down too many years, and everybody smelling.

As the children moved in around me, I could almost touch their unease with their life. Their unwashed odor. Their tangled hair. Their cast-down clothes.

These were children who were never dunked into a hot, soapy bath at night, never told a bedtime story, couldn't imagine the ecstasy of being tucked between clean sheets in a fresh bed, in a clean room, by a mother with soft hands and a happy and ordered life. So these were the outcast children, reared by uneasy parents who themselves never fit in with the rest of the world.

Here now, indeed, was this outcast family. In fact, I'd already dropped them in that category and assigned them a name, then let my mind roll:

Look at them, those awful, fat, dirty people. But *don't* look at my own fears: a marriage that needed work, a daughter who'd left the church, a mother I didn't always understand, and years of guilt.

Or as Carl Jung put it: "We hate the things we cannot explain."

So I hated how this family had somehow slipped through the clutches of order and let themselves go. If they did this, couldn't I? In a year's time, would I look like this mother: scratching at musty hair; yawning with my mouth open, teeth unwashed and missing? The father, meanwhile, his big stomach lopping over his sad, stained pants, had given up.

Would I go down this same road? Was it, indeed, closer than I dared to think?

Help me, Jesus. I'm drowning and I need help. That's what the Fat Family was shouting—at each other and at their children, and the children were shouting back. And the rest of us, crowded into the waiting room, just set our back, turned up our nose, and turned our head.

꒰ꕤ꒱

Well, I was fasting—just a few hours into it, in fact. And already here were some answers. At least here was the thing that Foster promised: The truth about who I was.

I was sated with negative judgments against others.

I longed to be loving and accepting. Well, I said I did. But here I was, drowning in nasty criticisms, ever quick to see others' faults, ever eager to feel superior. It was just as Foster predicted. When we fast, he said, our truth is laid bare: "More than any other Discipline, fasting reveals the things that control us." It's a secondary benefit of fasting, he said, "a wonderful benefit to the true disciple who longs to be transformed into the image of Christ."

The things that hinder our transformation will often "surface in fasting," he promised. "If pride controls us, it will be revealed almost immediately. Anger, bitterness, jealousy, strife, fear—if they are within us, they will surface during fasting."

And judging others?

Here it was, but there was more, just like the shrinks say. And I think they must be right: We judge others when we are afraid, when we know we can't control life. So we suppress our fear by diverting that energy into attacking others.

But fear and judging are sinful and small. My fasting shined the spotlight on this truth.

And yet? Love never fails.

꒰ꕤ꒱

I turned to the bigger kid, the one slumped next to me, eyeing his little sister, waiting for some mischief. The little girl sat next to her mother, curling into her mama's good arm. The father held the jumpy toddler.

They weren't expecting anything from me. But there it was. I spoke up: "You want something to write on while you wait?"

I looked to the bigger boy, holding up my notebook, holding out my pen. But this was like dropping a grenade on the carpet.

Instantly, eyes were moving. The boy looked at his father. The girl looked at her mother. The mother looked at the father. The father looked over at me.

"It's okay," I said. "It's kind of boring in here for kids."

"Don't break anything!" the father said to the boy.

I pushed a pen into the boy's hand, then handed him my notebook.

The boy examined the pen, then waved it in the air. He squiggled in the notebook.

"Look what I got!" he teased his sister. "I'm gonna make a picture of you."

The girl slid off her mother's arm, stopping an inch from her brother's chair.

"Let me see," she whined.

Her brother pulled back, taunting her with his new pen.

"Play with your sister!" the father shouted.

"I've got another pen," I half-shouted back, handing the girl another Bic.

I dug in my tote bag, pulled out another notebook. I had enough notebooks and journals and pens and junk in my bag for ten kids, let alone these two children.

The little girl smirked at her brother, then grabbed the pen from my hand with her precious, dirty fingers. She knelt on the floor, halfway between her mother and her brother, making designs on the paper with *her* new pen.

"Look, Baby!" she said, holding her notebook toward the toddler. The baby looked down and drooled, grinning, kicking his legs.

"Look, Mommy!" the girl said.

"Tell the lady thank you," the mother told her, her voice a little quieter.

The child turned, acknowledging me for the first time.

"Thank you," she said.

I looked into her eyes, transparent and hopeful. "Thank you."

⁂

So I was kind to somebody, a small thing perhaps.

But kind people who truly serve others are God's partners. Everybody says this—all the famous, good people: Foster and Warren and Gandhi and King and all the countless others. King said: "This is the judgment. Life's most persistent and urgent question is, What are you doing for others?"

Albert Einstein was good on this too: "Each of us is here for a brief sojourn; for what purpose he knows not, though he sometimes thinks he senses it. But without deeper reflection one knows from daily life that one exists for other people—first of all for those upon whose smiles and well-being our own happiness is wholly dependent, and then for the many, unknown to us, to whose destinies we are bound by the ties of sympathy."

Then Mother Teresa, writing from her little overheated office in Calcutta: "It's not how much you do, but how much love you put into the action."

Jesus, of course, took the teaching highest: "Whenever you did one of these things to someone overlooked or ignored—that was me—you did it to me."

My stomach growled. I was feeling hungry. Plus, I was minus two Bics and two notebooks. But even before lunch—or the lunch I would skip that day—I'd learned a clear and simple lesson: I was saved for one reason alone, to serve others. But first I had to become aware of others and then to stop judging them. More than that, I had to be available to give. On my campus, where I gave my all in the classroom, I rarely put out effort anywhere else. I wasn't smart enough. I wasn't good enough. I used whatever excuse I could to hold back from giving.

But people with needs were calling, getting closer.

Maybe if I had faith, God would give me another chance.

And all this from one hour of fasting?

I sat stupid with amazement. Countless millions already knew this simple thing and acted on it—that there's power in doing spiritual things as God asks. It's easy.

Thus, Jesus said *when* you fast, not *if*. *If* was for sloppy, doubting, disobedient followers. *When* was for disciples, the disciplined. For the praying, disciplined warriors. Lunch to lunch. Heart to heart. Bic to Bic. Spirit to spirit.

Dr. Goodbee walked into the waiting area, followed by Dr. Breeze, both of them scanning the faces in the room. They found me.

They were smiling. Even Dr. Breeze was smiling.

Everything looks good.

"Thank you," I said, nodding with them, agreeing.

Everything looks good.

Honor Jesus' Name: Model His Character

"From now on, whatever you request along
the lines of who I am and what I am doing,
I'll do it. . . . I mean it. Whatever you request
in this way, I'll do." JOHN 14:13-14

Dan's sister, Diana, was back in town. Two suitcases this time. She would stay longer this trip, and I was glad for the help. Dan was moving up to rehab. So Diana could share the workload, visiting Dan in the hospital, among other things, and keeping up his spirits.

Except Dan's spirits were already always up. For a man who ten days ago could walk and now couldn't walk one step—after having his head opened and his veins repaired and fiddled with—he seemed downright giddy.

Now he greeted us wearing regular clothes, a sharp, navy blue warm-up suit Diana had picked out at Target and a new pair of shiny, white sneakers. He was sitting in a wheelchair. He was thin. He'd lost at least fifteen pounds, maybe more. But he was smiling, his sneakers gleaming.

His legs and feet, in fact, felt tingly all the time, "like when you go to the dentist," he said, "and you can feel your mouth but it's still numb." As much as Dan wanted to walk again, he couldn't feel the floor with his feet. His legs weren't strong enough for standing anyway. So progress was steady but slow. A week after surgery, he still wore a catheter, still used an IV, still registered erratic blood pressures at times, and still couldn't stand. His little four-inch scar, snaking from neckline to midskull, looked like a zipper. Still he smiled.

So I was convinced that Dan would recover. I expected him to walk out of the hospital—smiling *and* rejoicing.

But prayer principles demanded I keep praying. Also I was learning: Problems on my prayer list often get harder before they get fixed. God, it seemed, wants us to remember he is sovereign. He decides timing. Moreover, God wanted time with me, it seemed. He must want time like this with everyone. "His longing for me is dearer than my longing for him," Mother Teresa wrote. So I didn't fight it.

Sure, I had "things to do." But the first thing every morning was to pray, to pause really, and enjoy the "sweet sinking into the Deity" that Madame Guyon described.

So I'd be like Martin Luther. He had so much to do every day that first, he said, he "had to pray three hours." For these faith pioneers, said Richard Foster, "prayer was no little habit tacked onto the periphery of their lives; it *was* their lives." For these, Foster added, "and all those who have braved the depths of the interior life, to breathe was to pray."

⚜

Dan took a deep breath and grinned.

"Free at last!" he said. "I get moved today. Going up to *rehab*."

He said *rehab* like he was going to Puerto Vallarta for some cool, tropical vacation, a cozy break in the frigid month of November. Instead, after warm good-byes to his nurses, Dan wiping tears, he was wheeled up to rehab on the seventh floor. It seemed like a good number, in fact.

Up there, he spent another ten days relearning everything.

Walking. Urinating. All of it. The truth is real. He was starting over.

But first he was content to figure out how to operate his wheelchair for himself. That was the morning of day one. By the afternoon of day one, he was wheeling himself around the rehab hallways, greeting the physical therapists and his young psychologist, socializing with other patients, spinning his way to and fro.

In between, Dan went to a therapy class with other recovering patients: stroke victims, trauma patients, and burn victims. The therapists arranged everybody in a big circle.

"Okay, this is simple," the therapist said.

Everybody groaned. Some people laughed. Dan eyed the therapist, focusing.

"Okay, kick the ball across the circle to somebody else. Stop the incoming ball with your foot. Then kick it."

"Like soccer?" one woman asked.

"Yes! Kinda like soccer," the therapist agreed.

Playtime as therapy. Dan braced his wheelchair, ready, eyes sparkling, watching the ball roll *slowly* from patient to patient across the circle.

Nobody had much strength. A nice ball. But *slowly* it rounded the lovely circle. Dan waited, hoping. He wanted to play. Some men are still boys. Then finally the ball *slowly* rolled his way.

Dan bit his lip, willing his right leg. It lifted an inch, two at most. Pretty new sneakers, barely inching toward the ball. Then with great, slow effort . . . contact!

"There it goes!" Dan said.

Well, barely. But the ball was moving. Crawling, in truth. It finally crossed the circle, finding another waiting, hopeful foot. Dan was beaming. Day one.

By day two, Dan was wearing his game face, warm-up suit zipped, sneakers on, tied tight.

"Look at you, sugar pie. You're a jock," I said.

"If kicking a ball across a circle is going to help me get better, I'll kick as long as I can," Dan said. To him, every game was like the Olympics. During the wheelchair races, on day three, he practically pushed people out of the way, trying to win.

"Look at him!" Diana said. "He's shoving people."

"Aren't you being kind of competitive?" I finally asked him after a race. "Do you have to win every time at every game?"

He raised a hand and pointed skyward.

"I'm trying to win *the* game," he said, "the ultimate race." Then he turned his wheelchair and broke out laughing. "Now step out of the way. I'm trying to get to the finish line."

This was the Dan I first knew, but bigger. In fact, the rehab floor was like a big reward for making it through the scary risks down in surgical ICU. Those who did best here had a spark about them. They wanted to live, wanted to get better, wanted to walk out of the hospital—even if the odds said they couldn't.

Dan was in the "spark" group.

"What's next?" he asked his therapist.

"Cooking," she said. "Occupational therapy."

"Thank you, Jesus," Dan said. He loved to cook. Even more, he loved to eat.

He wheeled his chair to the "mock" kitchen, listened to directions. Mix up a batch of brownies at this table. Then wheel to the oven. Place the brownies safely into the stove. Watch them while they cook, then eat them! Heaven. He showed off his misshapen brownies, tossed one in his mouth, licked his fingers.

"Just call me Sister Betty," he said, grinning.

Diana and I laughed.

"That would be *Betty Crocker?*" Diana asked.

"There you go! Betty Crocker," Dan said. "You can call me Betty, then call me for dinner—any day of the week."

Laughing. Laughing. "Oh, what a great attitude," the therapist said.

Ha. Ha. Ha. Aren't we having a grand old time?

That's how it seemed some days. Dan joking with everybody; winning most of his rehab games, kicking the ball so hard across the circle one day he had to be cautioned; joking around with other patients; then heading back to his room where he greeted a steady parade of visitors—prayer warriors and other church members.

Amazing church members, indeed.

Goodness, those people were faithful. They brought flowers. They mailed cards. They snuck in food: cheese rolls and fruit baskets and Krispy Kremes and Subways and whole home-cooked dinners. Fried chicken, hot biscuits, and collard greens. They brought their laughter. They delivered hope. Like good church folks, they left their pews and dug in. Praying and believing and sending love in get-well cards. The fellowship, indeed.

Soon enough, Dan started his walking exercises. In the gym, positioned between steel parallel bars, he grabbed on. With each hand, he pushed himself up, groaning, sweating, straining to a standing position.

His legs wobbled and shook, but he defiantly stood—for one minute, two minutes, three minutes, four minutes, *five* minutes—then he slumped, grunting with relief, back into the wheelchair, sweat gliding down his forehead, glistening.

"Wow, that's good, sugar," I said.

Breathing hard, Dan pointed upward with a finger. God at work. Not me, but God in me, he was saying.

"When I am weak, I am strong," Dan said, quoting Paul's Corinthian letter. My husband the Bible scholar.

⚜

Well. What comes over people?

When Dan and I met, nearly twenty-five years before, he was

a religious scoffer, a skeptic. But he had good manners, so he didn't out-wardly put down faith, not around me. But he didn't think much of it either.

And I was a churchgoer. Born-again. A divorced single mother with a four-year-old child who went to church every Sunday without fail. Never missed a week.

But Dan and I met on a Friday night. For lonely and single people, is there any other night?

I've written about this. But I'll say more. The first time I didn't tell it all—so, yes, it was a Friday night. Party night. A college campus.

Dan was mingling in the crowd packed in a professor's basement rec room. He looked over. Then he asked me to dance. Then he wouldn't go away. All evening, every few minutes, there he was, hovering at my side, talking, trying to joke with me, teasing with me.

People who know him will recognize this. This is how he works: Every-thing is fun and wordplay.

"What you up to, Dan?" he was asked by a friend.

"About five feet ten, five eleven," Dan shot back. He laughed at his own joke, and everybody was happy. So, joking, there he was all evening, teasing me, moving in for the slow songs, beating out anyone else who might be trying to score.

There was a bit of that going on that night: men pushing their charm and their interest at women. Talking their intellectual games—this was a university after all—but, in the end, simply trying to connect.

Joke. Joke. Joke.

"He masks," Dan's rehab doctor said to me now, twenty-five years later. Yes, that's it!

"You're right, Doctor," I said. "He does mask." Dan hides behind the laughter. That's how I first met him, liking at first how he loved to joke and have fun. I forgave his jokes about my religion.

And, anyway, he did go to church with me from the start. He was court-ing me, at that point, so in the evenings after my classes, I'd come back to my apartment and there he was, waiting in his car.

"Let's go eat." Okay. "Let's go to a movie." Okay. "Let's go to a game." Okay.

"Let's go to church," I said.

"To church?"

But Sunday morning, he picked us up—my daughter and me—and off we went to Second Baptist Church in Boulder, the black congregation in town, named "Second" because First Baptist was the "white" church. And may God forgive us for our separate praying grounds.

As for me, I wasn't Baptist. But after a week of classes on an upscale campus, I needed everything the black Baptists in Boulder could dish out. The big and audacious music. The assured and audacious preaching. The rocking hugs, the lipstick kisses, the sweet laughter, the bright sunshine. So there we were, Dan squeezed in next to me and Joi on a pew in crowded Second Baptist, with the saints shouting and singing and falling out slain in the Spirit.

I loved it.

He loved the music.

The rest of the week, however, he made fun of my Christian "thing." He joked about my Christian radio, my Christian TV evangelists, all the little weekday Christian ways that filled my nonschool, nonworking hours. Just give me Jesus, indeed.

But still we decided to get married. He told his jokes. He made me laugh. So after a short ten-week—crazy short, impossibly short, indefensibly short—courtship, we said "I do." I ignored, indeed, the apostle Paul's heartfelt exhortation not to "be yoked together with unbelievers."

So right away, this:

The first Sunday after we were married, I got Joi and myself dressed for church. But Dan was in the kitchen, joyously whipping up French toast or pancakes or scrambled eggs or bacon and wearing Saturday clothes.

"You go on without me," he said.

Millions of women have heard these words. Countless wives, girlfriends, mothers, sisters, daughters, granddaughters, and women in general have heard these exact words from a man.

I don't feel like going to church today. You guys go on without me.

So I had an answer.

"No," I said.

Dan looked up. Stopped scrambling the eggs.

"What did you say?"

Our first married fight.

"I said no."

"What do you mean 'no'? It's not a big deal." He started scrambling again. "I don't feel like going to church today. You can go without me."

I put down my purse. Set down my Bible.

Dan looked at me.

"You going to make a big deal out of this?"

I looked at him.

"Yes," I said.

I was so young then, just twenty-five. Also I was ignorant. About my man. About myself. I would never argue this way with Dan now. I know the basics now about my husband. Don't take the man on before breakfast, just for starters.

More than that, however, I have laid down that "everlasting burden of always needing to manage others," as Foster put it. The job of winning souls is the work of the Holy Spirit, not the work of an arguing wife. A praying woman will win a man to Jesus faster than an arguing woman ever will. I know that now.

The Bible is right: Believers shouldn't marry nonbelievers, no matter how "nice" or "good" or "fun" the other person is. But at age twenty-five—and not knowing these things, or deciding to ignore them—I set my mouth, arms crossed tight. Dan could see it. He tried to joke.

"C'mon, relax," Dan said, scrambling the eggs for distraction now. "No church? One Sunday. No big deal. And hand me that pepper."

I stood my ground. He reached for the pepper himself.

"Why'd you spend all those Sundays with me at Second Baptist?" I finally asked.

"Can I just finish cooking my eggs?" Dan asked.

"I thought you made a commitment to go—as a family."

"C'mon," he said again. "You act like I'm never going to church again."

Joi, age four, wearing her church clothes and Sunday coat, stood there looking at us, following the volley.

"You deceived me," I finally said to my new husband—and before he'd eaten his first bite of the day.

Dan got a look on his face that I'd never seen before.

"You really want to turn this into a big argument, when all I said was I am not going to church today. And you're going to *accuse* me of *deceiving* you!"

Voice close to shouting now.

My eyes started to water. Nothing rattles me more than shouting. Besides, I thought I was right. So I went to high drama.

"All of my life," I said, "I have seen women drag their children to church, husbands still at home, only showing up on Christmas and Easter—if then."

"Yeah, well, that's not me," Dan said. He poured the eggs in a hot pan, frowning over the sizzling noises, stirring like crazy. "To repeat," he added, "I only said that I did not feel like going *today*."

"That's how it starts," I said.

Dan dropped his fork on the counter, splattering half-cooked eggs.

"What is with you today, sugar? God's not sending me to a fiery hell because I don't feel like going to church *to-day*," he said.

I sighed. I was finished with it. I tried my logic, my parting shot: "Faith in God is the most important thing in the world to me," I said. "And church isn't something you do because you feel like it. When you *don't* feel like it is when you need to go the most."

❦

The saved and self-righteous wife.

Satan likes her better than the worst sinner. She prays in the name of Jesus. But she acts like hell—not winning souls to Christ, but pushing them away.

So we were both standing at the starting line. I had more church time under my belt. But Dan grew up with a redeemed, holy woman. His mother didn't just talk about Jesus. She died to Christ, as the church folks used to say, like Paul. "I have been crucified with Christ and I no longer live, but Christ lives in me."

That was his mother. So Dan grew up around the character of Christ, right in his own house, flying higher than the segregated schools and seg-regated movie theaters and segregated amusement parks and segregated churches in St. Louis County.

He could walk right off a segregated street into a house crippled by his father's alcoholism and still find Jesus. Inside his mother's blessed heart, Jesus lived.

But his own heart stayed closed to the invitation to Christ for years. Too much ego, he admits now. Also a certain portion of doubt. A little lack of interest. A lot of self-sufficiency.

"In all honesty, I hadn't studied," Dan said. "I hadn't done any research. Plus, I was part of the 'intellectual' community, engaged in 'intellectual' pursuits—till I found out nobody gets to Jesus by intellectualizing him."

His mama understood that, he said. "Mama planted the seed."

She didn't preach Jesus. "But she lived Jesus," Dan said. "And Jesus lived in her." So that seed waited in fertile soil.

"Then I met you," he said.

I looked up. He had caught me off guard. This was on a bright spring day, cool enough for jackets despite the glorious sunshine.

But I had started this chat with a question.

"When did you accept Christ into your heart? I mean, was there one moment that you remember when that happened?"

"What's this? Interviewing me?"

I laughed.

"I guess I am. Besides, I want to know. Was there one moment— a particular, singular episode, *the* moment—when you know you accepted Christ?"

I truly wanted to know. After all, I once had a husband who conspired to miss going to church. Now I had a husband who woke me up Sunday mornings, already dressed, sporting a Sunday suit and tie that had been laid out the night before, calling from the kitchen: I'll be in the car, engine running, waiting for you.

Once I had a husband who made fun of John Hagee and Charles Stanley and the other TV preachers. Now I had a husband who searched for Hagee and Stanley and T. D. Jakes and half a dozen others, a husband who cried when Hagee's sinners lined up to receive Jesus as Lord and Savior.

"That man is anointed," Dan said. "Isn't that the right word?"

The Word? Once I had a husband who couldn't find Genesis in the Bible. Now he owned not just one Bible, but three Bibles—all well used, underlined here to yonder in yellow, yellow, yellow—and he was looking to buy yet another translation.

"*The Message* Bible. Where can I get that?" Dan made a note on the grocery list. "Does Wal-Mart carry it, you think?"

"Wal-Mart?" I was ready to argue against the big retail giant in favor of a small, out-of-the-way Bible bookstore across town.

Then I stopped. My husband wanted to buy a Bible. Did I have to manage this too?

"Yeah, let's try Wal-Mart," I said to him. I got my coat. It's a bright spring day. We can walk. God help us. We can walk to Wal-Mart. I didn't know whether to laugh or cry.

⊹ᶘᶀ⊹

And Dan worked so doggone hard to learn to walk again.

On the rehab floor, he lay on his bed after breakfast many mornings and said to himself: *Why am I lying here? God gave me this body and he expects me to use it.*

He sometimes wanted to feel sorry for himself. But he knew the story of Jesus telling the man at Bethesda to "walk!" So one morning instead of calling the nurse, Dan determined to walk the three or four steps to his bathroom by himself.

"I figured I could hang on to the wheelchair," he told me later. "I'd use it like a crutch, wheel myself the three steps to the bathroom. And if I started to fall, I'd fall into the chair."

So he tried it. Step. Wheel. Step. Wheel. Step. Wheel. And finally there he was in the bathroom, under his own strength. He was walking again.

"My legs felt funny as all get out," he said. So when he got back in bed, he tried to exercise, moving his legs, raising them, rotating his ankles, wiggling his toes—whatever he could do to speed up the process of walking.

The rehab people became his partners. Every morning, they'd come in with their clipboard and review what he did the day before, what he would do that day. They made it known: You *will* become independent again.

So being in rehab was like having a job. And Dan's job was learning to walk again.

And it happened.

⧂

Gradually—from wheelchair to walker. Then to two hand crutches. Then to one hand crutch. Then one day: My husband, Dan, found himself in that delicate balance of mind, body, air, space, and movement called walking. Doing the dance.

"It's an amazing thing when you think about it, everything that goes into moving your body while you're standing upright," he said to me.

Dan had thought long about it.

"Feeling the floor. Discerning your body in relation to the space around you. Your mind sending nerve messages to your body and back again. Deliberately putting one foot in front of the next until you're propelling yourself along. In other words, you are now *walking*."

Walking in his name, indeed. In that closeness, you learn a few things, Dan said now.

He moved around our kitchen as he talked, moving legs and arms together, like a toy soldier, showing me—standing tall—that, look, this is *walking*.

Of course, most people don't think about it at all, he said.

"Most people just, you know, get up and walk," Dan said, still toy-soldier walking. "That used to be me. But starting again from scratch, to learn to walk all over again, it was the hardest and the best thing I ever did."

And God was so merciful, Dan said, preaching a bit now like Hagee himself.

"God was such a powerful presence in that hospital—prevailing over sickness—working on me and restoring my appreciation of what I'd been given: a second chance!"

Then the crazy thing: The therapists credited Dan's attitude.

But truly that was Jesus. That's what Dan said as we left our house that day and walked to Wal-Mart. It was a bright spring day. Puffy, happy clouds in a brilliant, blue sky. Sunshine beaming. A good attitude? "That wasn't *my* attitude," Dan was saying. "That was Christ in me. That was *his* character. Whoever I was and whoever I used to be is now dead. Crucified. And in exchange, there was Jesus. Christ in me—living in me, walking in me, walking with me."

But not with me alone, Dan said.

"God was with the other patients, also working on their temporary disabilities. So everybody knew, it took something bigger than yourself alone to get well."

Dan could walk again. But even better, he was a better person: Higher. Bigger. Grander—with a grander heart.

So praying in the name of Jesus meant, to him, more than saying the words: *in the name of Jesus*. Sure, some folks prayed those words, like a holy mumbo jumbo, hoping the words alone would open the door.

But praying in the name of Jesus seemed to mean praying in the character of Jesus, tenderly, grandly, majestically, "with the idea of changing the moral aspect of the whole earth, of recovering all nations to the pure and inward worship of one God and to a spirit of divine and fraternal love," as William Ellery Channing said it—praying with a certain knowledge of what God would do for a fellow traveler because that prayer warrior was taking time to listen to God.

Then God speaks. In that still, small voice.

And in that voice, God answers.

⊰⊱

As Dan and I walked down Chambers Road to Wal-Mart on that bright spring day, God walked with him. He had to walk with him. Dan didn't make his 100 percent recovery. At best, call it 90 percent. A good number.

So even today Dan moves like gangbusters, but his thighs and calves still have numbness. His feet still don't feel every inch of surface beneath them. Dan's gait is fast, but it wavers ever so slightly with each step. His mind is saying to his legs: *Move*—and saying to his feet: *Feel*. But the connections aren't 100 percent there.

"But Jesus makes up the difference. He fills in the spaces," Dan said.

At the stoplight, Dan pulled me close to him.

"You taught me that, sugar pie. Jesus fills in the spaces. Mama planted the seed. But you watered it."

I looked at him. "What do you mean?"

"You never gave up on me." He said this. So after a second, I accepted it.

"Thank you," I said.

"You were always consistent," my husband added. I allowed the compliment, loving it. But he wasn't finished. "You believed in Jesus and you believed in me, and you were always there. And you can quote me."

Well. That sounds nice, I told him.

Dan held my hand as the light turned.

"One day," he said, "I finally realized that whatever I was looking for, Jesus had it. And now I can talk about it!"

Suddenly he clapped his hands together, biting his lip, holding back tears. He still gets emotional, but he recovers quickly. So he laughed through his tears. Then with both hands pointed skyward, he asked: "How does that Scripture go? I'm not ashamed of the gospel of Jesus Christ. Well, free at last, I'm not ashamed."

On Sundays, we would sing about all of this in our church—a black church, yes—but not one full of angry people. I could hear the joy in the singing. In Jesus' name, the singing had purpose. Dan was a strong tenor.

"Woke up this mornin' with my mind stayed on Jesus."

I would stand next to him in our pew, listening to his nice voice, feeling him standing beside me. Hallelu. Hallelu. Hallelu.

Now whenever Dan prays for me, when I ask him to pray for me, I walk all day on air. That's how my day goes. In Jesus' name, I can fly.

Heed the Holy Spirit

But you, dear friends, must continue to build
your lives on the foundation of your holy faith.
And continue to pray as you are directed by the
Holy Spirit. JUDE 1:20

Then the year 2001. The best of times. The worst of times.

Didn't matter who you were. For everybody it seemed, the year was the best and the worst; the same calendar, hanging on the same thumbtack. Goodness, what a year.

For us, it started on a good note. Dan was home, getting stronger, working part-time as a substitute teacher in the Denver public schools. Driving himself. Working on his feet all day. Our own kind of miracle. A great start, indeed.

Joi's bookstore was bumping along, doing reasonable business for a small, independent shop in a struggling part of town.

Mama, now eighty-five after her birthday in December, looked good, was feeling good, and was still living in her home.

I returned to full-time teaching at CU–Boulder, still a bit shaky after Dan's roller-coaster year, but grateful to be working again. I was elated, frankly, to have a full-time paycheck and not ashamed to admit it.

Then the really good news: Alana decided to go back to college. In January 2001, she enrolled at the University of Northern Colorado in Greeley, formerly Colorado Teacher's College. She would be a teacher, she decided, settling on elementary education—a top major at UNC, respected worldwide. So after a year at her high-ticket university in New York, she was back on track now at a state college. And she had a graduation date: May

2004. It seemed like a long way off. But she had a game plan. And a graduation date! Moreover, she seemed happy and content.

Parents everywhere dream of such moments. Pray for such moments,
indeed.

Dan and I were ecstatic. We helped her haul her stuff into campus
housing, a one-bedroom apartment spiffed up with college doodads: posters, throw rugs, a bookshelf, spare lamps from home. We thanked God for
her return to school, an answer to prayer. Well, true, she still was following Farrakhan and his people, still draped in the long skirts and head-
covering scarves. But she was back in school. So we could be happy with
that. And that's a reasonable word for it: happy. When she called soon
after classes started, she sounded joyous herself.

"You sound good," I said.

"I am good," she answered. "I've made a decision about something."

Okay. This kind of talk always rings alarm bells. Even she agreed she
often chose paths outside "the norm." So here she was now, choosing a
path, making a decision about something.

I braced myself.

"I'm leaving the Nation."

"Hmm . . . ," I said, sounding as casual as I could. "The nation?"

I wasn't following her exactly.

"The Nation of Islam. I'm not involved with them anymore."

I pressed the phone tighter to my ear.

"Praise God," I said.

"I've decided to become an orthodox Muslim."

I was silent. My light heart was sinking. How to respond?

"Well . . . interesting . . . what does that mean exactly?" I finally
asked.

"The Nation isn't really 'orthodox' Islam."

"Okay," I said. I was holding back and she could tell.

"Mom, I've thought about this a lot. I've done a lot of studying, and
I'm now an orthodox Muslim."

"A 'Muhz-lum,'" I said, trying the word on my tongue.

"Well, you say it like 'Moose-lum,'" Alana said with a kind of Arabic
flair. "I'm a Muslim." Again, with the Arabic flair. "Orthodox."

I could feel my throat tighten. A mother of faith draws up when her
child rejects the family's deepest beliefs.

With Alana, in fact, this announcement meant she was moving away
from us further still, all the way to formal Islam orthodoxy, whatever that

would actually mean. I wasn't sure. In truth, I didn't even want to think about it.

And yet, I didn't say anything this time. No complaints. No criticism. No arguing. No debating.

"Well," I said finally, "thanks for letting us know." It sounded like surrender.

Indeed, on another day, I might have demanded answers: Why this? Why now? How did this happen? Or on another day, I might have quoted Scripture. Or called the prayer circle. Or e-mailed the prayer band. Or raised my fists to heaven, begging Jesus to bring her home.

But this time, after finally learning to meet the Father on his terms—in a relationship with his Trinity, with God's own Spirit living inside my old broken-down, humbled heart—I stayed quiet. The former words of my cast-off ways just weren't there anymore. Amazing. Instead, only love words came out of my mouth.

"So how are your classes going?" I asked Alana.

How is your money holding out? How's the car running?

Little love questions. God wouldn't let anything else flow up from my heart and out of my mouth. I loved this child, indeed, and I was unspeakably sad at this, her latest choice.

And, indeed, I reveled in hearing her voice across the phone line. But she seemed stolen, as if a thief had swooped in and robbed us of our own flesh and blood. I can't explain the feeling of the loss. Our daughter was close enough to hear on the phone—but still gone from our family's faith. And nothing I could say at that moment would bring her back.

I was heartsick. *I am dying,* I thought. *So why am I asking if her car's running okay?*

Indeed, I wanted to ask this: Why not Jesus?

After all, I had spent a lifetime in church, loving every warm bit of deep sweetness about it, sinking into the Deity, so grateful to know the man Jesus, to have been taught of his perfect and beautiful life, to share in his glory and his promise. Everlasting life with him and the Father, ushered into his presence and promises by the Holy Spirit. Eternity with the Holy Trinity. Could anything at all ever be better?

And yet I couldn't argue for the Trinity or eternity on this day. The words weren't there. God closed my mouth.

So short of special wisdom or points of argument, I offered what God gave me: love talk. We miss you so much. We're proud of you starting school again. Is your coat warm enough? Have you made any friends?

Please, God, let her have friends. Don't let her walk across campus alone—her dark Islamic head coverings whipped by the wind—drawing stares and frowns, people looking over their shoulder at her or, worse, throwing her dirty looks and catcalls.

Because what doesn't look familiar looks frightening. And Alana, now, would look to some like an enemy. For sure, she didn't look like a typical college coed.

Girls on campus wore their jeans tight and their sweatshirts baggy; they wore high-heeled boots and highlighted ponytails bunched high on pert, pretty heads, the whole look topped off sometimes with frosted lipstick and MTV makeup. Pretty American girls—black, white, Latina, Asian. On this campus, such girls looked perfectly at home. This was their turf, even if their young women's hearts wondered sometimes if they were doing okay. Even with those doubts from time to time, they looked like they belonged.

But Alana moved around life on the outside. She stood alone.

The cheese.

Race and religion put her on the fringes. I lost sleep over this. My daughter: the cheese? The other black girls on campus wore their tight jeans and baggy sweatshirts, their own highlighted ponytails, but always their heads were uncovered, showing their braids or some other breezy, confident style. Young American girls. Black and beautiful. Black and proud.

As a college teacher, I loved young people this age.

I loved their youth and openness—their young American style, their crazy blue spiked hair and eyebrow jewelry and tongue rings and all the ridiculous stuff their parents hated. But most parents weren't really all that worried, if they told the truth about it. Because all of us, parents included, know that soon enough the Kool-Aid hair and the stupid eyebrow jewelry will come off. One day soon, their children will become themselves again.

For now, while they studied and reflected, they could wear the blue hair and navel rings and nose jewelry and none of it hurt their studies or their chances.

So I met the students at UNC—black and white and others—and I liked their style too. They were finding their own way to fit in.

At UNC, black students met at the Marcus Garvey Center for their dinners and forums and luncheons and fish fries. They found a way to make the campus their home too. And they took Alana in, loving her.

They elected her president of the Black Women of Tomorrow, a campus students' club.

When they went bowling, they invited her. When they celebrated birthdays, she always went along. When they crowded into booths at Red Lobster and The Cheesecake Factory and The Egg and I, she went along too.

But when I stood back and looked at everything, she still seemed to stand alone. Nobody else wore *hijab*. Nobody else gave up the lipstick, the cute hairdos, the flash of youthful eye shadow, the seeming normalcy that I craved for her at her age, just twenty-one.

She was swallowed up inside Islam. I did not want this cross.

What more did God want? My husband had almost died. My oldest daughter was a struggling single mother. And Alana was the cheese? An orthodox Muslim in the middle of Colorado farm country?

⊹⊱⊰⊹

Good grief.

Sometimes Alana and I did argue.

She questioned why I believed the Bible. Who did I think Jesus was? How could I think that God would have a Son, as if God couldn't be God all by himself?

Good questions. But I didn't have answers. A Christian woman like me who always went to church never thinks the Bible isn't right. Never believes the Bible itself isn't a true and reliable source.

These were Alana's arguments, however, and she was well schooled. My every defense about Christianity was knocked down with one of her well-studied Islamic points of view.

The divinity of Jesus? "The Nicene Council *voted* him to be divine."

The authenticity of the Bible? "Please. The Bible has been changed, tampered with a zillion times."

The principle of the Trinity? "God does not need partners. God is God all by himself."

She could recite every counterargument and then some.

I was amazed at her devotion to this material—and there was a ton of it, reams and reams of it. It was as if Islamic scholars had spent entire lifetimes just thinking of arguments to disprove Jesus as God's Son.

But there was one problem.

To those who know him, Jesus isn't a theory to disprove. Jesus is a friend. I had a relationship with him. And who can disprove a relationship?

So, okay, the Trinity was hard for me to explain then. But I knew what the Bible said, that "the Father and I are one," as Jesus put it. I understood that the Holy Spirit was our Comforter, our Helper, our Intercessor, our Inspirer, the perfect completion of the blessed Trinity, and not just a concept. Besides, look at Dan. Wasn't he healed?

Sometimes I tried that argument. We were in the kitchen, sitting at the table, my Bible at my elbow. "It's like the Bible says . . . " I started in, but Alana never let me finish.

"The Bible? The Bible doesn't count here. It isn't reliable. It's been tampered with, changed over and over, by all kinds of people. Look at all the translations—King James this, Revised that, New Revised the other. Not like the Qur'an, which hasn't ever been touched since God gave it to Muhammad. Never, ever changed, ever."

She seemed so sure, and I didn't know one thing about the Qur'an. So I just sat there while she ran up her arguments and ran down mine.

"And," she was saying, "look at all the denominations in Christianity. In Islam, everybody believes the same thing, no matter where you go. I can go to any mosque in the world and they all believe the same thing, no divisions. Everybody in Islam believes the same."

She was ready. And I wasn't. Of course, now I'm aware of Sunni and Shi'ite and Sufi and everything in between. Oh, how things change, indeed. But back then, on the tip of her tongue, she could make every convincing claim for Islam and I couldn't offer a single slam-dunk counterpoint for Christ.

Worse, our theological tug-of-war dominated every visit. I spent hours in debate with Alana, it seemed, most of it going in circles. Then one Sunday night I watched from our driveway as my daughter climbed into her Honda Civic and drove resolutely back to Greeley, she and I both worn out from a weekend of theological battling.

Dan stayed out of it. "Not my battle," he said. A healed man picks his battles carefully, indeed. So I was always the heavy—or the lightweight, in fact.

"Three people?" Alana asked me one time, again questioning the Trinity, sounding so dramatically incredulous. "God is three people? That's crazy, Mom. It doesn't even make sense."

"Not three people," I said. "Three in One—God the Father. God the Incarnate Son. God the Comforting Spirit. Perfect and indivisible."

Why didn't she get it?

"That is so crazy," she said, walking away.

"But that's the point," I said, talking to her even as she left the room. "It's not about logic. Walking the Christian journey is about faith."

⊰⊱

But I wanted more. So I sat at my computer, surfing the Internet, looking up stuff.

The Nicene Council. The Council of Constantinople. The Apostles' Creed. Martin Luther. John Wesley. The Great Awakening. Pagan symbolism imbedded in Christianity.

The Nicene Council, indeed. Back in college, I'd taken a religious studies course and loved it. But now I felt like I needed a minor degree in Christology just to talk on the phone to my daughter.

I loved Jesus, yes. But I didn't know much about Christianity. Now, in the glow of my computer, I surfed through Web sites and blogs and this page and that forum, any Christian information I could find, points *and* counterpoints. There was much to read, all manner of philosophies bent on disproving the doctrine of Christ.

But the gospel faith I'd practiced all these years had a rugged and glorious history, as stunning as the Cross. Studying Christianity made me not just love my faith more, it also made me love Jesus more.

What a life. Our Emmanuel—"God with us," indeed. And what a God, to come to earth as a man to save our miserable, self-deluded, contentious soul. I could study and meditate and reflect on Christianity the rest of my own contentious life and never get tired of it.

It's like the friend Charles Spurgeon spoke of in his sermons, who said to him: "Sir, you say that Christ can save me. Well, if he does, he shall never hear the last of it."

Like that man, the more I learned, the more I couldn't stop talking about Jesus. When Jesus said from the cross, "My God, my God, why hast thou forsaken me?" he not only was quoting Jewish Scripture, which he knew backward and forward, he was also taking on the sins of the whole world at that moment, and those sins were too despicable for God the Father to look on. I loved that explanation.

Discerning that the Father God had turned away, God the Son used Scripture to pronounce his awareness. He even forsook the word *Father*, declaring instead: "My God, my God, why hast thou forsaken me?"

Jesus? I could say his name all day and all night and not get tired of it.

And yet, why did I believe?

⊰⊱

That was easy to explain.

It was after college. I had a baby and was heading to divorce. I needed a Savior. So what about Jesus? What about all the fifty zillion Sundays in church? They had to count for something.

So I just asked Jesus, *If you are real—if your Holy Spirit is real—if you are who you say you are, then show me some sign.*

That's how black people say it: God, if this is real, you got to show me a *real* sign. Real deal. So I was sitting in my childhood bedroom, surrounded by the real deal. All that blue—blue bedspread, blue walls, dark blue carpet that Daddy had let me pick out by myself at Sears. And, tell me, what black folks ever let a thirteen-year-old child pick out her own dyed-to-match carpet? So these were amazing people, Mama and Daddy. I mean, good black parents.

But now, some ten years later, there I sat in this same room. Same blue walls, blue bedspread, blue carpet—blue, blue, blue up and down and every which way, blue all the livelong day—blue looking downright dizzy and out of style, and bluer than blue should ever look.

College degree. A baby. Heading to divorce. A prodigal daughter back home. And I needed a Savior. Like nobody's business, I needed a Savior. So I asked: *Are you real, Jesus?*

And then came the peace.

The Holy Spirit moves like that.

Even without a Nicene Council, even without a "conspired" vote that Jesus was divine, the Holy Spirit moves like that. For all that day and all the next day and the next, peace that passed all understanding. Uncanny and unlikely peace. The real deal. My real sign. No logic to it. Not everybody's sign probably. But I learned: Just saying the name Jesus, calling the Holy Spirit, just speaking the name Holy Father, sends the peace.

But you have to ask. And logic doesn't have anything to do with it.

My daughter wasn't buying it.

⊰⊱

Easter week 2001. Alana was home for spring break. She looked good. Eating right. Studying hard.

This time, we didn't argue so much. She could tell that her Islamic journey made me too disconsolate for much more talk.

She apologized, in fact. I did too.

We had finished eating dinner, and she was helping me dry dishes. She did that a lot now, helping. Her Muslim walk had turned Alana into a Christian-like young woman, in that she showed that she loved me— all of us, in fact, especially Mama—now more than she ever had in her life. She was our own Mother Teresa, doing her good works and loving us. And we loved this about her.

"I want to tell you something, Mom," she said on Saturday night before Easter. She was drying a pan, helping me in the kitchen. "I'm sorry for all the arguments."

"Yeah, me too," I said.

"Arguing and putting you down is disrespectful to you and to what you believe," Alana added. "I'm sorry about giving you a hard time."

Okay, I said. We gave each other a quick hug. Détente in the kitchen. But it didn't salvage everything we'd lost. We couldn't share any more "kindred moments"—well, not holidays. She still sneered a bit, in fact, at the Easter bunny paraphernalia I dragged up from the basement.

"I know, paganism, right?" I asked.

She laughed, shrugged.

"Well, okay," I said. "Eggs are fertility symbols. Pagan, all right? But not anymore. Christians don't use them as fertility symbols."

I offered her a candy egg—a peace offering—but she refused.

"C'mon," I said. "It's just a fun thing."

But the fun that holidays once meant for our family was all over now. No longer Christmas with everybody, including Alana. No longer Easter with everybody, including Alana.

Lord Jesus. This was unbearable.

─ ⫤⫣ ─

She went upstairs to clean out her closet. She was taking clothes to the *masjid*, the mosque. In fact, there was a large mosque in south Denver on Parker Road, about ten minutes by car from our house. I'd passed it on Parker Road for ten years at least, never once even thinking about it. And now on Fridays, if Alana was home for the weekend, she rushed there for Friday *Jumah salat*, or prayers.

Good grief.

Was God doubled over somewhere laughing at me and my dilemma?

Wondering when I would understand that this business with Alana and Islam wasn't about me, it was about her and him?

She was on her journey, indeed. She was twenty-one and on her journey. My job was to stand back, then love her and pray. But that was the thing.

It was hard enough watching Alana reject Christ, using such beautiful energy to do it—praying, studying, contemplating God, helping the poor, loving her family—talents and strengths that would have been used, in a perfect world, in the name of Jesus.

So what to do?

What else? I helped her. Oh, the Christian journey.

If she collected clothes for the Muslim poor, I collected clothes for the Muslim poor too.

Once when she needed a ride to the mosque, *I drove her there*. I put both feet down on the promise: All things work together for good for those who love God and are called for his purpose. So, yes, I stuffed a ton of clothes into Glad bags—pretty good clothes, a lot of them—and helped Alana get them to her mosque. Yes, I did.

Because clearly Alana was making a statement and taking a stand, trying to live a better life, to be more than just another modern American girl. She'd been that: cheerleader, party girl, barfly, all of that. But the empty life is empty indeed. So now she longed to be modest and godly and good and deep.

These are good things. Great things, even. My dismay was that she didn't think she could be a deep and modest and good woman in Christ. Christian girls, she said, wore "tight jeans and low-cut tops just like hoochie-mama girls in the clubs. They don't look any different."

Well, some of them did. I couldn't argue.

Not so in Islam, she said.

I didn't know different, so I said okay.

In fact, she loved wearing *hijab*, the head covering, she said. And in truth, she looked lovely. Some days she even looked holy.

"For the first time in my life, Mom, men respect me. Mom, they *open doors* for me. They don't hang out of their car windows, yelling, 'Hey, baby' and all of that."

Well. Okay. "I appreciate that," I told her.

"But men respect me too," I said. "So I *don't* wear *hijab*. But I am modest in my dress. Men don't yell out of their car windows at me either."

She laughed. "Do men holler at fifty-one-year-old women?"

"If they dress like they want to be hollered at," I said.

We stopped then. Our arguments always circled around themselves, never finding their end. She thought Islam was best—and right. I didn't.

I couldn't win her back with arguments. But I could live like a true Christian. So I loved my daughter, *hijab* and all. I even bought her scarves. Pretty ones. The Spirit led me. The Holy Spirit was the key.

⸙

Charles Spurgeon, the great British Baptist preacher, said the things of Christ "are too bright for us to see till the Spirit shows them to us."

Isn't it wonderful, the great preacher added, "how the Holy Spirit can take a fool, and make him know the wonders of Christ's dying love?"

All this time, indeed, I had been a fool, pressing in my own strength toward my daughter, not to mention pressing toward God, in the name of Jesus. But I wasn't relying on the power of the Holy Spirit to lift and draw me there. And now, with my daughter in Islam, when I had run out of things to say and tactics to try to win her back to Christ, I turned to the Trinity, finally pleading, *Help me, Holy Spirit.* And my answer?

Buy her a scarf. A pretty scarf. And while you're at it, love her. That is, listen to her. Then, after you've listened, leave her to God. Leave her at the altar.

Yes. Well. Thank you, Holy Spirit.

Our "Divine Teacher" is how Spurgeon described him, the often forgotten entity of the Trinity.

"Some never think of him at all," Spurgeon said in a sermon preached from his pulpit in 1894. "How many sermons there are without even an allusion to him! Shame on the preachers of such discourses! If any hearers come without praying for the Holy Spirit, shame on such hearers . . . !

"And you, Christian people, do cry to him that you may not read your Bibles without his light. Do not pray without being helped by the Spirit; above all, may you never preach without the Holy Spirit! It seems a pity when a man asks to be guided of the Spirit in his preaching, and then pulls out a manuscript and reads it."

I'd heard sermons like that. A preacher reading off paper. You wanted to scream. The practical lesson, said Spurgeon, is this: "Believe what the

Spirit teaches you, and adore your Divine Teacher; then shall his instruction become easy to you."

Adoring the Holy Spirit? Easy?

Well, in truth, I barely spoke of the Holy Spirit. I was taught in Sunday school that to blaspheme the Spirit was an unforgivable sin, and I was afraid of messing up.

So the Holy Spirit seemed a deep mystery. Unlike Jesus, whom I knew from Miz Hall's kindergarten class. Unlike God the Father, the big presence in the clouds, in the flowers, all around. But the Holy Spirit?

Listen, said Spurgeon: The Father and the Son are glorified in each other, "the two evermore in that divine conjunction in which they are always to be found." But *the Holy Spirit must lead us to see this.* That was his emphasis, not mine.

But I was learning: Without this supernatural vision—this Holy Ghost sight—we can't pray right. We can't love right. Or discern right or serve right or preach right or teach right. We can't live right. Absolutely, we can't live with each other right. Moreover, we miss our calling in life without the Holy Spirit's revealing and leading.

When it came to praying for my daughter, or for anything else, even if I had everything else lined up right—motivation and intention, glorification and gratification, love and forgiveness, confession and denial, perseverance and faith, all prayed in the name of Jesus and under his precious and sanctifying blood—none of it would make one iota of difference if it wasn't inspired by the Holy Spirit.

The Holy Spirit is the key.

Torrey put it this way: "It is the prayer that the Holy Spirit inspires that God the Father answers."

And Foster: "The ideas, the pictures, the words are of no avail unless they proceed from the Holy Spirit who, as you know, is interceding for us 'with sighs too deep for words.'"

And Murray: "Surely, if there is one prayer that should draw us to the Father's throne and keep us there, it is this: for the Holy Spirit, whom we as children have received, to stream into us and out from us in greater fullness."

Murray was so sharp, so good. "Only the Spirit of God can enable us to do it aright."

Then Murray sealed it.

"The Father," he said, "gives the Holy Spirit to them that ask Him, not least, but most, *when they ask for others.*"

﹢⧏⧐﹢

I had been so confused about this.

For years, I called the Holy Spirit an "it"—and God help me. But all the Bible teachers were clear: The Holy Spirit is a person, the third holy person of the blessed Trinity.

Oh blessed Trinity. I'd never before in life said those words in prayer. But the prayer people used it all the time.

Every day, in fact, Torrey said, ask God to be filled up with God's Holy Spirit, and especially before trying to pray. "Or to translate more literally, 'Be getting filled with the Holy Spirit' (it is a continuous process, as is indicated by the tense of the Greek verb here used)."

Such a smart man. These warriors knew so much.

"If we are filled with the Spirit we will be guided by the Spirit in our prayers as well as in everything else," he said. "A Spirit-filled man will always be a *prayer*-ful man, and his prayers will be in the Holy Spirit."

So that person will be obedient, fervent, Bible ready, Spirit dependent—insightful of the will of God.

﹢⧏⧐﹢

September 11, 2001.

I was in the shower. The phone rang and went to voice mail. Rang and went to voice mail. Rang and went to voice mail. Rang a fourth time and finally I grabbed it, still dripping, answering, shivering.

Good grief.

Joi: "Mom!"

"What's wrong?"

Joi was shouting.

"What's the matter? Are you okay?!"

"Are you watching TV?"

"No—what's the matter?"

"The United States is under attack!"

"*What?*"

"Turn on CNN!"

I fumbled for the remote. *Good Lord.* Who can forget the day? The awful skies? The hellish sounds. Then the pictures. Replay and replay. Then the analysis: Islamic. Islamic. Islamic.

I called Dan. No answer. I called Mama. No answer.

I called Alana's cell phone. She was in class apparently. But I kept calling. All day. I could see her, rushing across campus, Islamic scarves whipping in the wind, a target for anybody's anger.

I fell to my knees.

The words wouldn't come. I stumbled for words, shouting into the covers on my bed.

"Oh heavenly Father, in the blessed name of Jesus . . . make this evil stop!"

What kind of prayer was this? Planes were falling out of the sky. But I couldn't find my words. All my pretty, glorious prayer talk. Gone.

But my Bible, the one my Muslim daughter claimed was unreliable and couldn't be trusted because it was tampered with and corrupt, that Bible knew about this moment.

And Paul, the "pugnacious" apostle, as Karen Armstrong described him, captured our 9/11 like this, writing in A.D. 58 to the church at Rome: "And the Holy Spirit helps us in our weakness."

It is deep help, indeed.

"For example, we don't know what God wants us to pray for," Paul said. "But the Holy Spirit prays for us with groanings that cannot be expressed in words."

The world that I knew was under attack. Hundreds and maybe thousands were dead, consumed by hellish evil. Islamic. Islamic. Islamic.

And my own child was walking around, swathed in her Islamic garments, defiant.

She finally answered her phone.

"Hi, Mom."

"I've been trying to reach you all day."

"What's up?"

What's up? Holy Spirit?

"Did you hear about the attacks on the World Trade Center?"

"Yeah," she said.

Yeah?

Didn't she remember? We went to New York on vacation once. Goofy tourists in the Big Apple. Diana and her kids and her husband. Me and her dad and our family. Cameras slung around our necks. Everybody in new tourist sneakers. Getting on the elevators, up and up. Forever ascending, infinitely rising. All the way to heaven on earth.

Then, above the clouds, the view! *God Almighty.*

The world of New York City, everywhere below us. And everywhere around us, the steel sheen of tall, tall towers. Gleaming, glowing above the clouds.

Now all of it gone. And all the people gone too.

Yeah?

"What are you talking about?" I said to my daughter.

"They keep blaming Islamic terrorists and . . . "

I interrupted her.

"Thousands of people are dead," I said. "Thousands of people, innocent people. Dead. Gone. Wiped out. Husbands and wives and daughters. This is a terrible, terrible thing."

She was silent.

Finally she said: "I know it's terrible. But it's so frustrating. The minute something bad happens, everybody starts blaming Muslims."

"Did you wear *hijab* today?" I asked.

"What do you mean?"

"I just think, until things cool off, you shouldn't walk around wearing Muslim clothes."

I could hear Alana shaking her head no.

"God will protect me, Mom," she said. "I'm not going to stop wearing *hijab* because people are mad at Muslims. And if something happens to me, that is God's will."

"No," I said, "it is not God's will for people to get hurt. The Bible says . . . " but I stopped.

"I love you. Be careful," I said.

"I love you too."

Then she hung up and I went back to CNN. It was the worst day of everybody's life.

So at bedtime on September 11, I didn't pray.

The Holy Spirit, helping me in my distress, prayed for me, with groanings and with sighs and with moaning too deep for words. Then when I woke up on September 12, after a night of not praying, I had new sight. For the first time in my life, at a time when everything seemed to be going wrong, I felt all right.

I didn't turn on CNN. Didn't turn it on for the next two or three months. In fact, anytime I saw a TV program with a crawl line at the bottom of the screen, I hit the remote, turning it off.

In the car, I traded my beloved NPR for an easy-listening station in Denver called KEZW. I clicked it on mornings, turned it off at night. So here was Frank Sinatra and Rosemary Clooney and Nat King Cole and Vikki Carr all the livelong day. I must have heard "It Must Be Him" and "All the Way" and "Unforgettable" ten thousand times forward, up, and back again.

The newspaper said Americans were struggling with the stress of 9/11—eating too much, crying for no reason, having trouble sleeping.

I was sleeping like a baby. Eating healthy. Taking long walks after coming home from campus, my Walkman tuned to KEZW, singing along as Vikki Carr belted out "The Big Hurt" and Engelbert Humperdinck kicked through "Quando, Quando, Quando (Tell Me When)."

Holy Ghost music? Had to be. When a black woman listens to Vikki Carr and Engelbert Humperdinck, the only way to explain it is the Holy Ghost.

So I was either crazy or sanctified, but mostly I had joy, and it didn't make any sense. And for the record, Vikki rocks.

So I had my last argument with Alana. I was through trying to convince her back to the blessed Trinity. That was Holy Ghost work, and I trusted the Holy Ghost to do the job in his own time in his own way. Moreover, I was leaving the war on terror to God.

And, yes, I understand that 9/11 rides at the top of the list of the horrific. As a trained journalist, I also know that CNN and the networks are great at covering the worst crises of our living and our dying. But I was done with crawl lines and All-Terror All-the-Time TV. God said leave it alone, give it to me and time to move on, by permission of the Holy Spirit—this wonderful "Gold Ghost," in Spurgeon's colorful words.

So for the rest of the year, that's what I did.

Then Christmas came and Dan and I put up the tree, loading it down with tiny white lights and gold-toned ornaments, plus every decoration my daughters had ever made in their life. It was beautiful. I bought gifts for everybody, Alana included, and she accepted her "holiday" packages with gratitude and grace and without complaint. Rocking around the Christmas tree, yes.

Mama turned eighty-six two days after Christmas. Dan and I celebrated our twenty-sixth anniversary. Then the year 2001 came to a close.

It was the worst year ever. Then it was the best year ever. So what if nothing that year made sense?

I ended it with Vikki and Frank and Engelbert: "Tell me, Quando, Quando, Quando."

I like that song.

The Holy Ghost keeps me on key.

Serve with Love

God loves it when the giver delights in the
giving. 2 CORINTHIANS 9:7

Mama wasn't feeling right.

She'd had shingles a few years back, a fairly bad case of it. Now the
"post-herpetic neuralgic" aftereffects were still giving her what for. Giving
me what for too. When Mama complained, I just folded. Her complaints
moved in and took me over. My sister was dutiful and loving, but she lived
in Atlanta. So when Mama complained, the complaints turned to me. I
never seemed to respond the right way.

My big goal in life was to make Mama happy. But rarely, it seemed, did
I get her to that soft place.

"What's wrong, Mama?" I asked. We were sitting in her family room.
Saturday afternoon. She was half-watching a baseball game on TV.
Dan was sprawled on the couch, enjoying a nap. I sat in the chair
facing Mama, unable to ignore her intermittent sighs, the occasional
grimace.

"Mama, what's wrong?" I asked again.

"No point in complaining," she said.

"About what?"

"Same thing: these shingles."

"It's hurting again?"

"It hurts all the time," she said. "But there's no point in complaining.
Nobody wants to hear complaining."

At moments like these, and there were a lot of them, I felt inadequate—totally and utterly ineffective as a daughter and as the comforter I was supposed to be. I knew that shingles can cause horrible post-neuralgic pain. I'd checked out the Web sites, talked to Mama's doctors, even taken her for acupuncture. When that didn't help, I took her to a hospital nurse who did "therapeutic touch" in her home on her days off. In the hospital, the doctors didn't believe in it, the nurse said. They thought it was weird and kind of kooky.

Mama thought so too. "A waste of time," Mama said, dismissing both acupuncture and the nurse. "Hands waving all around. She didn't even touch me."

"But you got better with that nurse, Mama," I said.

She shrugged, grimacing again.

"No, it was a waste of time," she said.

She grimaced again, still half-watching the game.

Good grief. What now? It wouldn't help to argue, to remind Mama that she *did* feel better lots of times—especially when she was out enjoying herself with friends. She went to water exercise three times a week, and she looked happy there. Those times, in fact, she didn't just look happy, she *moved* happy, laughed happy. Nobody would guess to look at her, during those times, that she'd ever even had shingles or that she'd be eighty-seven this year.

But the minute she was home with me, all that happiness seemed to vanish down the drain, like cold bathwater.

"I've got a busy week at work," I said, trying to change the subject. "We're hiring a new dean, and I'm on the search committee."

Mama looked over at me.

"What'd you say?"

"Next week at work should be really busy. We're hiring a new dean, and I'm on the search committee."

Mama turned back to the TV, not responding.

"You want me to call and get an appointment for your shingles pain?"

Mama shrugged. "The doctor said I'd always have this."

"He can prescribe pain pills. Or maybe some new treatment," I said. "I can call him on Monday if you want."

Mama shrugged. "Okay, if you want."

"Okay," I said.

I want.

I wanted a fairy tale.

I wanted a mother who felt better and who loved me. Or let me tell the truth: I wanted a mother who loved me—*and* I hoped she felt better too. But mostly I guess I wanted her to look at me and just drape me with hugs and kisses, with a fairy-tale portion of love and adoration. But she couldn't do that now. Never had, to be honest. And now she had post-herpetic neuralgia, for goodness' sake, and she couldn't care less about draping me in love or in anything else.

Also, she wasn't eating right. In the trash can in her kitchen, the discarded TV dinner packages were stacked in a telltale tower. She had stopped cooking real food. Stopped eating it too. The fruit in the bowl on her counter was gray and soft with mold. The cans in her cupboard were past the expiration date. Even the ice cream in the freezer was old, months past the best-if-used-by date.

"You can't eat this old food, Mama. It'll make you sick," I told her. She looked at me and shrugged. She closed her eyes to my concern, staying silent.

"She's depressed," my sister said, calling from Atlanta. "Ask the doctor to change her blood-pressure medicine. The medicine can make people depressed."

How did my sister know these things? Of course, she's a psychologist with a Ph.D. She knows a thing or two about pharmacology. More than that, however, she was keyed in to Mama like a tuning fork. From fifteen hundred miles away, she could hear on the phone what I couldn't see with my eyes from across the room.

"It's her medication," Lauretta said. "When you take her to the doctor, ask about switching to something else."

It sounded easy. Lauretta, in fact, always seemed to have the right answers. She is a servant. That is, she thinks of others first—and isn't that what Rick Warren said? "Servants think more about others than about themselves."

Lauretta did that. When she and Mama were on the phone, they talked for hours: laughing, gossiping. She gave Mama time.

Elders need that, Mary Pipher said: "The two main things that old people need are time and touch." I saw Pipher on PBS, talking, being wise. "Time and touch," she said. "That's what old people need."

But when I talked to Mama, maybe five minutes or so passed, if that much. We reviewed our to-do lists. Then there was nothing else to say. And touching? We never touched. Well, if I helped her across a street or parking lot, she tolerated my touch. But she didn't seem to like it.

I called my sister to talk about this.

"The wrong sister lives near Mama," I said to Lauretta. "Since you two get along so well, Mama should live with you. I'm not as good at attending to her needs, not like you are."

Lauretta disputed that. "You worry too much. You're doing fine," she said.

But I didn't feel fine. Instead I felt stretched.

With my full-time teaching job and my two-hour commute, a roster of students who needed my attention and their papers graded, my ongoing care for Dan and my role as his wife, reaching out to my daughters, visiting with my granddaughter, cleaning my neglected house, throwing together a meal or two, and my little ushering job at church, plus my prayer time for all the elements of my life, I had hit a wall.

So my sister's words sounded so easy: Change Mama's medicine. Take her to the doctor. Get some new pills.

But this little task—taking Mama to the doctor, asking for new pills—looked like the high peak of the world's tallest mountain.

I couldn't climb it. This service emptied me.

I will tell the truth.

I didn't want my mother to need me as she did. I wanted her to be her former self, to figure stuff out and just do it, like she used to. I wanted her to throw out old food and buy fresh fruit and change her own lightbulbs.

I will tell the truth.

I wanted her to see my mountain, to notice my hard job, my two-hour commute, my family demands. I wanted her to care that when I got to my office at work, students were lined up at the door, purple hair and nose rings, waiting with their questions. Their wants. Their worries. Their eyebrow jewelry and tattoos. Their unrequited love. And they wanted me to teach them and to love them, too, and the State of Colorado was paying me good money to try.

But in faculty meetings, I listened to the drone, and half the time I didn't know what was going on anymore.

I wanted a mother who knew how that felt.

I wanted a mother to understand the frustration of meeting with the young Latino office manager in my department who expected me, as a full-time, tenure-track faculty member *and* an African American woman, to help lead our unit's crusade for diversity. "We need more students of color," he had said, sitting at my desk, earnest and concerned.

He cared so much, and I wanted to care too. But there was this mountain. I'd never seen anything so high. I stood at its base and looked up. I didn't want to climb.

⚜

I'd seen the mountain before.

When Daddy got sick the last time and Lauretta was far away in Atlanta, I went to the hospital and saw the nurse give him the IV, and it looked wrong.

I'd never seen candy red medicine in an IV bag, and it did look wrong. But I didn't speak up.

I didn't say, Hey, wait a minute. I didn't ask, Hey, why are you injecting funny-looking candy red medicine into my father's veins? Instead I stood there and the nurse put in the IV and in a matter of minutes, he was sick. He never got well.

"Just as soon as they put in that IV," he mumbled to church members visiting him, "I started feeling bad. I haven't felt right since."

The church leaders wrinkled their brows. They grabbed his hand and prayed. But three days later he was dead.

The funeral was a glorious spectacle. Standing room only. Gospel singing for hours. Preachers from near and far lined up on the podium, handsome in their black clothes, deep voices thundering their accolades. Cleaves Church was packed, big people and little people, squeezed into the pews, standing in the back, not enough room for all the mourners. Mortuary fans flapping like birds. Folks coaxing down air with their fans, trying to draw up a breeze. Everybody in the family pews sobbing from the sorrow and the emotion and not enough cool air.

If I don't die right here from sadness, I thought, *I'll just die from the heat.* It was October, not a hot day really. But so many people crowded into the small, overheated church that it looked and felt hot all at the same time.

Outside the sun was shining like crazy. A brilliant October day.

God was smiling.

Mama and Daddy were supposed to be leaving that very day for a long-planned trip to China of all places. Black folks going to the Far East. The trip of a lifetime.

But Daddy's lifetime was over. He was just sixty-eight. Instead of China, we took him to the cemetery and left him there.

How did this happen? He took care of me when I was little. We had food on the table every day. We had a warm roof over our head. We had clean, good clothes. Eyeglasses. Orthodontia. A set of *World Book* encyclopedias. College money. Stacks and stacks of *National Geographic* magazines.

I cut out the *National Geographic* pictures, pasted them with white glue in my reports for school, copied facts from the encyclopedias, brought home the A papers. I showed the papers to Daddy who wouldn't accept anything less anyway. Of course it was an A.

But then the tables turned.

Children become parents of the parents. But I just wasn't ready. I didn't know how to do this. The mountain was too high.

Daddy's mountain was impenetrable. And look what happened. He was dead. Gone to Jesus, yes. But gone it seemed too soon.

❧

Now, almost twenty years later, the mountain was back. It was Saturday. I was at Mama's house with Dan, a short visit to say hello and change some lightbulbs. If any lightbulbs burned out faster than Mama's lightbulbs, I'd like to see them.

Every other week it seemed, she was calling about lightbulbs.

"The bulb burned out on the back porch. I hate to bother Dan. Could he come over to change my bulb?"

So there we were. A short visit and lightbulbs. Mama was sitting in her place, a big leather chair-and-a-half in the corner of her family room. The family room was buried in old newspapers. Every issue of the *Denver Post* and the *Rocky Mountain News* from the past three months was piled around her feet, circling her big reading chair. The papers were bone-dry, yellowing around the edges.

"This is a fire hazard, Mama," I said to her.

Mama ignored me, kept reading a newspaper. Her TV was turned to high volume, but she wasn't really watching. Instead, she was into her paper, turning the dry pages.

"You like reading old papers?" Dan asked. He was teasing her, something he liked to do.

"Yes," Mama said, laughing a bit. She liked Dan. Whatever he said, she laughed at it.

"But it's *old* news, Grandma," he said. He was standing by her chair. "You'll read something and think it happened yesterday—but, look, it happened way back in March."

He dug in the stack and picked up a paper. "Look, June 8."

Mama was smiling, acting as if she were ignoring him.

"And what's today, Grandma?"

"I don't know," she said. "And I don't care."

"It's September 5," he said.

"So?" Mama said, not looking at Dan.

"So? These are old papers and they're a fire hazard. If you dropped a match in here, the place would go up like a torch."

"I'm not dropping matches in here," Mama said, still reading.

"Seriously, Grandma," he said. "All these old papers are a hazard. Let me help you throw them out."

"As soon as I finish reading them," she said.

"Okay," he said, giving me a wink.

Mama changed the subject. "Look on the kitchen table and bring me those lightbulbs," she told him.

He found the lightbulbs, changed one on her back porch, then lay down on the couch and fell asleep.

I sat in the chair opposite Mama, pretending to watch the loud TV. She read one of her newspapers. But we didn't talk.

The sound of silence was louder than I could bear.

⚜

"I want you to think about moving in with us," I told Mama the next day.

"Why would I want to do that?"

"I don't think you're eating right. I am concerned about your safety."

"My safety? I'm fine," she said. "You sound like Dan."

"Today you're fine," I said. "But other days, you're not fine. Plus you're not eating right: TV dinners with expired dates on them?"

Mama ignored this.

After all, she was eighty-six years old, almost eighty-seven. She had never been sick a day in her life from eating an expired TV dinner. So she ignored me.

"Where would I sleep if I moved in with you?"

"That bedroom behind the family room. Right on the main floor. No stair-climbing."

She was silent for a while.

"What would I do with my house?" she finally asked.

"Nothing," I said. "You can keep your house."

"I don't know," she said.

"You wouldn't have to worry about fixing dinner every night," I said.

"I don't know. We'll see."

"What does that mean?"

"Nothing," Mama said. "I'll think about it."

❧

Did I pray about these things?

Not for a long, long time. A good, long time. Instead, I tried on my own to love Mama and meet her needs and climb my mountain.

For years I had done that. This year was no different.

At Christmas, she went to Atlanta to spend the holidays with Lauretta.

I bought too many presents for everybody, just piled it on. Mama's birthday is two days after Christmas, so I truly piled it on: Christmas gifts, birthday presents, cards, flowers piled as high as the sky. A mountain of love. But was it service?

It didn't feel like it.

But when we are weak, we are strong.

I was reading Rick Warren. Finally. The whole world was reading Rick Warren that year. In fact, a friend e-mailed me and asked if I wanted to study *The Purpose-Driven Life* along with her church group. But I e-mailed back, saying no.

"Anything with 'Driven' in the title doesn't work for me right now," I wrote. I didn't know then just how driven I needed to be.

I was buried with work, in fact.

Mama was back from Atlanta.

Alana was back at school.

I was back in school, too, teaching a full load, driving the freeway all the livelong day, grading papers every spare second, meeting the long line of beautiful students waiting when I unlocked my office door.

In the meantime, Mama's shingles was giving her what for again.

"Have you tried the new medicine?" I asked.

She didn't answer.

"The new medicine . . . does it help?" I asked again.

"Maybe a little bit. I don't know," she said.

"I'll stop by after work," I said. "So I'll talk to you later. Maybe we can go to the doctor again."

Service. Service. Service.

We serve God by serving others. Yes, Rick Warren said that.

I was reading his book now and underlining like crazy, the whole lovely book. Yellow. Yellow. Yellow. I was on chapter 33. The whole chapter was yellow now, underlining everywhere. It was like Warren wrote the chapter and then addressed it to me. Read this. Read it again. Read it a third time. Yellow on every single page.

I was haunted, in fact, by my failure to serve my mother with gladness.

I feared that if anything kept me from feeling God's presence—while also keeping me from my purpose on earth—it would be this lack of "servanthood love" for my mother. My attitude tripped me up every time, along with my impatience.

She needed time. I didn't have it. Or, in truth, I didn't want to share the time I *did* have, even though time wasn't even mine to share. It was a gift from God, and I was stingy.

Then Warren: "God often tests our hearts by asking us to serve in ways we're *not* shaped."

And surely that was me.

My extrovert mother could sit for hours, talking with friends about other people. She and Lauretta did the same.

But I hated the gossip. Maybe I thought I was "better" than the socializing she did.

Or maybe I was stuck on being the introvert, loving the solitary and only willing to talk about ideas. My friends were idea people. So was my daughter Joi. She and I talked on the phone every day, sometimes two or three times a day, often just thinking out loud. We loved this.

With Mama, it was Mars and Venus. But she needed me. She was eighty-seven years old now, for goodness' sake. She was happier with Lauretta, I was certain. But Lauretta was on another planet, way over in Atlanta. Mama needed me here and now.

Warren again. Yellow. Yellow. Yellow. "Your primary ministry should be in the area of your shape, but your secondary service is wherever you're needed at the moment."

Mama needed me now, indeed.

Help me, Father, I prayed, *to serve you by serving Mama and to serve Mama in a way that is pleasing in your sight.*

Amen.

⋈

Dan came home from Wal-Mart with batteries.

"I'm going to tape your mother," he said.

"Tape, as in tape-record?" I asked him.

"You know, preserve family history for future generations and fill in some holes."

"Okay," I said.

"Besides, Grandma loves nothing better than looking back—reminiscing. She'll enjoy this."

So soon, Dan and Mama were huddled around the kitchen table, laughing at her old stories, stories I'd heard ten thousand zillion times and back around again. She could tell the same stories every single day and never, ever get tired.

I will scream, I thought, *if I hear these same stories one more time.*

Soon as I thought it, however, I should have been on my knees. Forgive me, blessed Father, for annoyance, impatience, arrogance. Who do I think I am anyway?

Well, I am weak, and when I am weak I'm strong. How many times did I have to read *that* verse? Over and over, apparently, because I was weak.

Also I was stubborn. So I didn't want to surrender. I didn't want to just give in to Mama, to make peace with who she was, like I had when Alana turned to Islam.

Mama was getting old.

"Not *getting* old . . . I *am* old." Or as she put it: "Wait till you get to be eighty-seven. If you wonder why I act confused, just wait."

But the hard part, for me, was reconciling a physically active mother—who could swing a bat and kick a ball and swim a lap with the best of them—with the woman who shuffled around my kitchen.

This is who I am now, my mother said. But I was stubborn. I wanted the original mother to come back. The original mother was sufficient, orderly, capable, fun. Where did she go?

⋈

When I pray now, I am aware of God's patience. But how many days, months, and years had I been praying this same prayer? *Help me to love my mother right.* Those words have risen off my soul more times than I can count. So there I was, praying them again.

But laughter interrupted my prayer. Dan and Mama were huddled around the kitchen table downstairs, talking about her favorite subject: the past.

So the next day, I asked her to talk to me after breakfast.

"About what?" she said.

"I want to interview you."

Mama groaned, rolling her eyes. "You too?"

"For my book," I said. "I want to ask you about what happened after Daddy died."

But she didn't wait for after breakfast. Right away, Mama started in: "Well, Dan was so much help when Daddy died," she said, and I winced a bit. She thought Dan walked on water. As for me, well—she didn't think I did. Not even close.

But here she was talking, and not to me exactly. Mama was talking into her past, looking back, as she did on so many days, retelling her story to herself, repeating what happened on the night my father died.

"Dan stayed at the hospital with Daddy after we'd gone home to rest." And Dan this. Dan that. Dan the other. "Then Dan called and said Daddy had passed. Lauretta had come from Atlanta, and she answered the phone. Then I called Mr. Bell—I'm not sure why I called Mr. Bell—but Mr. Bell met us at the hospital."

Mama had a faraway look. She didn't notice that the interview hadn't exactly started. I hadn't planned, in fact, to ask about the night Daddy died. Instead, I wanted to hear about her life *since* he died. But then it was clear. Since he died, she didn't have life, not in the same way.

So his dying night was the freshest moment in her memory. Well, a few facts were wrong. Dan wasn't at the hospital when Daddy died. Our father's physician broke the news. Only after that did Dan and I call Mama. Lauretta answered the phone. Then Dan and I drove in the middle of the night to Mama's house, and the four of us cried together. Then together we drove to the hospital to see Daddy.

He was laid out on a bed in his hospital room under clean sheets. Tubes were removed. IVs were unhooked. The ordeal of the dying was cleaned up and taken away. The room was softly lit and quiet. Daddy was quiet like only the dead are quiet. Silent beyond silence, his spirit flown away to Jesus.

Nothing is more final on this side of heaven than a death. Mama sobbed onto Daddy's naked chest.

"He looks so cold," she said. "Cover him up, please," she said to a nurse, "so he won't be so cold."

The nurse hugged Mama and pulled the sheet up to Daddy's chin. Mama couldn't forget.

"Lauretta was so much help," she was saying. Somebody else was always better. More helpful. Well, weren't they? It seemed so. But I listened anyway. God helped me to listen.

"She stayed with me for weeks—I don't know, five weeks at least, I think. She sat on the floor and she went through every single one of Daddy's papers. Spread them all out," Mama said, spreading her fingers on my kitchen table. "Lauretta went through every paper, piece by piece. That was such a help."

Mama looked across the table, but not at me. She was talking still to her past. So I kept listening.

"Then Lauretta went back to Atlanta, and I remember being in the house by myself. Then the neighbors started coming to the house, bringing casseroles and things. I must've had five baked turkeys in that freezer, but I gave most of them away without people knowing it. I couldn't eat all that food by myself."

She looked sad when she said this, despite talking about something that had happened twenty years before. Being by herself, as she put it, was torment.

But you weren't by yourself, I wanted to say. I was right here, with my husband and children. We came over those first months, time after time, night after night, trying and trying to make you be okay.

"Nighttime was the worst," Mama said anyway. "I never wanted to go to bed. I sat up every night in Daddy's chair in the living room." Then one night: "I looked up and Daddy was standing there. I never told anybody that. But there he was, just as clear as day. Then I looked harder but he was gone. I never saw him again."

Grieving people see things. Mary Pipher talked about this, calling them hallucinations. For some, the grieving doesn't stop. They keep going back, trying to make peace, talking, talking, talking about it. The traumatized need to talk, the experts say. "They talk to work through the trauma," Pipher said.

But I had been unwilling to listen—to be, indeed, as Pipher said, what elders need: "The old desperately need natural healers in their lives, people who are not in a hurry and who care what they are thinking and feeling."

Instead, I only had another question. Mama watched me ask it.

"Why didn't you want to go to sleep? Why was that so hard?" I wanted a wonderful and reflective answer, but Mama looked at me like the answer was obvious *and* stupid.

"I was alone," she said, as if that should be obvious. "And houses make noises at night." She looked at her hands again. "I didn't want to be up in that front bedroom by myself."

She sighed a bit, then started in again, skipping over years and years of good and joyous moments, to describe the next hard deaths, the loss of her last two siblings, her brothers. The eldest, Frank, she'd always called "Brother." She still had his voice saved on her voice mail, from the last time he'd called.

"Then when Brother died . . . " she started in and suddenly I realized that this "interview" was all about the people in Mama's life who had died. From Daddy to the next person to the next person after that. Mama was saying that death was always the biggest thing, and she hated this.

"I was really scared then. Brother was the last in my family, except me, and it just scared me. When you think about it, it's kind of scary. When he died, it was the end of the road, the end of our family."

I listened, stunned.

"The end of the family?"

"Yes, my mother and daddy were gone. Both my sisters were gone. Both my brothers were gone now. Everybody but me."

"But what about all the cousins?" I asked. "What about the grand-children? What about Lauretta and her family? What about my family? And what about me?"

Mama nodded, not answering. Then she started talking about Missy, the dog she bought for company after Daddy died—and then Missy died.

"She was so much company," Mama was saying. Then she added, "And when Missy died, I really was in the world by myself."

The dog? When the dog died, she was by herself?

I asked again, almost shouting, "Mama, what about the rest of our family? What about all the cousins? What about the grandchildren? What about Lauretta and her family? What about my family—and me?"

Mama looked at me.

"You're not really immediate family," Mama said.

"What?" I said.

"Not like my sisters and brothers, not like my mother and father."

"We're *not*?" I said, my eyes big, trying to look incredulous.

"No," she said. "It was always the five of us and our mother and daddy. Then Daddy died. Then when my sister died . . . "

She repeated these stories, which I have heard more times than I can remember—all of my life. I didn't know how to listen again, but I knew I had to.

At the end, I said this: "Mama, it seems like you talk about the past so much."

Mama looked over at me. She nodded, shrugging.

"Well, the past has more meaning to me than the things that are happening now," she said matter-of-factly.

"Yes," I said. I sighed. Then I added: "Sometimes it feels like you don't care very much about what I'm doing now, like you're more interested in the past."

Mama considered this with another shrug. Then she said: "Patricia, I can't remember half the time what happened yesterday. But the past is just as clear as it can be. And other people, some of my friends, tell me the same thing."

Well.

"Yes," I said, listening, not sure what else to say. "Yes," I said again.

I wanted a fairy tale but I had a mountain.

So I surrendered.

—※—

"Dear heavenly Father."

I wrote those words in my notebook—Dear heavenly Father—not saying them out loud on bended knees, but while sitting at my desk. It's in my office at home, in my oldest daughter's former bedroom. It's painted blue for the little boy who slept here before we bought the house from his family. The room is the only one in the house that never got painted. So the blue paint is a bit faded. But the room gets east light from a good window, and it's roomy enough for a desk and shelves, for all my writing stuff, all my praying stuff.

A Bic pen rested in my right hand. A prayer journal, bought on sale at Ross Dress for Less, waited, opened to a clean page.

Mama was downstairs at the kitchen table, tired of talking with me on this day. So I came up to my office to write: Dear heavenly Father. In Jesus' blessed name, your name is excellent—higher above all other names, greater above all other names and . . . *blah, blah, blah.*

I *tried* to write, that is.

But God told me I was writing to the wrong person.

Your mother needs a letter more than I do, God said.

Yes.

Here it is.

Tell the Mountain to Move

And if I had the gift of faith so that I could
speak to a mountain and make it move, without love I would be no good to anybody.
1 CORINTHIANS 13:2

So finally, Mama.

Here is your letter. It took me fifty-four years to write it. My goodness,
God is patient. And so are you. I don't know how you hung on this long,
wondering if a daughter would ever learn to say the only thing that ever
matters: My goodness, I love you.

Satan tried to make me say something else.

That's his job, keeping folks apart who should be wrapped together,
making us think we're each other's enemy when the only enemy is him.
The Bible gets it right: For we struggle not against people made with flesh
and blood and all of that. In fact, the good apostle Paul said we are warring
"against evil rulers and authorities of the unseen world, against mighty
powers in this dark world, and against evil spirits in the heavenly places."

There's enough mysticism in that sentence to push some folks over into
atheism. But I'm so deep a believer that I can't help but buy it all.

I understand now: Satan wanted me to think I couldn't love you right
because I failed in the past, not just with you but in so many other ways in
life. So sometimes I think I can't love. Then sometimes I don't feel like it.
That's just the truth of it. I get tired and stretched thin and irritable some
days. Too many days maybe. On those days, therefore, I'm just plain worn
out. I don't feel like loving anybody. But love isn't a feeling. Love is a
choice. So in Jesus' blessed name, I choose to love you. It's that simple.

I love you not because you're warm and touching and knowing with me. I love you because most times you're not. In fact, you're crotchety sometimes and you bully me at times. But at eighty-seven, that's probably okay. Dan disagrees. He says even at eighty-seven, folks should be kind and touching and gentle.

But now I see that your kindness, or lack of it with me, is a piffle compared to what matters most: that God loved me first anyway. Just as he loved you. Some might call this soppy spiritual rationalizing. But this logic works for me. God loves us, indeed, so his love covers everything else. His love lets me love everybody else, including you, or *especially* you.

I owe you everything, in fact.

You did the hard things.

You grew up in the Jim Crow South in the bad days. You took the streetcar every day with your widowed mother to a rich woman's house on the other side of town, and you scrubbed floors.

You polished sinks and chopped vegetables and washed the sweaty clothes and starched and ironed the table linen and polished the silver and dusted the windowsills. You watched your mother call the people sir and ma'am, even though she was far older than they were. But they always called her Laura. Never called her missus. Her surname never crossed their lips.

So with "Laura" you cooked and served early breakfasts and late-night parties, all on the same day sometimes, walking on tiptoe with your mother in the kitchen so the privileged folks in the dining room wouldn't be disturbed by rattling dishes.

Then you took your earnings from the cooking and serving and window washing and clothes washing and clothes ironing, and you went to college. You forged a life that led you to your young husband—my beloved father—and together the two of you granted me a lifetime of relative comfort.

You did this all for me, and even before you knew me. You took pennies and dimes and hand-me-down clothes to a black college and you survived by your will, to make everything better.

And I reaped the benefits.

Not you, but I took piano lessons and cooking classes and enjoyed a birthday party with balloons and paper hats and more gifts than I could open every year of my childhood.

Not you, but as a little girl I slept in a new brick house—in my own bedroom—when you integrated a white Colorado suburb.

Not you, but I took cushy summer vacations as a child to Disneyland and Yellowstone and the Grand Canyon and the Atlantic Ocean, snapping photos with my own Instamatic, dressed in brand-new summer pedal pushers and tops that you bought on layaway at the downtown JCPenney.

I, not you, was dressed as a little girl in matching sandals and Celeste organza dresses and camel-hair coats that announced to the world that my sister and I were treasured in the eyes of our parents.

You made me royalty, as much as a black girl could be in the fifties.

So I love you, Mama.

It's that simple. And Satan is a liar. So I know that you love me too. Well, I didn't like the crotchety bullying. But now I know that the crotchety bullying doesn't matter anymore.

I can see you now, with full sight, when you walk into my house carrying your plastic bags with ice cream and soft bread and canned fruit and all the other things that I never eat.

I can see with full sight that you are limping. That arthritis or whatever it is in your ankle is giving you what for again. Therefore, any trip to the store to buy anything for me is a journey of love.

So I will go to Walgreens and buy something for you. Nothing fancy. Just a footbath.

I will use it tonight.

I will fill it with warm water and Epsom salts.

I will kneel at your feet and ease your weary leg into the warm water.

I will wash your feet, pour the soothing liquid over your limbs, rub your aching calves and ankles and insteps and your toes with my own hands, touching you and believing that the touching will be okay.

For an old person's feet, yours are kind of cute, in fact. I mean, how many eighty-seven-year-old women still go to the nail place to get a pedicure and frosted orange toe polish?

"I love that color, Grandma," Alana told you recently. You grinned. Then you lifted your legs, pointed your feet, and wiggled your toes, showing off your orange polish, and we all laughed together.

Eighty-seven and laughing and orange toenails.

I *have* to love you.

And I have to wash your feet.

Then I can say I'm sorry. For all the years I was angry. For all the years I wanted you to be somebody you're not. For all the years I got annoyed at your never-ending grief for Daddy. I wanted you to live your life *now*, not just grieve over the lost past. But I didn't understand that Daddy, in many ways, *was* your life. So when he was gone, life for you kind of ended. That part of your life was gone, and you were sad. Was that so crazy?

So forgive me for being impatient with your nostalgia and your grief. I wanted you to have hope—hope that you would see him again in eternity—and to believe the Bible when it says to live with this expectation because Jesus is our hope.

I wanted you to love Jesus as I do, but Jesus is *my* passion. Yours was another time, another place, another man. So forgive me for not understanding that it's okay for your passion to be different. God made you who you are, and my job is to love you the way God made you.

Forgive me—if you can, if you will—for taking so long to love that way, then walk into it.

If it's okay, I also forgive you.

For growing up in a generation whose members, as Mary Pipher said, "show love by being useful but are unschooled in the language of connection."

I'm like many adults of my generation who, Pipher again said, "are hungry for touch" from our parents.

That's why I married Dan. He petted me like crazy. And now, after our off years, he touches me again. I'm not ashamed to say that I love it and I need it.

I needed petting from you too. But I forgive you for not providing it. I didn't do a lot of touching with my children either, not even with my beloved first child. I didn't know how.

But, praise God, my children love me anyway.

In just the same way, I love you too. And I love that I can say it. I love even more that I mean it, so I can show it. Love is action. Didn't Rick Warren say that too?

But God said it first. Love is action and it looks like this: a bloodstained cross.

That's how to love, God said. Love with everything. Love despite everything. Despite mistakes and miscues and disappointments, be sure you just love as I love you.

I bear with you. I respect you. I bow before you. I kneel at your feet and I wash your feet. And look at this. You will let me touch you this time and you won't pull away. Maybe you'll understand. The past is over.

Jesus knew that about foot-washing. To do it right, you have to go down to the floor, to kneel there. You go low. Then looking up, from the grungy sadness of the other person's aching feet, what do you see?

You see gratitude. You see trust. The fear is gone. The lies that keep people apart have vanished. And now that I am on my knees, on the floor, I am amazed at what I see: It wasn't that hard to love.

All the little irritations and misunderstanding and miscues and wrong words crumble when you do what looks hard but isn't.

Once you're down there, it's easy to wash your loved ones' feet. Easy as pie. They can't move, for one thing. You've got their feet in your hands, just washing away, splashing water and soothing the aches.

So you sat there, letting me soothe. And it was nice. It was easy.

Then after the drying came the lotion. The lotion going on: a kind of heaven. Blissful for you. Heaven for me. Just stroking away. You, leaning back, trusting. Me, brave and happy, touching.

Finally I could see how you cared enough to teach me the beautiful details of your good, honest life. Not spectacular things. Just beautiful things: how to write thank-you notes and dress a table and help passing strangers and take food to funerals and hug necks and iron a man's shirt.

So I did those things. But I did them because you showed me they were important. Love is action. Words would be nice, Mama. But like Jesus, you *did* the words. Love is action. Don't talk so much about love, you were saying. Instead, *do* the love things.

After I married Dan, and before he and I had money to have his shirts laundered, I stood at the ironing board and gave him a gift: a clean shirt ironed on a high setting with light spray starch.

I didn't know then that Dan actually irons better than I do, a lesson taught by his father, his family's fashion maven. So Dan was being nice, letting me iron a shirt that he could iron in less time and with more flair.

But I stood at the ironing board anyway, just like you taught me, and I pressed the wrinkles from the shirts of my husband—loving him by doing the work, defying every argument that I shouldn't love him with an ironing board and a steam iron and spray starch.

You taught me how to fix dinner for eight or ten or twelve and get everything on the table, well cooked and still hot at the same time.

You insisted on serving hot food on warmed plates. So I still do that, not knowing if anybody really cares about warmed-up plates, but warming the plates anyway. Why? Because, well, love is action.

That's how you showed love, by "doing for folks the right way."

Jesus wanted that. You know the way to the place where I am going, he told his beloved friends in that beautiful chapter, John 14. But Thomas spoke for all of us: Wait a minute, Lord. We don't know where you're going, so how can we know the way? Then Jesus explained it.

I am the way.

⚜

Now, praise God, yes. We understand that the way of Jesus, with his self-less, forgiving, all-giving help, was the right way to be in this life.

So I thank you, Mama, for showing me how to do for others the right way. How to show up at the never-ending funerals and take food to the grieving and bring flowers and hug necks and sit tight until the minister says the final amen.

Thank you for reminding me to say good morning in my household when people wake up and say good-bye when they leave for the day. Thank you for showing me how to say please and you're welcome and thank you, and to say yes and no—not yeah and nah—and, at the end of a long day, to crawl into bed only after telling the people in my household good night.

Good night is the last hard thing to say, of course. I was afraid for a long time that I wouldn't be ready to say it. Make sure you can say it without regrets, my friend Denise always said. Well, I can say that now. *Thank you, Jesus. I wake up now with no regrets.*

So good night becomes a beautiful song. Good night to the past. Good night to old mistakes and longtime hurts and lost chances and old stories and older thinking. Good night to all the stuff we should have been to each other but weren't. Good night to yesterday's millstones hanging around today's necks.

This good song ends like this with fresh grace: Good morning to forever.

Now when you reach this page in these memories, you will understand and be okay. Then you can sing the same song.

Good night and good morning.

And then look at this, Mama!

God is answering our prayers.

Be of Good Cheer

"I have told you all this so that you may have peace in me. Here on earth you will have many trials and sorrows. But take heart, because I have overcome the world." JOHN 16:33

Winter 2003 came with sunshine, mild days, and a surprise—a big one. It started with a phone call. Alana was on the line.

"I have something to tell you."

I started to laugh.

"Okay," I said. Tell me something. Tell me anything. The mountain is always high. But God always reigns. Still, Alana had some news.

"I met this guy. My friend introduced us."

"A guy? Oh really?" That was nice. "That's nice, Alana," I said. Then I added: "And?"

"And . . . I think I might be getting married."

I laughed out loud.

"Just want to keep me on my toes, little girl—right?" I said.

Alana laughed too.

"Seriously, Mom. I met this guy and he's *so* nice and I really like him."

And that is how it started. Praying mothers should know this. Lightning can strike and not make a sound, nothing more than the trill of laughter and a daughter's smile on the other end of a phone line.

"A guy," I said.

"Yes," Alana said.

"A guy," I repeated.

"Yes," Alana said, "a guy."

"Well," I said, "what's the story with this guy?"

I was sitting down then, leaning back in the chair in my office, eyes closed, holding in the panic or the resignation or whatever it was that was rising up in my chest. Would I ever have a normal day in life?

"And what's this guy's name?" I finally asked.

"His name is Iesa."

I didn't say anything. How do you respond to a name you've never heard before?

"It means Jesus—in Arabic," Alana said.

"Jesus," I said. "And he's Arabic."

"No, Mom. He's not an Arab," Alana said. She was correcting me, but gently. "Actually, he's white. Well, his father is white. Iesa converted. He's from America. He's from Texas."

"Texas," I said. "A white guy," I said. I closed my eyes tighter. "So how did you meet a white guy from Texas named Iesa—and now you want to marry him?"

"Actually you say it like 'Ay-esa,'" Alana said, the name rolling off her tongue with a warm sigh.

I know that sigh. To the praying mother of a young twenty-three-year-old daughter, that sigh can mean that long nights of prayer and meditation are soon on the way.

"Ay-esa. Well, okay. But start from the beginning," I said. We had stopped laughing, but I was listening. Alana could hear me trying, like Mother Teresa, who said to listen with our eyes. "Even if my mouth is closed," Mother Teresa wrote, "with my eyes I can talk to you for a whole half hour."

So with my eyes, I looked at my daughter over the phone line and I could see she was trying to tell me something important.

"He's nice, Mom. Really nice," she said. "And I want you and Dad to meet him."

"How old is he?"

"He's twenty-eight," she said.

"Okay," I said, glad he wasn't older. "So you want us to meet him?"

"Yes. And Mom, actually his father is white and his mom is Latina. She is Hispanic American. Their family is from San Antonio but they live in Germany."

"Iesa lives in Germany?"

"No, his parents live in Germany. They work for the U.S. military."

"As civilians?"

"Yes. And they're almost ready to retire and move home to Texas. And Iesa lives in Houston."

"He's a Muslim?"

I was trying to keep up. *Help me, Jesus,* I was praying.

"Yes, he's a Muslim. He was raised a Catholic, but he's a Muslim now. Like me!"

And my head spun a bit, but I was trying not to lose my balance. Jesus was holding me down—or holding me up. The direction didn't matter. But Jesus was holding me. That's what counted.

So next I wanted to know where Alana had met this Iesa.

"Well, he e-mailed me and . . . "

My breath tightened. That is, I looked with my eyes and I could see another big, big hill. But then I moved to the right, closer still to Jesus, leaning on the Savior so I could move on up to the next point.

"Wow, Alana. E-mail," I said, taking a deep breath. Then I spoke: "Is it okay if I say that sounds a bit dangerous?"

Was that too crazy a question?

"Actually, it wasn't like that, Mom," Alana replied, taking in her own deep breath.

"Well," I said. More deep breathing. "What was it like?"

What's it like to meet a white guy whose mother is Latina, whose name is Iesa, who is a Muslim, and who lives in Texas? I wanted to hear.

So she told her African American Christian mother the story.

"You know my Egyptian friend, Hoda? Well, she's been talking to this guy, a friend of Iesa's, and this friend of Iesa's came out to Colorado about a month ago to meet Hoda's family."

"Hoda and Iesa?"

Goodness, these names. Wasn't anybody named Jane and John anymore? Not in America apparently, and it was time I got used to it. Meantime Alana was being patient.

"No, Mom, not Iesa. Hoda and Iesa's friend—we all went skiing: Hoda and her friend from Houston and Hoda's sisters and a bunch of other people and me too."

Alana was telling this story happily now, painting the picture: It's a beautiful Colorado day, and she and her Muslim friends are skiing. Skiing on a beautiful Rocky Mountain morning. Sunshine and white snow and laughing. The girls are wrapped in *hijab,* falling down on the bunny slopes. The boys are poised on short skis, flying down the mountains. A fun Colorado day.

"So Hoda's friend goes back to Texas and he told his friend Iesa about me," Alana said, smiling. I could see her smile over the phone.

"What did he tell him?"

"I guess he said that I was a nice person and that he thought Iesa should meet me," Alana said, sounding pleased.

It feels good to be liked, to be approved. I understood.

Alana. A real nice girl, he said. An interesting young woman. Smart. Attractive. Modern. I think you would like her.

Iesa remembers first hearing about her. "My friends," he told me several weeks later, "were always trying to find me a wife."

Iesa told me this on the phone after I calmed down and found out the whole story—how he was raised a Catholic but converted to Islam and changed his name from Paul to Iesa.

"Paul is a good name," I interjected. "A very good name."

"Yes, ma'am," he said.

But now he was Iesa.

So as Iesa, he had e-mailed Alana to introduce himself. She might be someone he would like to court.

A Muslim boy named Iesa, which means Jesus, who wanted to court my daughter, and he didn't even know her?

I don't want this, I told God in my prayers. I want a regular life with people I know, names I can pronounce, and everybody in church. But God stayed silent except for one thing: Love them and trust me.

Iesa went on with his story, how Alana wrote him back. She said thanks but no thanks. "I'm trying to finish my degree. I have a year and a half to go. I just want to focus on school," she told him.

So Iesa said okay. Besides, he said, I have a son. Alana read this, looking at the words. My boy is five years old, he wrote Alana. He lives with his mother. We were married but now we're divorced. And I want to focus on him, on being a good father.

This was complicated. So they both agreed to say thanks anyway but close it down. But they kept writing the e-mails.

Then the e-mails got longer. Every few days. Then every other day. Then every day, the e-mails went back and forth. After a month or so, they decided that they should meet face-to-face with parental permission.

"So Iesa wants to talk to you and Dad," Alana said.

"Talk to us?" Dan asked it like that. "Talk to us about *what*?"

He said it with a father's look in his eyes. You don't know this boy, Dan's eyes were saying. We don't know him either. He's just somebody on the Internet e-mailing you from Texas. Somebody who's changed his name to Iesa, which means Jesus. And you're already talking about *marriage*?

This was America in the winter of 2003 for our little Christian family. Dan and I sat at our kitchen table, contemplating this scenario, looking out at falling snow. The snow was beautiful, falling into our backyard trees, quiet and wintry and traditional.

So during this winter, I wanted good Christian daughters who would marry good Christian men in a quiet and traditional way: a long courtship, a nice engagement, and a lovely wedding—in a church. Is that too much for a mother to ask?

But my prayers kept giving me surprises.

So a guy named Iesa called us on the telephone.

Alana was right. He was a nice guy. A lovely human being, in fact. His Latina American mother had taught him well. Beautiful manners. Beautiful speech. Sincere heart. In love with his son. Working in the community on civil rights for Muslim Americans.

The only hitch was that he was sold out to Islam. In love with Allah.

"Is that the same as God?" I asked anybody who would listen.

"Allah is the Arabic name for God," Iesa said. "The same God."

That's what the news reports said on TV.

I wasn't sure. I prayed: *Jesus, God Almighty, what do I do now?*

But the Holy Spirit gave only one answer: I give you this commandment: Love one another. Show the world Christian love.

So my husband and I talked on the telephone to Iesa. We were gracious, as Jesus would be. We reached out, as Jesus would reach. What would Jesus do, indeed? That's what we did. We extended ourselves. We were kind. We were polite.

He wanted to court our daughter, Iesa said, explaining that the process is expected to lead to marriage. In Islam, "there is no 'dating' as such," he said. "So after two people meet, if they decide it won't work, that's the end of it. But, as it goes, I shouldn't continue to communicate with your daughter without your permission."

Dan and I listened.

This young man sounded sincere and good, even if there were the complications.

"I have a son," he told us. "He's five years old."

Alana had told us this, of course, and everybody has a past and there is no condemnation in Christ.

"Is he a good boy?" I asked.

"Yes," Iesa said. "He is a very good boy."

So there we were.

❧

So Iesa came from Texas to visit Easter weekend 2003. Iesa came bearing gifts; talking about Jesus, his new namesake; and brewing Arabian tea purchased in Mecca in Saudi Arabia. He'd been there the past year for *hajj*.

Is that how you say it?

Jesus, help me say these things I don't understand. That's how I prayed.

Then I sat in my family room in Aurora, Colorado, on Resurrection Sunday and I drank the Arabian tea.

This was really happening.

In truth, Iesa was everything Alana said that he was. He was polite. Attentive. Engaging. Well-groomed. Handsome. Well-read. Pleasant to know. Kind to my mother. He helped Mama in and out of the car when we went to restaurants. Took time talking to her. They hit it right off, in fact. So she liked him. He hit it off with Dan and me too. We did like him, in fact. We even liked the courtship style, a true family affair. That's how it worked. This young man and Alana didn't spend time alone. If they went anywhere, the whole family went with them. Our African American Christian family and Iesa and Alana, with him acting like this was as natural as the livelong day.

He kept unpacking gifts.

For Alana, he brought a beautiful scarf, a bracelet, a rose, a beautiful card. The gifts kept appearing. For Dan and me, there was a tiny silver teapot and a box of glass teacups.

Iesa also brought Mexican vanilla ice cream, packed in dry ice, from his favorite creamery in Houston.

"I thought you might like this," he said, unpacking the ice.

I looked at this young man—dark hair, white skin, trim beard, clear eyes, wide shouldered from years of competitive swimming in middle school and high school.

He was standing in my kitchen on Fraser Street, this home where our good Christian friends have gathered for Christmas Eve and Easter dinners, birthday celebrations, and Dan's recent retirement—all prayed over in the name of Jesus. Mostly these were gatherings of black Christians, folks like us.

Iesa wasn't black. He wasn't Christian anymore. But the Holy Spirit was all over him. That is, his Latina mother had prayed him into this world, raised him in the Catholic church, called him Pablocito when he was a toddler, hugged and kissed him, and taught him good manners. But now he was a Muslim. She had cried. Like I had cried for Alana.

Interfaith may be just a word. But it's more than a notion. It's a hard thing.

But love him anyway, God said. So with Christian gratitude, I thanked Iesa for his lovely gifts.

"You didn't have to do this," I said.

"There is an Islamic tradition," he said. "Upon meeting people and entering their home for the first time, you bring a gift."

Well, okay.

But the news out of the Middle East rocked everybody. The war on Iraq was going full bore. Alana took an antiwar position, went to campus forums on the war, and even got her picture in two local newspapers.

My daughter dressed in *hijab*, putting down the war.

I looked at her picture, not really believing that this was the little girl I took to Sunday school and taught how to sing "This Little Light of Mine" and to say Now-I-lay-me-down-to-sleep-I-pray-the-Lord-my-soul-to-keep.

She was an antiwar sympathizer *and* she was a Muslim and she was in love.

Her grades in school were excellent. She would start her student teaching in the fall, teaching little third graders. But first Iesa called and asked if he could come to visit, so now here he was, standing in my kitchen.

This was a big weekend.

Alana was nervous. She had come home from school the night before Iesa's arrival and scrubbed everything I had already cleaned—not just in our house but in Mama's house too.

"What's this? Is he doing the white-glove test?" Dan asked.

"I just want everything to be supernice," Alana said.

"What should I wear?" I asked Alana. "Long skirts?"

"Just wear what you normally wear," Dan answered.

So there I was in khaki pants, a white blouse, and black flats, welcoming Iesa to my superclean house, but not shaking his hand because Alana reminded us that Islamic men don't shake the hands of women who aren't related to them.

Mama forgot so she shook Iesa's hand anyway, then gave him a little hug. Oh well.

Iesa laughed, shaking her hand and hugging her back, and the sky didn't fall in. So the weekend started.

I prayed a long prayer beforehand.

Help us, Lord, to show Christian love. Help us, Lord, to look like Jesus.

Help us, Lord, to know that in these challenging times, when children are leaving their churches and rejecting your beloved Son, that you have your hands around them anyway and you know how their stories will end.

Help us to have faith and to believe that.

But until then, help us to love them anyway.

So love is what we did. I knew how to do that now. But how did I feel that Alana's guy wasn't a black guy? No, wrong question. How did I feel that Alana's guy wasn't a Christian?

Well. I felt as I did about Alana's religious journey. I must release this matter to God and move on and trust God. And, yes, this was hard. Can a Christian mother sleep at night, knowing her beloved younger daughter has rejected Jesus as Christ and turned to another faith—and now might marry in that faith?

This was my ongoing distress.

In fact, in our church, other college children had drifted from church for a while. Not everybody's kids. But a few. Drifted from Jesus. Drawn to the world. Dipping their toes into New Age this and that, but eventually jumping back.

Every one of those kids, in fact, had come back. I'd see this one or that one walk quietly into the sanctuary on a Sunday morning, maybe sitting in a back-of-the-church pew, conspicuous and alone. Then in a few Sundays, the child moved closer. Then in a month or two, there was the wanderer, back in the family pew, next to Mom or Dad. Soon that son or that daughter was clapping hands with the choir. Then singing along with the choir. Then pretty soon, singing *in* the choir. Lifting up hands to the good Lord—even saying amen, not to mention shouting amen. At least two of those kids had become ordained ministers of the gospel themselves. Preaching and teaching and rocking with Jesus, bathed in joy by the Holy Ghost. Everybody's child but mine. All but my daughter. All but mine.

I held back tears every Sunday, walking into our soaring church sanctuary, knowing Alana wouldn't be there, looking with sadness on sons and daughters safely sitting with their families. Her absence hurt me but maybe it also indicted me. To tell the whole truth, I felt embarrassed that my daughter had turned from the gospel. If other people could pray their children back to Jesus, why couldn't I?

That's what I asked the Lord. Why *my* child?

I was like the old prophet Habakkuk, asking the same questions.

"How long, O Lord, must I call for help? But you do not listen! . . . I cry, but you do not come to save." I wasn't sure I could pronounce Habakkuk either. But I understood his plea.

How, indeed, could I lay my head down at night, knowing that my prayers for my daughter's salvation in Christ were in spiritual limbo?

Here is a surprise: God said sleep. Her life and her choices, God said, are *my* business.

So go get some sleep. Pray for her as you would pray for yourself. Then sleep, because Jesus himself already did the work for her redemption and her salvation. Trust *that*. Then get some sleep.

Rest well, in fact, because the days of life are hard. And, of course, life doesn't always go as we plan. Look at Habakkuk. Besides, Jesus understood that.

"In the world ye shall have tribulation," he told his disciples after his Last Supper. Then he added his remarkable lesson: "But be of good cheer."

Take heart! Be encouraged, he said, and for one good reason: "I have overcome the world."

⌘

So Iesa came to visit again. It was July. This time, after the long weekend, he asked our permission to marry Alana.

We were sitting in my kitchen, surrounded by the debris of a renovation. Mama was moving in, needing more help at age eighty-seven with her meals and doctors' appointments and pill management and bill-paying and all the other details of being Mama at eighty-seven. She also wanted our company, especially at night. Her house, without Missy the beloved dog, felt empty to her after dark. So we asked her to move in with us. After months of wavering, she finally said yes. But our efforts to turn the front of our home into one of those mother-in-law suites had somehow turned into a full-fledged overhaul of the entire house. Walls were down. Floors were naked. Construction dust hovered.

And to make it interesting, my daughter wanted to marry a Muslim man from Texas named Iesa.

"When exactly?" Dan asked.

"We were thinking about December," Iesa said.

Five months away. I blinked, stayed silent.

I still had questions. It was because I had grown to like Iesa so much. I'm sure that was it. It would be easier if I didn't like him, easy to say no.

But he was a lovely young man. Nothing riffraff about him at all. Reared right. Upstanding. Folks in Texas, calling us, saying the same thing—confirming what we already believed: He was solid. But even without any calls, I liked how he stood. I admired his character and respected him. Alana respected him and loved him.

And he loved and respected her.

We could see it in their eyes. And love *and* respect is that remarkable mix. That's how marriages last.

And yet?

"He wants to marry our baby daughter, Dan. *Our youngest child.* What do you think about that? I'm looking to you."

Dan and I were sitting in our kitchen-in-progress, after Iesa had returned to Texas. Alana had returned to school. Dan was sitting in a chair, in the middle of the in-progress jumble, eating Mexican vanilla ice cream.

"I think they love each other," Dan said. "And I think he is a good man."

"So you're saying yes?"

"I'm saying have faith. That's what we had when we got married."

"Faith?"

Dan put down his spoon.

"Faith. I support them by faith." He picked up his spoon, started slurping ice cream again.

I watched him eat. He looked relaxed and happy instead of worried and tense, as he should have been looking. And that slurping was a killer. This matter was critical. Perhaps the most critical decision we would help our daughter make. And he was busy with Mexican ice cream?

"We should pray about this again," I said.

"I have," he said. He slurped again.

"And?"

"God said have faith."

But that was too easy, wasn't it? Where was the sour pill?

So I turned to Mama. At eighty-seven, she'd have an opinion and good wisdom. Surely she would. Mama was eating ice cream too.

"Mama, what do you really think about Alana and Iesa getting married?"

Mama looked at me. She put down her spoon.

"Well . . . I really like him," Mama said.

"I do too," I said, "but the thing is, he's not a Christian. Well, he was raised in the church. But he's not a Christian now."

Mama was quiet for a moment.

"Some things you leave in God's hands," she said. "In the meantime, I like him—and Alana loves him. And he's a good young man." Mama finished her ice cream, letting the spoon rattle in the empty bowl.

"Yes," I said. Good young people in love.

So that was it. A wedding in December. A beautiful daughter. A beautiful man. White snow and blue sky and sunshine and cheer on a lovely Colorado day.

Is this how a prayer story ends?

Get Quiet with God

He withdrew about a stone's throw beyond
them, knelt down and prayed. LUKE 22:41

Mothers dream of weddings. But this was now and this was real. I was
wide-awake. So after Iesa left for Houston, I went to a Christian bookstore
and bought a big stack of prayer journals. I could talk to friends, and on
many days I did. But mostly I talked to God.

As always, I wrote out my prayers:

"Jesus, I don't know how to do this."

That's what I wrote. Several times, in fact, I spelled it out for God and
God just listened:

"Father, we will be an interfaith, interracial family," I wrote—"and, oh
blessed Father in heaven, here is the truth: I don't know how to do this,
to do this right, that is. Not with my daughter out of church, and with her
husband-to-be out of church, too. But you know everything. So I have
faith you will keep on teaching me. You'll help me rise, to be everything
good that you want me to be. And praise your holy name for your lessons.
In Jesus' blessed name. Amen."

Short prayers. Long prayers. I just prayed, prayed, and prayed some
more. I listened to God's peace. Then I got up from my desk and got back
to it.

Alana was calling every weekend, meanwhile, about wedding details.

She would go with Dan and me to Texas in November to meet Iesa's
parents, who were home now from Germany and almost ready to retire.

Mama had moved in. The renovation was successful and finished. But Dan and I were still painting. This bathroom. That baseboard. Those ceilings. Every spare minute, it seemed, we were rolling on paint—Benjamin Moore Linen White paint. We rolled out 10 gazillion gallons of Linen White on doors, cabinets, baseboards, ceilings. Dan and I were poster kids for Linen White paint. That "pearl finish" was the limit, in fact—smooth as milk, cool as silk—and, yes, that is a paint endorsement in a prayer journal. But, in truth, our dingy, old woodwork was transformed. Our brand-new woodwork was stunning.

Our house looked new and beautiful.

I was also teaching again.

My beloved course on magazine writing, my favorite class to teach, met on Monday mornings on the Boulder campus. My students were smart, funny, productive, and on time for our weekly morning seminar. Every Monday at 9 A.M., they clocked in and took their seat—beautiful and scholarly and prepared. I loved them. They loved me back. I thanked God for each of them, in fact. I told them the truth about my life. They told me the truth about theirs. So their writing was good. It was a great semester.

Dan was teaching part-time at a career college. His students were non-traditional adults, some with a hard background but all with a good heart. So every Monday at 9 A.M., they clocked in and took their seat—beautiful and scholarly and prepared. Dan loved them. And they loved him back. He thanked God for each of them. He told them the truth about his life. They told him the truth about theirs. So their writing was good.

It was a great semester, indeed.

Joi, meantime, was doing bookkeeping part-time for a publishing company in suburban Denver. She also joined a small church in northeast Denver with a minister who could preach flame out of fire. The man was anointed, and so was his lovely gospel-singing wife. Within six months of joining the church, Joi had started tithing, closed her failing bookstore, landed a position as a financial analyst with a city municipal government, and was on her way with Jesus.

"I finally get it," Joi said one day.

"Get what?" I asked.

"Being a Christian means having a relationship with God—a friendship with all of the rights but also all of the obligations. So you have to spend time with God, to keep the relationship going."

Oh yes.

I knew about that. Night after night. Morning after morning. Not a day went by without morning and nighttime prayer. No day was complete, in fact, if I didn't start it with fervent prayer of praise and end it with fervent prayer of thanksgiving. Hours and hours of prayer some days—thank you, Jesus, all the livelong day.

Then as the wedding drew closer, I paused some days to go upstairs midday to pray yet again. Upstairs, my little room was jumping with prayer. All prayer all the time. Prayer without ceasing. Then after the praying, sitting quietly and listening—praying without ceasing and listening.

Is that what Paul was talking about?

⊰⊱

Alana came home from school almost every weekend. She couldn't find a wedding dress—a modest wedding dress, that is, not in Denver or Greeley or Fort Collins or Aurora or anywhere in Colorado, or anywhere on the planet. At one point, she searched online for dresses from India.

But on closer look, the midriffs were cut out.

"Jesus," I whispered. It was a Saturday. We were standing inside a national-chain bridal store, fighting for air against racks jammed tight with strapless, plunging dresses. Girls and women of every size and shape were squeezing flesh into revealing gowns. Lord, give me patience and give me strength, I prayed. And even as I prayed, I recalled the name of a local seamstress, a good Baptist woman named Bobbie Jean whose specialty was wedding gowns. Her phone number was in the white pages.

We left the store and Alana called her. "I'm a Muslim," she explained to the seamstress. "I'm getting married, but I can't find a modest wedding gown."

"Hmm . . . " Bobbie Jean, the good Baptist seamstress, listened. She looked at Alana over the phone line. Then she said: "I'd love to make a dress for you, sweetheart. Come on over next Saturday."

So the beautiful Baptist seamstress welcomed Alana and me into her wedding-fantasy home, a dollhouse not much bigger than . . . a dollhouse. In fact, it *was* a dollhouse. Pretty as one, indeed, with its pink velvet couches and pink velvet chairs and snowy white carpet and pink silk-flower arrangements and crystal lamps and mirrors gleaming floor to ceiling and a sparkling glass chandelier the size of a small car suspended and fully lit over the woman's white dining-room table.

"Wow," Alana said, stepping inside carefully, taking in the scene. "Your house is . . . beautiful."

Bobbie Jean, gracious and welcoming, smiled at Alana.

"Aren't you pretty," she said, gesturing us inside, not worrying at all about Alana's Islamic clothes. Bobbie Jean invited her to sit down on a pink velvet couch. So I followed, sitting next to Alana in the pink velvet glittering, gleaming splendor.

And not a drop of Benjamin Moore Linen White had been spilled by Bobbie Jean in *this* house. At Bobbie Jean's, we were in pink heaven glory.

"Wow," I said, looking around, echoing Alana. "Your home is amazing."

"Pink is my favorite color," Bobbie Jean confirmed, laughing and demure. She was a tall drink of mahogany with a round chignon at her neck accenting her sleek black hairdo and a sizable diamond wedding ring lighting up her exquisite hands. Bobbie Jean carried herself like a fashion model, in fact. Her hostess skirt and cashmere sweater were picture-perfect. "I always have loved beautiful clothes," she said.

"Alana, let me show you something," she added. "I'll be right back."

Bobbie Jean was gone for a minute into another room. Then, with a rustling sound, she returned with a huge garment bag. Then smiling and regal, Bobbie Jean unzipped the vast bag to reveal a great froth of wedding gown that was not only one-of-a-kind beautiful, it also was *pink*. A fluffy masterpiece of candy-colored chiffon and rustling silk and ruffling Chantilly lace, the dress outdid the diamond ring and the velvet couches and the huge chandelier all put together.

Bobbie Jean lifted the grand gown out of its vast bag with flair and drama and love, arranging the endless lace train with grace and care across her snowy white living-room carpet.

Alana opened her mouth to speak, but she looked speechless.

"Wow," she finally managed. "Wow," she said again.

She turned to me and our eyes locked, saying everything.

"Wow," we both said in unison.

"That is amazing," I said for the second time in our visit.

"This isn't a style for you," Bobbie Jean said, and I could see Alana visibly relax. "But I thought you'd like to see it. It's for a woman who loves pink like me!" and she laughed, and we laughed with her.

This was nice. Bobbie Jean looked like Jesus and she created pink wedding gowns. For a nervous bride and mother, does it get any better?

Bobbie Jean returned the dress to its room. Then she joined us and sat on a velvet couch to talk to Alana about her wedding gown.

She flattered my daughter. She asked her to stand. She took her measurements.

"You have a beautiful figure," she said, turning her around. "And you are a nice height. You will look beautiful in any wedding gown."

So Alana showed her magazine pictures. Alana's choice was a floor-length sheath with a long overcoat—a duster—with a high collar.

In the magazine picture, the outfit was a stunning lemon-colored fabric.

"Dupioni silk. This is gorgeous," Bobbie Jean said. "A classic style. A little plain for a wedding. But what about lace on the sleeves, around the cuffs?"

"I'll have on a scarf," Alana said, "wrapped like I'm wearing now."

Bobbie Jean looked at her.

"Well, okay," she said, contemplating the *hijab*. She didn't look too happy about one of her brides being hidden under a scarf. But she makes wedding dresses and she knows brides and her brides have to be happy, to have things like they want them. So she gave Alana a sincere and assuring smile.

"We'll make it beautiful, Alana. You will be a beautiful bride. Come back next Saturday and I will have some fabric samples."

So that's how it went.

The next Saturday Bobbie Jean showed us fabric within our budget, some silk-*looking* polyester in three different colors: cream, champagne, and ice white.

Alana chose the cream and it was easy. The dress would be finished in three weeks.

⧉

"Heavenly Father, you are excellent."

I wrote this. I was on a second wedding prayer journal by this time.

On the inside front cover, I wrote down a wedding checklist: invitations, flowers, favors, cake, gift registry, food, limousine, photographer, and this thing and that thing and on down the line. None of it was in our December budget, not even remotely.

In fact, *where* would this December wedding take place? Would we go to a mosque? I was willing, but I couldn't visualize it.

Then, to fix it, Alana called to ask if she and Iesa could have their wedding at home.

"At our house?" I asked.

"Well, actually, yes. Is that okay, Mom?"

Was it okay? Did I roll out 10 zillion gallons of Linen White for nothing?

Never, in fact, was a humble house more ready for a wedding. So there we were.

Back upstairs to pray. What did I lift to God this time? The truth: That I was having fun.

But that didn't seem right. My younger daughter was getting married outside of the church. So why did I have this joy? Why, despite every bit of logic and the obvious problem—a daughter and future son-in-law living outside of the Cross—did I feel not just okay about everything, why did I feel wonderful?

It didn't make sense. It seemed too good to be true, always a worrisome sign.

So I prayed the hard prayer, and my friend Denise helped me.

"I'll just be blunt," Denise said on the phone. "When I'm not sure about something, I ask God for one thing: to bless it or blow it up."

"Oh Lord," I said.

"I know. It's a hard prayer," Denise said. "But do you want this marriage to go forward if it's not in God's will?"

"For my daughter? No," I said. I was absolutely sure of that.

"Then let's ask God together: Bless it, Lord, or blow it up. And make it plain, Father God, absolutely plain, if this process should move forward or end."

"You and your hard prayers," I said.

"Well, what are friends for?" Denise asked, not budging.

But that language—bless it or blow it up—challenged me for real.

That is what I wrote that night in my prayer journal.

"I am challenged, Lord," I wrote. "This is the hardest thing I have ever tried to do." Then I added "my deepest confession, Lord, and here it is: that Dan and I are saying okay to Alana's wishes and plans for this marriage because we don't trust you enough to encourage her to wait for her true life partner—if it's not Iesa—and to insist she return to church, even if 'insisting' would actually work. Meanwhile, oh Father, I know how hard it is to blend a family, and Alana already is stressed and the train keeps moving! So in Jesus' name, oh Father, and for your glory, I pray for peace in these matters, even as I thank you for the portion of peace and joy that I'm already experiencing in this, her wedding preparations. So, Father, I will rest in your sovereignty, in Dan's blessing on this union, and in Alana's desire to be a wife and eventually a mother, and in Iesa's desire to be her husband."

I kept on:

"You said in your Word, oh blessed Father, that a man who finds a wife finds what is good and receives favor from the Lord. In that manner, oh Father, I will move forward with faith, following the example and the blessing of my husband, who says he will support this marriage by *faith*—trusting in you, oh Father, to take it where you want it: back to you, in your own time and in your own way, so in that manner, I will support it too.

"I will trust, oh Father, that this union can find favor with you, and that all of the complications that I see in it have fallen under your feet, because you are bigger than all of them, singly or combined. Hallelujah. So, Father, thank you for bringing a godly man to the hand of my daughter—a man who says he loves God and wants to serve others. Help her to respond in kind and to always have favor in your sight, and also in his sight, all of this for your glory. For your glory and in Jesus' blessed name, bless them to be holy, loving, kind, gentle, forgiving, united, and returned together to Christ. Cover us all tonight, indeed, in Jesus' wonderful name, with your wings of mercy and peace, for your glory, blessed Father. I pray this prayer with all gratitude and joy. In Jesus' mighty name. Amen."

Then I turned out my light and I went to sleep. That's what the Holy Spirit had instructed me to do: to dwell in the shelter of the Most High and in that peaceful place to rest in his big shadow.

So the invitations got ordered and mailed. The list had 110 names. Six weeks to go until the wedding. Alana and Iesa invited Muslims. Dan and I invited Christians. Together we invited black, white, Latino, immigrants, homegrown Coloradans, Texans—blessed friends and family all.

Iesa was calling regularly. He had ordered a ring to surprise Alana, and he wanted our opinion on the design—a marquis-cut diamond on white gold with two baguettes.

"What's a baguette?" Dan asked.

"The little accent diamonds. They sit on the side of the center stone."

Dan looked at me like I was speaking in a strange tongue.

"Never mind," I said.

Then he gave me a hug. "Are you the diamond expert, sugar? The wedding coordinator?"

"Yes," I said, "I am the wedding coordinator, but God is in charge."

"Hallelujah," Dan said, "and praise the Lord."

So November came. The caterer was booked, thanks to Joi, who knew a friend of the owner. I got a good price. The cake was ordered from a local bakery. Another good price. The dress was almost finished—with a Baptist good price from Bobbie Jean. The rings were getting made without the baguettes. The favors were finished, thanks to my friend Jane and her skillful way with a craft glue gun.

It was time now to go to Texas. Time to meet the parents. Thanksgiving dinner. *Jesus, help us.*

"I'm scared," Alana said.

"God is bigger," I said.

Indeed, the plane ride from Denver to Houston was easy and smooth.

Iesa picked us up. His son was with him. A beautiful child. A boy sent from heaven. Aren't five-year-olds supposed to be cranky, pouty, selfish, and whiny?

But this child was smiling. He was gentle. He sang songs half the way to San Antonio. Then he announced that his eyes were tired and he was taking a nap. An hour later he woke up and sang the rest of the way to his grandparents' house.

Iesa's father, George, met us outside.

This was a modern American moment.

A white American father. Two black American parents. A Muslim bride-to-be. Iesa, whose Catholic American family still calls him by his birth name, Paul. Iesa's sweet little son. The blessed Holy Spirit.

Everybody breathed deep and shook hands.

Dan and George talked cars right off the bat, standing in the driveway. Iesa's father restores old cars. On top of that, he'd just bought a new Texas-sized truck. Deep red and pretty and worth talking about.

Dan dabbles in old cars too. He dreams about them, scouring the car magazines. Dan's old '71 Cougar convertible isn't a classic. But on this day the Cougar and the truck and their mutual interest was a spectacular icebreaker.

In minutes, the two men were laughing over car mishaps. Two vintage American dads. Car guys from the same era. Plain talk. No nonsense. Breaking ground in the driveway. Balding but still vintage handsome. Car talking. Rolling with the punches. Thanksgiving afternoon.

Iesa looked more relaxed.

Alana looked like a dream. She had given Iesa's father a hug and nobody had fainted and the sky didn't fall in.

If she was nervous, she didn't look it. She was wearing a pretty, new ivory-colored scarf and, as usual, a matching long skirt and long-sleeved blouse buttoned to the neck. She was covered but she was glowing.

So we went inside the small house that Iesa's family had rented for Thanksgiving weekend in an old resort area near San Antonio. The house wasn't fancy. But the area was nice. Trees everywhere. Country quiet. Birds singing in the Texas sunshine.

George was the cook for this Thanksgiving dinner—a family tradition. Great smells were coming from the kitchen: The baking turkey. A barbecued brisket. George went back to putting the finishing touches on a pumpkin pie, ready to slide it into the oven among the meats.

"Where's Mom?" Iesa asked his father.

"She'll be coming," his father said.

So while we waited, we made small talk. Soon Iesa's eldest sister and her husband arrived from Midland with their two children, sweet little boys. Shaking hands. More small talk. The kids playing outside. A TV on but nobody watching. The dinner cooking. The aromas smelling wonderful.

Around dinnertime, the front door opened. Iesa's youngest sister and her husband entered. Smiling and warm, good handshakes all around. Then they stepped aside. The waters parted. A slow, slow motion. Everybody holding his or her breath.

Now. Here was Delphina. Iesa's mother was now amidst us, holding her newest grandchild, maybe the cutest six-month-old little boy ever born in Texas.

Alana melted. She reached for the child. Iesa's mother let him go into Alana's arms. Then the two women—Iesa's mother, silver haired and young looking and stylish, and my younger daughter, beautiful and glowing and brave—met over this baby. Slowly and together they warmed the room.

Not high heat. But warmth.

So two American families, Protestant and Catholic, black and white and Latino—and their two newly Muslim offspring—found a way to have Thanksgiving dinner and nobody choked. In fact, we rose above ourselves. That's how you do it.

❖

"Wow." Iesa was beaming, driving us back to Houston two days later. "That went really well. I mean, that was great."

I sat in the car's backseat, watching the flat Texas hills roll by, looking at God.

Iesa's son sat between Alana and me, playing with his toys. Dan sat up front with Alana's future husband.

"Yes," I had to agree with him, "it couldn't have gone better."

I was amazed, in fact. I had asked God to bless this weekend or to blow it up—whatever *that* might mean—so all of us could know for certain if this impending marriage should go forward.

I had been ready for the worst, indeed. Our bridges were so tall. Faith and race. Are any two things in life, in America at least, ever higher or bigger or filled with more fear? But everybody walked over the bridge. By grace and with prayer, we walked.

In America, this is what we have to do these days, I guess. We walk over the hard things or else we roll up and die. And none of us that weekend were ready to do that: to give up and turn in yet. Most of us aren't ready for that, in fact.

So I cinched on my whole armor and walked out on faith. Back in Houston, I even went with Alana and Iesa to his coworker's wedding in a big downtown mosque. When Iesa asked me to cover my head before going in, I draped on one of Alana's scarves and went with it. That afternoon, with the scarf removed, I rolled with them again. All of us—Dan, me, Iesa's son, Iesa, Alana. This time we schmoozed through a wedding reception in the garden of a bed-and-breakfast near downtown Houston. Pretty old house. Roses all over the yard still blooming. Lovely Islamic people, immigrants from you name it—and sick and tired of extremism in the name of their faith—greeting Iesa and his new fiancée.

I ate the lamb and the rice and the vegetables and drank the sweet hot tea and smiled a Christian smile. Dan did the same. What would Jesus do? He would go to the wedding. So there we were.

Coming around a corner of the restaurant, Iesa greeted a friend and then introduced us. "This is . . . my family," he said, and it was starting to sound right. "My fiancée. My son. My future in-laws."

Then I looked up.

There was Jesus. The Savior was there and he said to have faith and to trust him and to love one another. Easy, if you don't fight it. Love one another and don't stop.

But first pray. Prayer is how we rise.

Imagine the Answer

Pray also for me, that whenever I open my
mouth, words may be given me so that I will
fearlessly make known the mystery of the
gospel. EPHESIANS 6:19

So we stopped arguing about religion.

At first Dan and I debated religion with Iesa at almost every turn. But
those talks went nowhere. Clearly, God did not intend for us to evangelize
our future son-in-law.

Our assignment was first to help us all be a family.

The family part was lovely, in fact. Iesa is a beautiful man. Earnest.
Smart. Hardworking. Self-sufficient. Kind. Strong. Gentle. Godly. He
would be a wonderful husband for my daughter and a lovely son-in-law
for us, and I told him so.

Holding my tongue on religion was another thing, however. Big differences mark Islam and Christianity, even if some Muslims say that we're
all related through our father Abraham as the "people of the Book."

But my book—my Bible—was also called unreliable by some of those
Muslims. They argued that the Bible had been changed over the years.
Some Gospels weren't even included in the Bible, they argued some more.
So from the Nicene Council to Martin Luther to Vatican II, the Christian
church was corrupted and built on our "manipulated" book. Well, this is
what some seemed to argue anyway.

But my book—my Bible, sitting so mighty and burnished on my nightstand, underlined from here to yonder, prayed over and held and read and
loved so much—was all about two big things: faith and friendship.

Indeed, the God of my Bible was holy and mighty, but also he was a matchless friend. I wouldn't argue with Iesa. But friendship with God wasn't on the table for Muslims, or didn't seem to be. Islam seemed to stand at arm's length from God, revering God, but revering him through Islam's many, many rules for every possible aspect of life. Goodness, so many rules. Iesa said they were liberating.

"If you aren't allowed to drink alcohol, you don't have to worry about what might happen if you do drink it," he said, for example.

I could see that, I guess. But overall, rules in Islam looked to me like legalism. Moreover, God in Islam looked unapproachable. The theologian Caner brothers, Emir and Ergun, confirm this: "The greatest difference between the two faiths," they wrote in *Unveiling Islam*, "is the personal quality of God."

They explain: "One must love Allah in order for Allah to love that person in return. In Christianity, God loved people first in order to secure their salvation."

These two brothers are eloquent and knowledgeable. And bold— good witnesses in every way. In contrast, I was timid and unknowing in witnessing.

At dinner one night, when Dan was extolling good ol' gospel music, Iesa said that Muslims would probably "walk out" of an event featuring music and singing and instruments.

I sat there, nodding and listening, saying "Hmmm . . . interesting."

But if I had known—oh Lord, if I had remembered and if I were bold— I would have responded boldly. I can see myself now: lifting up a great "singing" Scripture, inviting Iesa to consider the Bible's reminder to "come before his presence with singing" and to "sing to the Lord, you saints." I would shout, in fact, like David: "I will sing a new song to you, O God! I will sing your praises with a ten-stringed harp."

Good ol' gospel music, indeed.

Muslims never would sing like this, it seemed. Instead, they had their rules.

"If Allah wills" is what Alana so often said about everything, but she seemed to say it so tentatively. The phrase just drove me crazy.

So I battled at first.

"Alana, if something is good and proper, then God wills it," I had argued. "And yes," I told her, "I know that God is sovereign. But if something that you want *doesn't* happen, then praise God for his wisdom and move on."

Night and day. Mars and Venus.

We were reading our marching orders from different scripts indeed. And I knew the stakes. My daughter's eternal salvation, and her fiancé's eternal salvation too, were in danger of being eternally lost, I believed. But there was something else.

I longed for them to know heaven on earth. That's what I had found in Christ. Despite all the hell I had raised, Jesus had redeemed me. And his redemption was heavenly, right here on earth. That's where eternity starts, in fact, Jesus said, as soon as we understand who he is. No idle statement. He said this in the garden on his last night: "Now this is eternal life: that they may know you, the only true God, and Jesus Christ, whom you have sent."

⊰⊱

Well. Families can't argue these things. Soon-to-be mothers-in-law surely can't. So I saw clearly that God was not assigning me to preach Alana and Iesa back to Jesus. Not now, anyway. I was still learning, for one thing. Learning to praise. Learning to *be* a sermon, not preach one. My job now was to love them and trust God and hold them close in the bosom of our family. To be a mother. And now to be a mother-in-law.

I couldn't argue and bicker and dis and be those things. Not in a good way.

If God ever changed this arrangement—that is, if I grew bold and knowing, I would be ready to accept a new role. Iesa even wondered out loud if I would conspire, along with *his* mother, to convert him back to Christianity.

"No, not me," I said. I didn't explain God's clear direction to me to leave that alone—for now, anyway.

I also didn't explain that, by faith, I was more convinced than ever that Iesa and Alana would one day return to Christ. But this is the assurance that I have in approaching God about their salvation.

My Bible, waiting on my nightstand—with all of its yellow markings and all of its answered promises—promises me "that if we ask anything according to his will, he hears us. And if we know that he hears us—whatever we ask—we know that we have what we asked of him."

And Jesus did that. He thanked God *before* the victory. "Father, I thank you for hearing my prayer," he declared. Then he turned to the grave and told Lazarus, "Come forth." And the grave opened and out walked Lazarus.

So Lazarus lived again, living above his circumstances, living above his own death, for goodness' sake.

If Jesus could be so confident, why couldn't I?

Salvation in Christ for these beloved children would come.

When? Where? How? I didn't know that.

But, blessed assurance, I was standing on the promise. Besides, God had other work for me right now. So I got to work and believed and moved on.

And we stopped debating religion. We had other common ground.

More than that, we had a wedding soon. Two weeks to go.

⊰⊱

My latest prayer journal had a sky blue cloth cover with red accents and a painted white-iris design in the middle. It wasn't really that pretty. But Mama had bought it for me. A gift for her writing daughter, with lots of light-blue lined pages—and, man, was I writing in it now. My little journal was getting prettier by the hour, in fact.

My wedding-day worries kept trying to nag at me. So I wrote them all down, every single worry, making a list. Then I gave the list a name: a "Give to God" list.

Thus, I gave to God:

The stress of the interfaith choice of Alana and Iesa. The stress of welcoming and receiving a former Christian young man into our family, even though he was solid as a rock *and* tenderhearted, a great combination.

The stress of hosting people of different faiths and backgrounds in our home, especially those with Muslim backgrounds who normally don't mingle with the opposite gender at wedding parties.

The stress of worrying that our house would be too crowded, or that people wouldn't circulate or socialize well, or that the food wouldn't be delicious or plentiful.

The stress that folks would socialize *too* well, rendering disapproval by Iesa's imam, Zubair, with fallout negatively impacting Iesa and, by extension, Alana.

The stress of worrying, again, that Iesa and Alana would struggle with marriage because in truth they didn't know each other well, not in terms of spending real time together.

The stress that Alana would be overwhelmed by her last semester of school, marriage, stepparenting, budgeting, and other challenges.

The stress of trying to finish and put the house back together "perfectly" before the wedding. Some days it felt as if we were getting nothing done, even though I knew we were—it just felt as if there was so much more "to do," and our budget was tight, nonexistent some days, in fact.

The stress of worrying whether or not anybody would show up!

The stress of worrying about whether Alana and Iesa would make it through the rough patches of marriage. Bless their hearts. This was a mountain.

Bad weather during the wedding weekend. What if it snowed? No, what if there was a *blizzard*? The weather. *What if it snowed and nobody could get here?*

Snow on Sunday? For his glory, I asked the heavenly Father to help us with: catering and ceremony planning, finding the two male Muslim witnesses we needed for the ceremony, our meager finances, and flowers!

⸎

"I can get the flowers," Denise said. "What's your budget?"

"Budget. What if I don't have a budget?"

"Yes, you do. How about a hundred dollars?"

"A hundred dollars for flowers. That won't buy much."

"Maybe, but leave it in my hands. Me and God."

"You and God. I can do that."

"Okay. What color?"

"Creamy white. You know the look: a houseful of creamy white wedding flowers."

"Okay. It's done."

And may God bless and keep you, my wonderful and remarkable friend.

Denise had prayed so much with me, not just now but over the years. She stood with me during Dan's illness. Believed with me when the doctors looked sober. And now, after looking Alana "in the eye"—and deciding that Alana was truly in love with a godly man—Denise prayed with me about this wedding.

She listened when I said I couldn't visualize this wedding celebration, prayed with me when I said I didn't know how to prepare my home for the ceremony.

Then as we prayed, God answered in that moment: Give the party for me.

Instantly I knew exactly how I would welcome God into my home:

Flowers on every surface, all over the house. Trays of kosher food so every guest would feel okay eating it. Tiny, white lights sparkling over everything: the fireplace mantle, the staircase, the front porch, the juniper bushes out front—and out back, lights sparkling on the bare lilac branches and wintering cottonwood trees. So from inside the house, the outside would be ablaze with white lights, like a winter wonderland.

Well, that was my fantasy. A few strands of lights on my budget wouldn't blaze. But I could dream. But would anybody come? Do all mothers of the bride worry about such nonsense?

Well, praise God, our guests were stepping up. With two weeks to go, we had eighty "yes" responses—including my sister, Lauretta, flying in from Atlanta. "Frequent-flyer miles!" she said. And Iesa's parents were flying in from Texas. The parents would bring Iesa's son. Also, Iesa's imam in Houston would fly in for two days and perform the Sunday afternoon ceremony. A Houston school principal born in Algeria, Zubair was known as a man who could pray all night, and he had the air of a man who spent a lot of time with God. Calm. Peaceful. Joyful. No worry lines. Always a gentle smile.

"It will be beautiful," he told me on the phone. "Beautiful wedding. Beautiful marriage. Iesa is a wonderful young man. If I knew anything about him—anything at all that would be unacceptable—I would be obligated, as his spiritual leader, to tell you. But what I see in him is only good. You can be proud to have him as a son-in-law."

A beautiful endorsement.

But what about rules for the wedding? "Is a mixed reception okay, with men and women in our house at the same time?" I asked Zubair.

"It is not typical, but it is okay," he answered. "But no alcohol."

Not a drop, I promised.

Then the week of the wedding was here.

Upstairs at my desk:

Our heavenly Father, holy is thy name.

Thy kingdom come, thy will be done, on earth as it is in heaven. So in Jesus' perfect and mighty name, I come tonight, oh Father, first praising you for who you are: the only sovereign, good, mighty, worthy, majestic, creator, and all-sovereign God. In your name, oh blessed Father, I thank you, indeed, for the privilege of calling you Father. I thank you for the mercy of forgiveness and for your forgiveness, already accomplished by

Jesus, for all I might have committed against you these past weeks, or even today, even as I receive with thanksgiving your mercy. Hallelujah.

So, oh blessed Father, thank you for forgiveness as we go into this week, this wedding week. Oh Father, in the mighty name of Jesus and for your glory, I pray that you be magnified in this week, in everything that we do, for your glory.

In Jesus' blessed name, send your Holy Spirit into each of the hearts of all involved. Keep us prayerful, reflective, hopeful, joyful, productive, efficient, caring, kind, patient, gentle, good, faithful, peaceful, and loving—all for your glory.

Heavenly Father, for your glory, keep us balanced, harmonious, trusting, and attuned to your blessed Holy Spirit, in Jesus' wonderful name.

Help us to know when we've done enough—enough planning, enough preparation—for your glory. Then quicken us to love, in Jesus' perfect name I pray.

Amen.

<hr />

Alana took her last final at school.

"How'd you do?"

"I did great," she said. So have faith. She was right.

Meantime, my class ended on my campus. My magazine students gave me my best evaluations ever, not just As but A+ ratings. They said they loved the course. I loved teaching them. *Praise God, and Jesus, thank you.*

Dan organized airport pickups.

I cleaned house. I purchased four boxes of tiny clear lights with white wiring, plus an armful of silk-flower wedding garlands from Hobby Lobby. Good price.

The weather report. Chance of snow 60 percent on Friday, 50 percent on Saturday, 50 percent late on Sunday, the day of the wedding.

I reviewed my "Give to God" list. Weather was now at the top. Then it started to snow, lightly all day Thursday, all night Thursday, still snowing lightly into Friday.

"We need the moisture," the weather report said.

Yes, but not right now!

Then by Friday afternoon, the snow petered out. So Iesa's plane arrived on time. Lauretta's plane arrived on time. Denise pulled up at five o'clock sharp with a carload of glorious fresh flowers—lush creamy blossoms bursting with wedding beauty—sitting on her car's backseat in clear glass vases, stems in clean water.

"Wow," I said.

Denise was grinning, standing in my slushy driveway in snow boots and a big coat, car door open, gesturing at the flowers. "Well, how'd I do?"

"Amazing," I said. "How on earth did you pull this off?"

"I have faith," she said. "I could see it."

So she went to a florist—"not the grocery store," she added, grinning at me. The florists offered two for one, half price for every stem.

"She said come by after three o'clock. I could have all the white flowers left over from the week at two for one."

"Amazing," I said again, admiring the bouquets.

I hugged her. We moved inside and she shrugged out of her coat.

"Okay, let's arrange flowers," she said. "I've got all night. Where's Lauretta?"

So my best friend and my sister filled the house with wedding bouquets. Jesus helped them. The house was bursting with scent and beauty and Holy Ghost peace and joy and Linen White paint, all of it looking like a garden.

Now where was the bride-to-be?

The snow had stopped hours ago, and Alana was driving home from Greeley, a ninety-minute trip. She was late but God is faithful so I didn't worry. Refused to worry. In fact, I was sure she had stopped to visit friends, get a manicure, pick up Iesa's ring, this and that and the other and who knows what else. Then eight o'clock. Then nine o'clock. Then ten o'clock.

Then the key in our front door turned and there she was.

Iesa greeted her, looking into her eyes, holding her hands. I wasn't sure if this was okay in Islam. But they stood in my foyer, gazing into each other's eyes, smiling and talking and laughing and they held hands.

Alana was beaming. Iesa was beaming. Love one another.

One day to go.

⊰⊱

Upstairs at my desk, Saturday night:

> *Our blessed heavenly Father. Sweet Jesus:*
>
> *This is really happening.*
>   *I thank you for traveling mercies for our friends and family. Everybody is here safely. I thank you for your safety in our lives.*

I thank you for good weather, and for a good weather prediction for Sunday afternoon. You order the snow. You stop the snow. You will order what you will. It's your own weather. So whatever we get on Sunday afternoon, I praise you for it now!

So now, oh Father, thank you for beautiful people and beautiful fellowship. What a lovely dinner tonight and what lovely people. Well, my lasagna wasn't perfect. And yet . . . your Holy Spirit was. So thank you for allowing such different people, from such different backgrounds, to sit together at my kitchen table and eat and laugh and talk and listen to each other—black American, white American, Latino American, Protestant American, Catholic American, Muslim American, Algerian American, Lebanese American, I can't even name all the Americans, but all in good and perfect harmony.

So thank you for moments of prayer, this blessed time with you, this consecrated moment to say thank you: the only all-wise, all-merciful, all-powerful and all-loving Father God, to whom we bow and praise and worship.

We come in your mercy, indeed, oh Father, confessing what is true: The Raybons aren't a perfect family. So we don't pretend that. It's in our imperfection, indeed, that we still are saved and still joyous in your merciful care, anyhow. So oh Father God, in Jesus' wonderful name, we confess our sin against you: any doubt, any fear, any unbelief, any attempt to be in control when all of our control is by you. Help me, perfect Father, for your glory and in Jesus' blessed name, to let go and let God. To release every anxiety about tomorrow to you and only you.

But first, thank you, Father, for people to love. Praise God, help me to love them well, even as I watch and anticipate how you will unravel our problems, for your glory. So for tomorrow, our sovereign Father God, I invite—humbly and boldly—your problem-unraveling power on this wedding day, now almost here. Be ye magnified in it. Be ye glorified in it. By your sovereign might and power, be bigger than anything, anybody, any problem, any fear, any apprehension, any conflict, any dissonance, any distance, any potential misunderstanding—any misspoken thought, word, or deed—any complication, any missed signal, all in the sweet and wonderful name of Jesus, for your glory.

Assist me, indeed, oh Father, to let go, for your glory. You can't get the glory if I don't let go.

For this day, I ask the blessed help of your loving Holy Spirit so that I may let go. Pour out your Holy Spirit on this day—into my heart—to speak and act only with love, all day and all for your glory.

I pray today for your people in the world—missionaries and teachers and healers and believers, as they do your work, for your glory, all over the world. Bless and comfort our brave young soldiers, such brave young people, serving with trust all over the world, in faraway places.

Then assist, as you will, Alana and Iesa to be examples today of your love for the world, right here in our home, by reflecting their love for each other. Remind us all to show appreciation to our guests, along with gratitude and love, for the time they will take to be here with us. Help us for your glory, to show these things.

Thank you, in fact, for the complications, whatever they may be, so we can see you and only you unravel them because of your might, but also because of your great love for us.

His name is Jesus. So for your love, on this—a special and remarkable day—and in the name of Jesus, envelop Alana today in our Holy Spirit. Help her to walk in that spirit all day. To glow with peace, calm, maturity, womanly grace, and beauty, with every thought, word, and deed, in Jesus' name, spoken for your glory.

Envelop her soon-to-be-husband, Iesa, today in your Holy Spirit—helping him to walk with confidence, assurance, a sense of duty to Alana, kindness, patience, love, and surrender to you, for your glory.

Use us all, oh Father, to send a message of unity and harmony and diversity, all of it a reflection of you. Help us, indeed, to be the message that you our God are love, letting this message glorify not us but you: our Source, our Inspiration, our Hope, our Help, our blessed Rock of Ages.

Bless Joi for loving her sister even while her own business is draining away, and draining her. But here she is anyway. Supporting her sister, cheering her on. So bless her richly for that, as only you can bless, indeed.

Lastly, blessed Father, help me today to be and live and glow and go for Christ, in that good A.M.E. way, just glowing for the Savior, our Lord, our Friend, our Brother.

In his perfect and wonderful name I pray. So like this, I say with peace: Amen.

Trust God

Do not be anxious about anything, but in everything, by prayer and petition, with thanksgiving,
present your requests to God. PHILIPPIANS 4:6

So we had a wedding.

The sky was dry and Colorado clear. That sky looks like this: Not
a cloud, or a hint of a cloud, anywhere. Overhead everything is crisp,
brilliant, clear as glass. Nothing but blue to blue, from here to yonder.

In sharp contrast, the snow-blanketed earth on this wedding day was
electric with its white. Piercing sunshine reflected off everything, lighting
up everything. The ground was cold but the air was hot with the sunshine, and this was December. A brilliant after-the-snow-stops-falling-
and-the-sun-comes-out-in-Colorado-in-December day.

"Well, you got your good weather," Dan said this Sunday morning,
swinging open our front door, standing in the brilliance, looking out at
God's own gift. Sunshine poured past him into the hallway, spilled into
the kitchen and right out the back windows.

"Boy, did I ever," I said. "This weather is gorgeous." I looked at him.
He saw my eyes.

"God is in charge, sugar pie," Dan said. "Everything will be wonderful."
He hugged me. We kissed, husband and wife. He held me.
Our younger daughter's wedding day.

Soon Iesa and Zubair arrived. Zubair wore his dignified, gentle smile. Iesa was splendid in his wedding clothes: navy blue wool coat, a long tunic over creamy white pants, and gold braid on collar and sleeves. A prince.

He stood outside in the sunshine, waiting for his parents and son to arrive.

Joi and her baby pulled up, the baby gussied up and pretty, pretending to be shy. I went inside and showered, took a deep breath and gussied up too—changing into a ball gown, copper colored and worn at Alana's request.

"I want you to *look* like the mother of the bride," she had said. So I gussied up. I wore a ball gown in my own house. Bobbie Jean would be proud.

Then Alana, standing in her bedroom—the room of her childhood, this place of slumber parties, phone calls, slammed doors, open confessions, late studying, and long struggles—lifted with a rustling sound her Bobbie Jean wedding ensemble from its zippered bag. If we had splurged on anything for this wedding, this was the splurge. Bobbie Jean hit the high mark. The dress and matching coat—creamy and silky and regal, adorned with a cream-colored silk scarf bordered in Chantilly lace—were matchless. Alana was beautiful. A princess.

Then Najat, Iesa's coworker from Houston, pulled a rhinestone pin from her own scarf and pinned it onto Alana's.

"Something borrowed," beautiful Najat said, and we all laughed.

Then there was Alana at the top of the stairs.

Dan, who two years ago couldn't walk down those same stairs, took his daughter by the elbow and led her gallantly to her husband-to-be.

The ceremony was short and much like a Protestant Christian wedding.

Do you take? Do you take? Will you honor? Will you honor?

Alana and Iesa sat in chairs on opposite sides of a table set up near the family-room fireplace. Zubair sat between them. Then papers were signed after a brief talk by Zubair on the sanctity of marriage and the role of the family.

The wedding rings, new and gleaming, were exchanged. Alana's diamond was stunning with promise. Iesa's band was silvery and shining. Our families stood for pictures. Together, there we were: our blended American family, relaxed by God's grace and smiling.

Then the shadows lengthened and the 4 P.M. wedding reception began.

Muslim guests were right on time. Doorbell ringing like crazy. *Ding dong. Ding dong.* The women were modest but beautiful, some wearing light coats over their gorgeous dresses all evening when they saw that men were in the same rooms too. The men bore the gifts, big packages, beautifully wrapped. A lot of families toted in little children.

About a hundred people came, filling the living room and den and family room and kitchen and little room off the family room, and everybody greeting and talking and smiling. The women kissing each other's cheeks. The men gathering in the den, greeting Iesa and Zubair, exchanging men's talk and immigrant stories. Children holding their mother's knees, then later eating cake and sipping punch and playing, skipping from room to room.

By six o'clock, the black Protestants and Latino Catholics and white neighbors and Alana's school friends and anybody else who was coming were in the house.

The caterer announced the food was all kosher, so the buffet line was hopping.

The day that might have killed us instead blessed us with genuine joy. Congenial. Loving. Laughing. Shining. Beautiful.

To my Christian friends, I can only say this: God was in the house.

Maybe some friends aren't convinced. Maybe they wanted a different ending. Maybe they still have questions. Are we bad Christian parents for taking this road? Was there another way?

There always is. But God told us: Go this way now and love. Then leave the future to me. You know how to pray now. So keep praying and just never stop. Face life and let me bless you. As for happy endings? Look to God to write the final chapter. And in the meantime, live in love. And, Patricia, *trust me.*

At sundown, the Muslims all stopped to pray—women in the living room, men in the den, with my son-in-law's imam calling the prayer in Arabic. Then the husband of my good friend Marsha gathered everybody around the buffet tables and lifted a prayer of praise and adoration in the mighty name of Jesus.

The punch and food never ran out.

The bride and groom were beautiful and so happy, so excited about starting their life together. Next day, guests were still feeling the glow, calling with their thanks: What a beautiful, wonderful wedding. All those people, together. Bride and groom so perfect. An extraordinary day.

Mother Teresa said this: "I love all religions but I am in love with my own. If people become better Hindus, better Muslims, better Buddhists by our acts of love, then there is something else growing there. They come closer and closer to God. When they come closer, they have to choose."

Well, I already chose. So I opened my house to a wedding. Then Jesus held me all day, praying with me, filling every room.

Jesus understands weddings like nobody in the world.

Abide, Praise, and Celebrate

Enjoy God, cheer when you see him!
PSALM 68:4

Mama loved the footbath: Orange-painted toes wriggling in the warm water.

Actually, it wasn't a plain foot basin like the ones in Bible days. For Mama, Dan went online and found an electric bubbling "foot spa" with aeration jets, vibration and heat, two loofah disks, and five whirling attachments, including a buffing stone and a revolving arch massager.

"Goodness!" Mama said.

"It was on sale," Dan said.

So we wrestled it out of the box and sat it on the floor in front of Mama. Then Dan started unpacking everything while I read the directions.

"Never plug or unplug the footbath while your feet are in the water."

Mama's eyebrow shot up.

I read the next instructions: "To start, push any of the three push buttons; you can also use two of three or all three buttons at the same time."

"What do they do?" Mama asked.

"Number one is vibration and heat. Number two is bubbles and heat. Number three is water jet."

"I want all three," Mama said.

So Dan filled the basin with warm water and set it in front of Mama.

"Get a towel," Mama said.

"Already have it," I said, helping Mama out of her shoes.

"Okay, in you go," Dan said.

Then Mama placed one foot, and then the other, into the warm water.

Dan set the plug and hit the three buttons. All systems go. Bubbles and vibration and heat and splashing all over the place.

"Oh, that feels good," Mama said.

Everybody laughed.

"Fifteen minutes," I said. "That's your time limit." Me, the timekeeper, still trying to be in control. *Lord Jesus, will I ever learn?*

But then I tried to act like Jesus and rinse Mama's feet and rub her calves while she sat in the water. But she wouldn't let me. She even stopped me from drying her feet with a towel—as Jesus had done, indeed—when her fifteen minutes were up.

"Don't you want me to help you?" I asked.

"Just let me sit here," she said, leaning back in her chair. "I can dry my own feet, like I do when I take my shower."

Well, I tried. And I was willing. And the Father knows my heart. I hope he found it clean.

So Mama was still cranky some of the time. I was, too, I guess. Elder care is hard. Having people fuss over you or having to do the fussing— either way it isn't easy.

Later we found out that fancy vibrating foot spas aren't good for elders with high blood pressure or circulation problems, and that was Mama.

"Well, it was good while it lasted," she said.

So back we went to a plain, big bowl. Jesus had it right after all.

Indeed, every day that Mama lived in our house, she blessed us. Every good thing that happened to our family in recent years happened since we invited her into our home and she moved in, joining our family on a wintry, blizzardy day and never leaving. And now, with her settled in for the count as it were, the sun kept shining.

So it was time to celebrate.

We were doing a lot of that now it seemed, getting invitations to lots of anniversaries, weddings, baby showers, birthday parties, retirements, graduations, surprise tributes. Celebrating other people's happiness like crazy, or celebrating the people themselves. That's what we were doing. I was sending e-cards and buying greeting cards and mailing them off from here to yonder. Every morning that I opened my eyes, it seemed there was somebody else to love with a card or a gift or a call or a smile or an open-armed hello.

Celebration, said Richard Foster, is at the heart of the way of Christ.

Jesus entered the world with good news "of great joy." And that's how we should live, Foster said, with great joy, celebrating "when the common ventures of life are redeemed."

Our life seemed ordinary, indeed. Washing my mother's aching feet? A common venture. But when I got stuck at a hard place—and stopped to pray—right there came a miracle. If I was looking, yes, I saw the miracles.

In the meantime, there was something uncommon and wondrous that I loved about prayer: Daily contact with the Holy Spirit had lifted me above my common circumstances. I was standing on the mountain-top. From there, the Holy Spirit brought other people's ventures to mind: sick people to call, grieving people to comfort, lonely people to hug, faithful people to thank, victorious people to celebrate, cranky people to love. So you buy a stamp, put a card in the mail, and before you know it, somebody who needed some love and appreciation and acknowledgment is feeling it.

But was this a ministry? Is showing people that you see them and love them—celebrating them—part of the great commission?

Indeed, could I become a hero by praying as Jesus taught?

The answer was clear. I'd never get close to a heroic life without the heroic habit of prayer. Maybe my praying hadn't led me to Calcutta to feed the hungry or clothe the naked, not yet anyway. But sending a card to a friend across town in the name of Jesus, or turning off the TV and calling another friend instead, seemed mighty close to giving a heroic cup of cold water in his name.

Prayer is about abiding, indeed. Jesus laid out the plan: "If you remain in me and my words remain in you," he promised, "ask whatever you wish, and it will be given you. This is to my Father's glory, that you bear much fruit, showing yourselves to be my disciples."

Only abiding disciples pray prayers that God can answer? Oh yes. The fruit of prayer. Torrey insisted it is the most effective work that anyone can do, adding: "We can often bring more to pass by praying than we can by any other form of effort we might put forth."

All the prayer warriors say this. Then they say it again.

Bill Bright: "Prayer is God's appointed way of doing God's work."

Richard Foster: "Prayer is the means by which we move the arm of God."

Jill Briscoe: "God wants all of us to be so in touch with him that we are tuned into heaven's wishes for earth."

Kenneth Taylor: "God, for reasons of His own, wants His will and work known and empowered by the Word and by prayer."

Vashti Murphy McKenzie: "It is in prayer that God guides and gives directions to our destiny."

George Muller: "Patient, persevering, believing prayer, offered up to God in the Name of the Lord Jesus, has always, sooner or later, brought the blessing."

Oswald Chambers: "When you labor at prayer, from God's perspective, there are always results."

George MacDonald: "This is and has been the Father's work from the beginning—to bring us into the home of his heart. This is our destiny."

Andrew Murray: "The inner sanctuary is our home, we dwell there."

⊰⊱

Now in my own life, if something hard stood up, I sat down. I went to my desk, that is, to pray. Sinking like butter into the Deity, resting in God's amazing invitation to meet him in prayer. Then when I really got stuck, with seemingly no way out—words wouldn't even come sometimes— I remembered to stop and conquer in prayer. At the hardest moments, it looked like praise. *Praise you, Lord, for what I can't see but what you will do*—that kind of praise. In a hard place, this lifted me every single time. Then suddenly there I was: a prayer hero. Imperfect me. *Sweet Jesus, thank you.* And, no, I couldn't imagine the lives of people who don't pray.

But sometimes I forgot, reverting to my old, small, worrying ways. So the weeks after Alana's wedding, when Joi closed her business and was searching for a job, my older daughter was calm but I got panicky, calling her on the phone: Did you contact so-and-so? Did you follow up with this, that, and the other?

Then she spoke a word: "I'm not worried, Mom."

I took a deep breath. I listened with my eyes, watching my beautiful daughter's emerging faith.

"God promised he would take care of me, Mom, and I am standing on that."

"That's beautiful, Joi," I told her.

"I'm not worried about a thing," she added. "My job is out there."

Then out of the blue, a job announcement—financial analyst needed— showed up online. Joi responded. The employer responded in turn. Joi took their test and passed it. They called her in to interview, flying high. She took their second test, flying higher. They called her again, the follow-up interview. And soon, without any intervention from me—except for my prayers on her behalf—she had the offer.

She turned it down.

"What?" I asked.

"I'm worth more, Mom," she said. "So I asked for more."

"You turned it down?"

"Mom, 'You have not because you ask not.' Isn't that what you've been saying?"

As I started to protest, the insight hit, of course. Her words were an answer to a prayer, offered years ago, that my beautiful daughter in Christ would grasp her full worth in Christ.

She was saying that now: I am worth more. Not because she wanted to buy more things with a bigger paycheck. She wanted instead to witness to more people by testifying that in Christ they are worth more too.

"This is a ministry, Mom," Joi said. "And other people will get blessed by it and God will get glorified."

Yes, Lord. My child was teaching me. A hero herself.

The employer called again, offering a higher salary. This time Joi said yes.

A month later, Alana finished college, completing her bachelor's degree in education, a solid accomplishment and something wonderful to celebrate. I watched her beaming in her cap and gown, blowing kisses to her waving husband, to her friends, to us, letting her professors hug her, making it a good day.

She wasn't back in church, but God said have peace. Abide with me. Then keep asking—ask to my Father's glory—and bear much fruit, thereby showing the world that I am coming. So keep on believing. Live in hope and abide in this discipline of prayer.

My daughter was in Houston now with her husband, searching for a teaching job. Then right away she faced a hurdle. The Houston school district announced a freeze on all new hires. *Lord Jesus, here we go,* I thought.

So again I forgot. I panicked. I called Alana on her cell phone: Did you update your résumé? Have you contacted so-and-so? Did you follow up with this and double-check that? And, Alana, *is your car working okay?*

Then one night I just stopped. A quiet night. Too peaceful for worry. Dan was teaching a class. Mama was downstairs watching a baseball game on TV.

So I went upstairs to my desk and I sat down in the peace and I wrote at the top of a page: "A prayer for Alana's job search."

And like that, I gave it back to God.

Just have your way, Lord, I prayed. Use this job process, as you did with Joi's, to stir up Alana's openness to your Holy Spirit guidance. Move me out of the way. Then use the process of searching for a job to stir up your gift of faith in her, so that you are magnified in the process in her. Amen.

Then I could rest.

I moved on, believing the job would come. Whatever the Lord had set aside for her, and whatever would glorify him, was the job I petitioned on my daughter's behalf—all for *God's* glory. Moreover, I was freed up to get back to my own work.

Alana got hired, yes. Got three good job offers, in fact. She took the hardest and most challenging, a fifth-grade position in a rising district near Houston.

But there was more. I'd finally come to realize that my adult children were *adults* now, indeed.

I could step back. My hands-on work was done. Sure, I could bake cookies and muffins and make encouraging phone calls and do hands-on grandmother things, of course. I could give them advice when they asked. I could tell them about Jesus when the Lord said to tell. But the *best* thing I could do for them now was to lift them in prayer.

In fact, when I was tempted to interfere with unsolicited advice or even with handouts or bailouts or other false help, I knew the better choice was to hold them up with prayer. That was the better way. When the mountain got high and refused to move, I knew then to praise. A crazy thing. Praising God as troubles piled up. Praising God anyway.

Then the mountain moved. Some mountains even crumbled. When God speaks, I heard a preacher say, "get out of the way so the mountain can move."

We are more than conquerors, indeed. Well, it was time to celebrate.

⚜

We'd have a little fun. A beautiful thing. Christians having fun. We have trials, yes. But as Paul told the good folks at Philippi: Don't forget, brothers and sisters, to have some fun. And he was writing from prison when he said it: "Rejoice in the Lord always. I will say it again: Rejoice!"

So we would rejoice in the Lord at a baseball game. A game for cheering, for hoping—for having fun.

My friend Denise's son was competing the next afternoon in the state high school championship. My praying friend's son, yes—the lead batter in the state championship game. We'd show up with faith and joy and maybe with posters. "Go, Etienne!"

That is his name, an unusual name. A family name, so he's learned how to wear it tall. And now he was a tall center fielder, six feet–something and powerful, a fast power player. Using that power, Etienne and his varsity team would compete against their archrivals for the state's biggest baseball honor. The Eagles vs. the Grizzlies. Go Grizzlies.

I knew nothing about this team, in truth. But Denise said they were very good boys. Look, she said, they were seeded number seven. And now, in an eight-team tournament, the humble Grizzlies had outlasted every team but one.

So here they were, one game away from boxing up the number-one-seeded team to win the state prize. Their big rivals, the Eagles, would fight to the death. A big, fun battle.

"So how do I pray for my son's game?" Denise asked the night before. "I mean we're talking *state* championship."

"So this is huge?" I said.

"Bigger than huge," she said.

Dan and I were at her house, celebrating at Etienne's high school graduation party. I listened with my eyes, as Mother Teresa taught.

Then I said: "I pray that he be covered to play his best."

Obvious, yes. But Denise said it was a good prayer.

But then during the night, I understood there was more. The Holy Spirit helps our feeble prayers, indeed. About 3 A.M., I was stirred awake. The house was dark. Dan lay next to me, sleeping with even breathing.

I eased out of the covers, trying not to wake him. Then I padded down the hall to my little office. I turned on a lamp. I opened a prayer journal, found a clean page.

Then I sat there and waited. The best prayers have the fewest words—Martin Luther's reminder. I'm not sure that's always true. But tonight I would be a woman of few words.

Father, I am praying for Etienne. Then I sat still. I would just listen. I would enjoy the presence of God.

Then the Holy Spirit spoke.

And, yes, maybe God loves baseball. Getting us back home is his intent, after all. Besides that, however, the sport is a good game.

And my friend's son is a good son. Never caused her a bit of trouble. Never asked for anything for himself, Denise said, not when other boys these days beg for so much. But Etienne only wanted to please his parents, it seemed, and to be a good citizen, to be a good witness for Christ.

So he wore his silver cross around his neck with ease, with pride. And now he was asking: He wanted his team to win the state championship.

Does God hear such prayers?

I didn't know. But I knew this: The Holy Spirit offered a word for my praying friend's son. Moreover, it was a good and perfect word:

Tell the boy he's already a champion.

In fact, his whole team is a championship team.

They have fought the good fight. They have played like their good coach taught them. Year after year, when others doubted, they played the game with integrity and fairness and discipline. Better still, they played this good game with a good heart.

They practiced hard. Fought right. Played fair. Competed well. They studied to show themselves approved.

So today when they walk on that field—before the first pitch flies—they are champions.

Tell the boy these things. Then he can play with power and joy and the authority that comes from knowing he's already a winner.

And the game?

The game will take care of itself.

Saturday afternoon. Goodness, those Colorado-perfect days.

Dan threw on his sunglasses, slung his camera around his neck. Mama grabbed her cane and a cowboy hat. Mama, the sports lover until the end, wouldn't miss this for the world. I hustled up the bottled water. We were set.

At the ball field, the parking lot was full but not packed. In Colorado, I guess high school baseball isn't a hot ticket like football, especially in the big city. But a state baseball championship is no chump game either.

So the stands were filled—if not in numbers, with fervor. Go Grizzlies! I hadn't shouted such words since high school. But when you feel the spirit, shouting just seems right.

Then in the first inning, with the score 0–0, the Grizzlies went to bat. And there was Etienne. Leadoff batter. Tall and confident. Watching the pitcher wind up.

And here came the pitch. Etienne swung hard. Dust flew. Strike one.

That's okay. Settle it down. Take your time. Another pitch. Strike two. Deep breathing. The sun was shining. Third pitch. Etienne swung from his heels and *crack!*—it was a double off the left-field wall. Crowd up and yelling. Moms and pops praying. Then two more Grizzlies went to work. And here we were, just like that: one, two, three runs. The score was 3–0, Grizzlies.

As I said: Go, Grizzlies.

Then the second inning: The Grizzlies' second baseman reared back. His bat was dynamite. It was a two-run single and, look, it's 5–0. Then two more runs stormed in. When the inning broke, it was 7–0, Grizzlies. My goodness. The bleachers were jumping. Moms and pops screaming their heads off.

Then bottom of the third. The Grizzlies' left fielder pounded a two-run single, and then it was 9–0.

Grizzlies' fans went wild. The bleachers were jumping. Their boys did believe. They did understand. They really were champions.

I looked at Denise. She was standing, eyes skyward, arms outstretched, praising God.

Dan's camera was firing. He was quick on the trigger, recording the moment, loving this baseball face-off.

"Look at that score!" he shouted to Denise's husband, Louis. "This game is over!"

But Louis still wasn't breathing easy. Too early to celebrate, he shouted back. He turned to the field, cupped his mouth with his hands.

"We're not done yet, boys!" he yelled to the Grizzlies. "You're doing good, boys. *But we're not done yet!*"

He looked at my mother. "They have to watch it! This other team can explode!"

"But our team's ahead 9–0!" my mother shouted, fighting the noise. "You can relax!"

"Not yet," Louis shouted louder. Then he stood up. "Good job, boys. But *we're not done yet!*"

This is why believers keep the prayers going. There is always work to do, and until it's over, we're not done.

Sometimes we give up too soon. Pray without ceasing, Paul said. But that's what is compelling about prayer: The talk with God never has to end. And he is always there. Listening and leading us home.

Even in his silence, Oswald Chambers said, are actually his answers— and the sign that "he is bringing you into an even more wonderful understanding of Himself." Indeed, his silence promised that I "could withstand an even bigger revelation."

So I sat on my bleacher, pondering other good baseball reminders—to keep my eye on the ball, to scramble for first, to steal bases, keep running for home, and as I go, to just leap in and slide, baby! Slide!

Foster said to celebrate, indeed. Devout folk get too stuffy, he said. Jesus rejoiced in life, and so should we, Foster declared, then he ended *his* book.

There was much to celebrate this day. Mama was wiggling her toes. Joi was walking in the way. Dan was walking—living and breathing and having his being. Alana and Iesa were happy together, hearts still forming, blessing the bosom of our blessed little family.

And me?

I would be fifty-five in a few weeks. And a party? Like nobody's business.

But now, it was the fifth inning. The Grizzlies' big pitcher, a kid named Kozloski, who everybody called Koz, stepped to the mound.

"He's a big guy," my mother said. She pushed back her cowboy hat. "C'mon, big man!" she yelled.

"Yeah. Kid's got an arm on him," Louis agreed. "All right, Danny! Let's do it, Koz!"

And Koz was working it, burning through the inning, throwing out hitters. Quickly, the Eagles had three outs. Koz wasn't even sweating, it seemed, not much anyway.

Then the bottom of the fifth. The Eagles didn't die easy. Their pitcher, clawing for a comeback, threw out hitters himself. One, two, and three outs, and he wasn't sweating much either.

Then the top of the sixth. If a tide would turn in this game, the turning would come now. For both of these teams, it was do it now or die.

Etienne was in position, deep in center field. He'd had a solid day. He was two for three at bat with two runs so far in this long day's game.

Now he waited deep in center field, facing the setting sun, glove ready, eyes set.

Koz took the mound. Maybe Koz was tiring. One player got on first. Another moved along. Then a player made it home. It was 9–1. One more Eagle got by Koz, landing hard on first, dust erupting. Bases loaded.

Then the Eagles' first baseman came to bat. He stood down Koz. He wouldn't strike. Koz eyed this batter. Then he hurled a curveball toward the plate. The batter connected. The ball was a rocket. It sliced the air. It went screeching past the pitcher, past the infield, ramming into center-field air. The batter dropped the bat and scrambled for first. The other two Eagles turned tail, too, flying for home.

Every fan was hollering now—moms and pops and fans screaming for glory.

One ball was their destiny.

"THAT'S ETIENNE'S," Mama shouted into the noise. Then she was yelling. "CATCH IT, ETIENNE!"

Then everybody: "Etienne! ETIENNE! E. T.!"

Some of us were praying.

Father in heaven, please let your boy catch that ball.

Etienne was racing toward his target. He took a bead on this rocket. It was his alone—his to capture. Or his to lose forever.

Then at the second the ball should have sliced right past him, this good young man of God leapt into the air. Then he dived. His baseball mitt was raised toward heaven, saluting the fading sun. Then as he was skidding and hurtling and hammering into the grass, there it was.

The catch.

Bleachers wild.

The ball sat like a rock in Etienne's outstretched glove. In the next day's paper, the photo spanned the top half of the page. A six-column picture in living color: Etienne suspended above the field, reaching big with all he's got, the ball slamming into his trusting hand. Dan's camera didn't catch that shot, but Dan was alive to try it. This day was its own kind of miracle.

In the bleachers, the whoops were deafening.

"Did you see that?" Mama yelled. "A *diving* catch! That's my boy! Go, baby. *Go, Etienne!*"

Dan was shouting with her, grabbing for his camera.

I was hollering like crazy myself.

"Way to go! Etienne, way to go!"

The boy was racing for the dugout—fast and confident—eager to finish this race on top. In that manner, Etienne scored one more run before his great game ended. And why not? We go out swinging.

The Grizzlies nailed the state championship, 11–1. Not a perfect ending. But it was the right ending. It was decisive.

Denise's husband was crying, eyes shining. He ran on the field, high-fiving and jumping and whooping with players and their moms and pops and coaches and other fans. Everybody rejoicing, slapping each other on the back, celebrating the joy. In this lovely noise, the father searched for his son. But the crowd was a happy blur. It was hard to sort through, to find a loved one. Then Etienne saw his father.

⚜

A father understands: It has been a long road. Playing this game since childhood. Getting knocked down. Crawling back up. Getting dragged under. Battling away fear and doubt and lies and trouble and bad choices. But listen, if you believe and keep on rising, there it is. *The win.*

The boy leapt into his father's arms. From the stands, Denise savored the moment. Dan's camera flashed in the fading daylight. Both understood what had happened here. The victory.

Prayer is like that, of course. The best part comes with understanding: We don't pray to get, we pray to love. Then when we come forth, bleachers go wild. And then? This is how it ends: Jesus welcomed Mama a few beautiful weeks later—just swept her into his loving arms, erasing the leg pain and the hospital stays and long surgeries and, finally, all that ended. She was *home.*

But, oh, I prayed. We all did. *Let her stay, Jesus.* The e-mail list was hopping, good folks praying for my beloved mama, the woman I loved now with everything. In the hospital, I petted Mama like crazy. Sometimes I just held her hand. She let me. Her hospital room was plastered with get-well cards, the phone ringing steadily, Lauretta here to help, Etienne's newspaper photo taped big on one wall.

"Give Grandma a kiss for me," Iesa said, calling with Alana from Houston. "Is she better?" they asked in unison. Joi asked the same, rushing in after work to pray. Is she *better?* Oh my goodness. We all were. But we sobbed without control that final hour. Then came the peace. Our beautiful mother was gone.

The psalmist said it right: "We have escaped like a bird from the fowler's snare; the snare has been broken, and we have escaped." Indeed, if we keep praying—never ceasing, always abiding, the living Word treasured and growing in us—the enemy *doesn't* win.

That's why we loved that final game together. We liked that feeling of triumph, of finishing right—celebrating together, enjoying each other's peace, enjoying Mama, resting in Jesus, savoring the sight of a good team accepting its trophy.

The coach lifted the big prize, holding it toward the sky, letting it catch the fading daylight.

The trophy was big. "Look at it, Mama!" I said.

Her smile was gold. "Yes!"

My goodness, it was beautiful. And look at it glow. Look at its mighty radiance. Shining and gold and like a cross. Oh it is!

It's a crown.

ACKNOWLEDGMENTS

Thank you, blessed Trinity, for teaching me that learning to pray means learning to love. Thank you for showing me that praying is praising in *all* circumstances—and that when my prayers are delayed or denied, your sovereign will is being done. Thank you for convincing me that my best time every day is time spent with you. So thank you, Holy Spirit, for speaking to a believing heart—and for letting me play this part in glorying you.

I thank you, God, for the amazing circle of support for this book, especially for: Brenda Quinn, my Colorado writing friend and prayer partner, for introducing me to the works of Andrew Murray, Richard Foster, and other great prayer warriors; the amazing Ann Spangler and Linda Peterson Kenney, my literary agents and friends, for their untiring advocacy, support, and prayers; the visionary Knox Group at Tyndale House for their extraordinary enthusiasm and support; and Jeff Wright at Urban Ministries Inc. for his visionary expertise and support. Bless them all, Father!

In particular at Tyndale, thank you, Lord, for: Doug Knox, for his wise, congenial, and visionary leadership; Jan Long Harris, for her visionary management, advice, support, and prayers; Lisa Jackson, for her guidance, patience, timely advice, great editing, and friendship; Sharon Leavitt, for her kindness and prayers; Kim Miller, for her timely copyediting assistance; Caleb Sjogren and Beth Sparkman, for their untiring design guidance and creativity; Nancy Clausen, for her enthusiastic publicity management and vision—and for introducing me to media-relations maestro Kelly Hughes of DeChant-Hughes Associates. Thank you, Father, for all others in Doug Knox's smart, professional, and very loving team, who welcomed me into their fold and believed in this book from the beginning.

Thank you, blessed Lord, for beloved friends, especially my praying soul mate Denise Materre, my writing supporter Janet Elyse Singleton, and for the praying saints in Denver at Shorter A.M.E. Church and Cleaves Memorial C.M.E. Church—including my late pastor, the Rev. J. Langston Boyd Jr.—whose support, friendship, and prayers have lifted me daily. Very kind thanks also to Dr. C. T. Lin for clarifying medical terms and conditions. Thank you even for supporters over at Zondervan, including John Sloan, Lyn Cryderman, John Topliff, and Scott Bolinder, whose gift—a copy of R. A. Torrey's *The Power of Prayer*—was such a mighty inspiration.

Finally, I can't write without my spectacular family. So, wonderful Jesus, I thank you for each of them, especially: my beloved husband, Dan, for standing with me and encouraging me every step of this journey; for my beautiful daughter Joi, whose book knowledge was timely and priceless and whose prayers lifted me every day; for my beautiful daughter Alana, for her grace and for so loving me enough to let me tell our story, then reminding me always to aim higher; for my beautiful son-in-law, Iesa, for his kindness and love and for his always-thoughtful support, approval, and feedback; and for my precious *and* smart grandchildren, little Nia and little Anthony, who make me laugh, smile, and feel great whenever I am with them. Thank you, God, for my beautiful sister, Lauretta, and beautiful sister-in-law, Diana, for their unwavering support, love, and kindness and for trusting me with our families' story.

Finally, blessed Father, I thank you for Mama. Our darling is now with Jesus. What an amazing shock to all of us. We weren't ready for her to go, and we miss her. But she looks down with love. We can feel it! Thank you, God, for giving her time to read through these pages and give this story her blessing. Now thank you for graciously allowing one shared final game. Well, we loved that diving catch. And, look! Mama made it home. Thank you, Jesus. Amen.

DISCUSSION GUIDE

1. For starters, what is prayer? Patricia offers several definitions of prayer in
   I Told the Mountain to Move. Which definition is correct? Is prayer enjoying
   God's presence? Or listening to God's voice? Or seeking God's thoughts?
   Or relying on the Holy Spirit? Or asking God's favor, or even knowing
   God's thoughts? Which definition of prayer feels right to you? Is your own
   definition of prayer altogether different?

2. Patricia sought to learn about prayer during a period of personal stress and
   crisis. What do you think was wrong with her praying before this time? What
   impact has prayer had on you during periods of personal struggle or crisis?

3. What about your praying? What in your prayer life, if anything, do you think
   needs to change?

4. When mountains rise up, why does God want us to pray to move them?

5. If God knows everything already, why does he ask us to bring our burdens
   to him in prayer? What did Patricia learn about God during the course of
   her prayer journey?

6. Patricia's human relationships—with her husband, her mother, and her daughters—were sometimes strained. How do relationship problems affect your prayer life?

     Conversely, how does your prayer life impact your relationships?

7. Patricia usually prays at her desk and at her bedside by writing out her prayers in a journal. How do you feel about writing prayers? What are the benefits? Are there drawbacks? How does this practice differ from your prayer style?

8. As Patricia's prayer journey began, she was surprised to realize that prayer, in some ways, is actually easy. What about prayer is easy? At any time, has prayer felt easy to you? If it sometimes feels hard, as it did later to Patricia, what makes praying feel hard?

9. Prayer scholars often emphasize the idea of making precise requests during prayer. Why do you think precision in prayer is so important? If it's important to be precise, what role does faith have in praying?

10. A nurse in the hospital prayed for Patricia's husband. Can you think of a time when God wanted you to pray for another person? How did you know you were being asked to pray? How did you respond?

11. What about collective prayer, or praying with others? Patricia was led to reach out by e-mail to a community of prayers on the Internet. How do you feel about "online" community prayers?

12. Along her journey, Patricia discovered an interesting truth—that learning to pray is about learning to love. What does this mean exactly? In what ways is learning to love interconnected with learning to pray?

13. Moving mountains always means moving ourselves in some way. What mountain in your life would move if you made a move first in a higher, fresher, fearless direction? Explain.

14. If Patricia is right, that "telling the hard truth" is one requirement for effective prayer, what truth do you need to address in your own life? Why is telling the hard truth so difficult?

15. What role does gratitude have in prayer? For example, when Patricia thanked God for her husband's successful surgery, she suddenly began to remember the plight of poor and sick children in Africa. How did this train of thought affect you as you were reading this story?

16. Patricia struggled with the fact that her mother wasn't perfect—but who is? What relationship challenges are you facing in your own life?

17. Patricia's shocking confession is a major turning point in her story. Were you surprised by it? How did it affect you? Now read James 5:16. Do you think James meant that public confession is required of all believers?

18. When she fasted, Patricia was confronted with a judgmental streak in her personality. Have you ever fasted? What have you learned during the course of the fast? If you haven't tried a fast as part of your spiritual growth, why haven't you? Do you think fasting is expected of believers? If so, why?

19. One of Patricia's biggest challenges was her younger daughter's turn from the Christian church to Islam. What do you think of the way Patricia handled this challenge? What would you have done differently?

20. What inspired Patricia's letter to her mother? Do you think the letter, arriving so late in her mother's life, said enough? Do you need to write a letter to someone in your life? What is stopping you from writing it?

    What are other ways you would choose to reach out to a loved one to say "I love you," and why?

21. If you pray in Jesus' name, what does this mean to you? Has your understanding about "praying in Jesus' name" changed since reading Patricia's book? If so, in what ways?

22. Patricia's prayers didn't move every mountain in her life—at least not in ways she had expected. Does that mean she prayed wrong? When our mountains don't move as we would like, how can prayer still make a difference?

23. Patricia cites twenty-four prayer lessons in this book. Do you agree that prayer has such rules? Are there others she might have included? Does she include any that you wouldn't follow? Of the twenty-four prayer lessons in I Told the Mountain to Move, which lesson had the biggest impact on you, and why? Which were new to you? Which are you applying now in your prayer life?

24. At the end of I Told the Mountain to Move, Patricia takes her mother to a baseball game. While the trophy is being awarded, Patricia reveals one final surprise in this story. What did the ending suggest is the outcome of a life of prayer? Did the ending, and this book, make you want to pray more?

    List here, in precise fashion, the most important petitions on your prayer list:

    _____

    _____

    _____

    _____

    _____

    _____

_____

_____

_____

_____

_____

_____

Thank you for participating in this discussion, and for sharing these questions with others. God bless you and your loved ones as you continue to seek the Lord—and seek to glorify him—by moving your mountains in prayer!

ENDNOTES

Climbing

6   "we cannot give to the outside" Mother Teresa, A Simple Path (New York: Ballantine, 1995), back cover.

7   "O my God, I cry out" Psalm 22:2

7   "the withering winds of God's hiddenness" Howard Macy, Rhythms of the Inner Life (Old Tappan, N.J.: Fleming H. Revell, 1988), 95.

7   "long silence . . . pulls into darkness" Renita Weems, Listening for God: A Minister's Journey through Silence and Doubt (New York: Simon & Schuster, 1999), 25, 36.

7–8 "icy cold . . . God was, in fact, to conquer me" Richard Foster, Prayer: Finding the Heart's True Home (San Francisco: HarperSanFrancisco, 1992), 38.

8   "The tragedy . . . is not that things are broken" Alan Paton, Cry, the Beloved Country (New York: Scribner, 2003), 56.

9   "When our hands are tied" Frederick D. Haynes III, "Prayerfully Handling Situations beyond Your Control," in No Other Help I Know: Sermons on Prayer and Spirituality, ed. J. Alfred Smith (Valley Forge, Penn.: Judson Press, 1996), 35.

10 "The highest part of the work" Andrew Murray, With Christ in the School of Prayer (Belfast: Ambassador, 1998), 10.

10 "in which He trains His redeemed ones" Murray, With Christ in the School of Prayer, 17.

11 "Then Jesus looked up" The story of Jesus raising Lazarus from the dead is found in John 11:1-44.

11 "We work, we pull, we struggle" Evelyn Christenson, Gaining Through Losing (Colorado Springs: Chariot-Victor, 1980).

12 "enjoying the presence of God" Steve Wingfield, Live the Adventure (Nashville: Nelson, 2001).

23 "ever liveth" to pray, Hebrews 7:25, KJV.

24 "is the deepest and highest work of the human spirit" Richard Foster, Celebration of Discipline: The Path to Spiritual Growth (San Francisco: HarperSanFrancisco, 1988), 33.

25 "the movement and the traveling" Renita Weems, Listening for God, 32.

Prayer Lesson 2: God Is Bigger

37 "can only be learned in the school of much prayer" Andrew Murray, With Christ in the School of Prayer (Belfast: Ambassador, 1998), 18.

43–44 "In Abraham, we see how prayer is not only, or even chiefly, the means" Ibid., 132.

44 "We do not once find Abraham praying for himself" Ibid., 132.

44 "Prayer is not merely the cry of the suppliant for mercy" Ibid., 133.

Prayer Lesson 3: Look for Jesus

51 "lay down the everlasting burden . . . to set others straight" Richard Foster, Celebration of Discipline: The Path to Spiritual Growth (San Francisco: HarperSanFrancisco, 1988), 10.

52 "generous to those in need" 1 Timothy 6:18, NLT

56 "On Sunday mornings" James Baldwin, Go Tell It on the Mountain (New York: Dell Publishing, 1953), 15.

59 "And the Word was made flesh" John 1:14, KJV

Prayer Lesson 4: Have Faith but Be Precise

62 "wants you to sense his presence" Rick Warren, The Purpose-Driven Life: What on Earth Am I Here For? (Grand Rapids: Zondervan, 2002), 110.

62 *"God is always present, even when you are unaware of him"* Ibid.

62 *"when we least feel like praying"* R. A. Torrey, *The Power of Prayer and the Prayer of Power* (Grand Rapids: Zondervan, 1971), 66.

62 *"Simply be quiet and look up to God"* Ibid.

63 *"that it almost seemed that if I opened my eyes I could see Him"* Ibid.

69 *"we may most confidently believe"* Andrew Murray, *With Christ in the School of Prayer* (Belfast: Ambassador, 1998), 236 in the notes section.

69 *"The power to believe a promise depends"* Andrew Murray, *With Christ in the School of Prayer*, 87 (emphasis in original).

70 *"Have faith in God"* Mark 11:22-24

Prayer Lesson 5: Love Each Other

72 *"Are you still sleeping and resting?"* Matthew 26:44-46 (emphasis added)

73 *"My prayer will depend on my life"* Andrew Murray, *With Christ in the School of Prayer* (Belfast: Ambassador, 1998), 161.

74 *"This is my command"* John 15:17

74 *"To forget oneself . . . opportunity for His being glorified"* Murray, *With Christ in the School of Prayer*, 226.

74 *"We must love one another"* W. H. Auden, from his poem "September 1, 1939."

75 *"we do not know what we ought to pray for"* Romans 8:26

75 *"And we will receive from him whatever we ask"* 1 John 3:22-23, NLT

75 *"He demands that we listen to His Word"* R. A. Torrey, *The Power of Prayer and the Prayer of Power* (Grand Rapids: Zondervan, 1971), 77.

75 *"If we have a sharp ear for God's commandments"* Ibid., 77.

76 *"T-I-M-E"* Rick Warren, *The Purpose-Drive Life: What on Earth Am I Here For?* (Grand Rapids: Zondervan, 2002), 127.

77 *"the kingdom of the sick"* Susan Sontag, *Illness as Metaphor & AIDS and Its Metaphors* (New York: Picador USA, 1989), 1.

78 *That made me a cousin to the woman at the well* The story of Jesus and the Samaritan woman comes from John 4:6-10.

80 *"There is therefore now no condemnation"* Romans 8:1, KJV

80 *"And we know that all things work together . . . If God be for us"* Romans 8:28, 31, KJV.

Prayer Lesson 6: Tell the Hard Truth

83 *it's obedient love—the evidence of a "living faith"* R. A. Torrey, *The Power of Prayer and the Prayer of Power* (Grand Rapids: Zondervan, 1971), 100.

85 *Mary Pipher says adults of my era carry a deep longing* Mary Pipher, *Another Country: Navigating the Emotional Terrain of Our Elders* (New York: Riverhead Books, 1999), 75.

86 *"Love one another, even as I have loved you"* John 13:34, NASB

87 *"Honor thy father"* Exodus 20:12, KJV.

Prayer Lesson 7: Try Again to Love

92–93 *"I simply argue that the cross"* George MacLeod, as quoted in Charles R. Swindoll, *Come Before Winter* (Carol Stream, Ill.: Tyndale House, 1985), 321–322.

99 *"Dear friends, if we don't feel guilty"* 1 John 3:21-22, NLT

100 *"The point of life is learning to love"* Rick Warren, *The Purpose-Driven Life: What on Earth Am I Here For?* (Grand Rapids: Zondervan, 2002), 125.

100 *"Anyone who does not love"* 1 John 4:8, NLT

Prayer Lesson 8: Persist

105 *"to the silent thunder of the Lord of hosts"* Richard Foster, *Celebration of Discipline: The Path to Spiritual Growth* (San Francisco: HarperSanFrancisco, 1988), 39.

105 *"vain repetition"* Ibid.

106 *"If our prayers are to mean"* Frederick D. Haynes III, "Prayerfully Handling Situations beyond Your Control," in *No Other Help I Know: Sermons on Prayer and Spirituality*, ed. J. Alfred Smith (Valley Forge, Penn.: Judson Press, 1996), 35.

107 *"Keep on asking"* Luke 11:9

107 *"If you sinful people know"* Luke 11:13, NLT

107 *That is, the prayer that the Holy Spirit inspires* R. A. Torrey, *The Power of Prayer and the Prayer of Power* (Grand Rapids: Zondervan, 1971), 137.

Prayer Lesson 9: It's Hard

112 *"maintaining our own Christian life"* Andrew Murray, *With Christ in the School of Prayer* (Belfast: Ambassador, 1998), 10.

114 *"Prayer does not equip us for greater works"* Oswald Chambers, *My Utmost for His Highest: The Golden Book of Oswald Chambers, an Updated Edition in Today's Language*, ed. James Reimann (Grand Rapids: Discovery House, 1992), October 17th entry.

115 *"hears the prayers of the righteous"* Proverbs 15:29

Prayer Lesson 10: So Ask! Then Get Moving

119 *"Pick up your mat and walk"* John 5:8

119 *You have not because you ask not* See James 4:2-3.

119 *"It must be our prayer that the Lord"* Andrew Murray, *With Christ in the School of Prayer* (Belfast: Ambassador, 1998), 72.

119 *"Whatever you do, work at it"* Colossians 3:23

121 *"All you have to do is die spiritually"* Joseph Campbell, *The Power of Myth* (New York: Anchor, 1991), 141.

121 *"I say, follow your bliss"* Ibid., 150.

121 *"Ask and it will be given to you"* Matthew 7:7

123 *"We pray not to get something . . . because a relationship with him is what we desire most"* Jerry Sittser, *Why God Doesn't Answer Your Prayer* (Grand Rapids: Zondervan, 2003), 138.

123 *"Prayers are not tools for doing or getting"* Eugene Peterson, *Answering God: The Psalms as Tools for Prayer* (San Francisco: HarperSanFrancisco, 1991), front matter.

Prayer Lesson 11: Thank God

133–134 *Africa had more than 11 million AIDS orphans . . . "Some 200 million people in the world are infected with the tropical disease known as schistosomiasis"* AIDS statistics come from UNAIDS, UNICEF, and USAID, *Children on the Brink 2004: A Joint Report of New Orphan Estimates and a Framework for Action* (Washington, D.C.: U.S. Agency for International Development, 2004) and UNICEF, *Africa's Orphaned Generation*, 2003. Statistics on measles, trachoma, and schistosomiasis come from the World Health Organization and UNICEF.

135 *"To pray means to stop expecting"* Henri Nouwen, *With Open Hands* (New York: Ballantine Books, 1992), 44.

Prayer Lesson 12: Forgive

138 *"Dear friends, do not be surprised"* 1 Peter 4:12

138 *"We also rejoice in our sufferings"* Romans 5:3

138 *"When troubles come your way"* James 1:2-4, NLT.

140 *"ordinary human beings: people who have jobs . . . our friends and neighbors"* Richard Foster, *Celebration of Discipline: The Path to Spiritual Growth* (San Francisco: HarperSanFrancisco, 1988), 1.

140 *"Love begins at home"* Mother Teresa with Jay Chaliha and Edward LeJoly, *The Joy in Loving: A Guide to Daily Living with Mother Teresa* (New York: Penguin Books, 2000), 154.

140 *"The streets of Calcutta lead to every man's door"* Ibid., 125.

140 *"love and peace and compassion in our own homes first"* Ibid., 57.

145 *"Against you . . . a willing spirit, to sustain me"* Psalm 51:4, 10-11

145 *"And when you stand praying"* Mark 11:25

145 *"for our own spirits . . . rediscovering the humanity"* Lewis Smedes, *The Art of Forgiving* (New York: Random House, 1996), 125.

Prayer Lesson 14: Confess

153–154 *some 1.3 million legal abortions* Abortion statistics come from Physicians for Reproductive Choice and The Alan Guttmacher Institute, *An Overview of Abortion in the United States,* January 2003.

154 *"We must not be surprised when we hear of murders"* Mother Teresa with Jay Chaliha and Edward LeJoly, *The Joy in Loving: A Guide to Daily Living with Mother Teresa* (New York: Penguin Books, 2000), 88.

154 *"Confess your sins"* James 5:16 (emphasis added)

154 *"We are saved to serve"* Rick Warren, *The Purpose-Driven Life: What on Earth Am I Here For?* (Grand Rapids: Zondervan, 2002), 229.

156 *Against you only, oh Lord, have I sinned* Psalms 51:4

Prayer Lesson 15: Fast

159 *"Ministry to God must come before ministry to people . . . letting that overflow pour into their lives"* Elizabeth Alves et al., *Intercessors: Discover Your Prayer Power* (Ventura, Calif.: Regal, 2000).

161 *"You dress in burlap"* Isaiah 58:5, NLT

161 *When you fast . . . "your Father, who sees everything, will reward you"* Matthew 6:16, 18

161 *He ticked off the different methods of fasting. . . "to glorify our Father which is in heaven"* Richard Foster, *Celebration of Discipline: The Path to Spiritual Growth* (San Francisco: HarperSanFrancisco, 1988), 55.

163 *"We hate the things we cannot explain"* Carl Gustav Jung, *Man and His Symbols* (n.p.: Laurel, 1968), 82.

164 *"More than any other Discipline"* Foster, *Celebration of Discipline,* 55.

164 *"If pride controls us, it will be revealed almost immediately"* Ibid.

165 *"This is the judgment"* Martin Luther King, *The Words of Martin Luther King—Selected by Coretta Scott King* (New York: Newmarket Press, 1983), 3.

165–166 *"Each of us is here for a brief sojourn"* Albert Einstein, *Living Philosophies* (New York: Simon & Schuster, 1931), 3–7.

166 *"It's not how much you do, but how much love"* Mother Teresa with Jay Chaliha and Edward LeJoly, *The Joy in Loving: A Guide to Daily Living with Mother Teresa* (New York: Penguin Books, 2000), 96.

166 *"Whenever you did one of these things"* Matthew 25:40, *The Message*

Prayer Lesson 16: Honor Jesus' Name: Model His Character

168 *"His longing for me is dearer"* Mother Teresa with Jay Chaliha and Edward LeJoly, *The Joy in Loving: A Guide to Daily Living with Mother Teresa* (New York: Penguin Books, 2000), 102.

168 *"sweet sinking into the Deity"* Madame Guyon, *A Short and Very Easy Method of Prayer,* chapter 22. See http://passtheword.org/dialogs-from-the-past/methodofprayer.htm.

168 *"had to pray three hours"* Martin Luther, as quoted in Richard Foster, *Celebration of Discipline: The Path to Spiritual Growth* (San Francisco: HarperSanFrancisco, 1988), 34.

168 *"prayer was no little habit"* Ibid.

170 *"When I am weak"* See 2 Corinthians 12:10.

172 *"be yoked together"* 2 Corinthians 6:14.

173 *"everlasting burden of always"* Foster, *Celebration of Discipline,* 10.

174 *"I have been crucified"* Galatians 2:20

175 *But he knew the story of Jesus* The story of Jesus and the man from Bethesda can be found at John 5:1-15.

177 *"with the idea of changing the moral aspect of the whole earth"* William Ellery Channing, "The Character of Christ" in *The World's Greatest Sermons*, vol. 4, comp. Grenville Kleiser. See http://hippocampusextensions.com/gs.

Prayer Lesson 17: Heed the Holy Spirit

184 *"the Father and I are one"* John 10:30, NLT
185 *"Sir, you say that Christ can save me"* Charles Spurgeon, "The Holy Spirit's Chief Office." This sermon can be found at http://www.spurgeon.org/sermons/2382.htm.
185 *"My God, my God, why hast thou"* See Psalm 22:1, Matthew 27:46, and Mark 15:33, KJV.
188 *All things work together* See Romans 8:28.
189–190 *"are too bright for us to see . . . the Holy Spirit must lead us to see this"* Charles Spurgeon, "The Holy Spirit's Chief Office."
190 *"It is the prayer that the Holy Spirit inspires"* R. A. Torrey, *The Power of Prayer and the Prayer of Power* (Grand Rapids: Zondervan, 1971), 137.
190 *"The ideas, the pictures, the words are of no avail"* Richard Foster, *Celebration of Discipline: The Path to Spiritual Growth* (San Francisco: HarperSanFrancisco, 1988), 42.
190 *"Surely, if there is one prayer that should draw us to the Father's throne . . . when they ask for others"* Andrew Murray, *With Christ in the School of Prayer* (Belfast: Ambassador, 1998), 58, 16, 60 (emphasis in original).
191 *"Or to translate more literally . . . prayers will be in the Holy Spirit"* R. A. Torrey, *The Power of Prayer*, 144.
192 *"And the Holy Spirit . . . with groanings that cannot be expressed in words"* Romans: 8:26, NLT

Prayer Lesson 18: Serve with Love

197 *"Servants think more about others than about themselves"* Rick Warren, *The Purpose-Driven Life: What on Earth Am I Here For?* (Grand Rapids: Zondervan, 2002), 265.
203 *"God often tests our hearts by asking us to serve"* Ibid., 258.
203 *"Your primary ministry should be"* Ibid.
206 *"They talk to work"* Mary Pipher, *Another Country: Navigating the Emotional Terrain of Our Elders* (New York: Riverhead Books, 1999), 187.
206 *"The old desperately need natural healers"* Ibid., 190.

Prayer Lesson 19: Tell the Mountain to Move

209 *"against evil rulers and authorities of the unseen world"* Ephesians 6:12, NLT
212 *"show love by being useful but are unschooled in the language of connection"* Mary Pipher, *Another Country: Navigating the Emotional Terrain of Our Elders* (New York: Riverhead Books, 1999), 75.
212 *"are hungry for touch"* Ibid.
214 *I am the way* See John 14:5-6.

Prayer Lesson 20: Be of Good Cheer

216 *"Even if my mouth is closed"* Mother Teresa with Jay Chaliha and Edward LeJoly, *The Joy in Loving: A Guide to Daily Living with Mother Teresa* (New York: Penguin Books, 2000), 115.
223 *"How long, O Lord, must I call for help?"* Habakkuk 1:2, NLT
223 *"In the world ye . . . I have overcome the world"* John 16:33, KJV

Prayer Lesson 22: Imagine the Answer

238 *"The greatest difference between the two faiths"* Emir Caner and Ergun Caner, *Unveiling Islam: An Insider's Look at Muslim Life and Beliefs* (Grand Rapids: Kregel, 2002), 31.
238 *"come before his presence . . . sing to the Lord . . . I will sing a new song"* See Psalm 100:2, KJV; Psalm 30:4, KJV; and Psalm 144:9, NLT.
239 *"Now this is eternal life: that they may know you"* John 17:3
239 *"that if we ask anything according to his will"* 1 John 5:14-15.

Prayer Lesson 23: Trust God

250 *"I love all religions but I am in love with my own"* Mother Teresa with Jay Chaliha and Edward
     LeJoly, *The Joy in Loving: A Guide to Daily Living with Mother Teresa* (New York: Penguin Books,
     2000), 124.

Prayer Lesson 24: Abide, Praise, and Celebrate

253 *"when the common ventures of life are redeemed"* Richard Foster, *Celebration of Discipline: The Path
     to Spiritual Growth* (San Francisco: HarperSanFrancisco, 1988), 193.

253 *"If you remain in me"* John 15:7-8

253 *"We can often bring more to pass by praying"* R. A. Torrey, *The Power of Prayer and the Prayer
     of Power* (Grand Rapids, Mich.: Zondervan, 1971), 27.

253 *"Prayer is God's appointed way of doing God's work"* Bill Bright, *The Christian and Prayer:
     Unlocking the Secrets of a Successful Prayer Life* (Orlando: New Life Publications, 1994), 7.

253 *"Prayer is the means by which we move the arm of God"* Foster, *Celebration of Discipline*, 195.

253 *"God wants all of us to be so in touch with him"* Jill Briscoe, *Prayer That Works* (Carol Stream, Ill.:
     Tyndale, 2000).

254 *"God, for reasons of His own, wants His will and work known"* Kenneth Taylor, *My Life: A Guided
     Tour* (Carol Stream: Tyndale House, 1991), 352–353.

254 *"It is in prayer that God guides"* Vashti M. McKenzie, *Strength in the Struggle* (Cleveland: The
     Pilgrim Press, 2001), 54.

254 *"Patient, persevering, believing prayer, offered up to God"* George Muller, as quoted in Andrew
     Murray, *With Christ in the School of Prayer* (Belfast: Ambassador, 1998), 249 in notes section.

254 *"When you labor at prayer"* Oswald Chambers, *My Utmost for His Highest: The Golden Book of
     Oswald Chambers, an Updated Edition in Today's Language*, ed. James Reimann (Grand Rapids:
     Discovery House, 1992), October 17th entry.

254 *"This is and has been the Father's work from the beginning"* George MacDonald, *Wisdom to Live By*
     (Eureka, Calif.: Sunrise Books, 1996).

254 *"The inner sanctuary is our home"* Andrew Murray, *With Christ in the School of Prayer* (Belfast:
     Ambassador, 1998), 228.

256 *"Rejoice in the Lord always"* Philippians 4:4

259–260 *"he is bringing you"* Oswald Chambers, *My Utmost for His Highest: The Golden Book of Oswald
     Chambers*, October 11th entry.

260 *Foster said to celebrate, indeed* Foster, *Celebration of Discipline*, 193.

262 *"We have escaped like a bird"* Psalm 124:7

Patricia Raybon's personal essays on family, culture, and faith have been published in the *New York Times Magazine*, *Newsweek*, *USA Today*, *Guideposts*, *Country Living*, and in many college-writing texts and other publications. Her critically acclaimed first book, *My First White Friend: Confessions on Race, Love, and Forgiveness*, was awarded the prestigious Christopher Award for "artistic excellence affirming the highest values of the human spirit." A frequent contributor to National Public Radio, Patricia has been a guest on national and local television shows including NBC's *Today*. Formerly a features reporter at the *Denver Post* and the *Rocky Mountain News*, she also served on the journalism faculty at the University of Colorado at Boulder. Patricia and her husband, J. Daniel, live in Colorado; they have two grown daughters.